KNOW YOUR STORY

KNOW YOUR STORY

CONFIRM YOUR FAITH

CONFIRM YOUR FAITH

LIVE YOUR COMMITMENT

LIVE YOUR COMMIT

CREDO

WRITERS

Tim Gossett
Kevin Alton
Rev. Dee Dee Azhikakath
Rev. Karen Kluever
Kara Lassen Oliver
Mark Ray
Rev. Chris Hughes
Rev. Taylor Burton-Edwards
Lanecia Rouse

EDITORIAL AND DESIGN TEAM

Josh Tinley	Development Editor
Andrea Roth Murdock	Development Editor
Jennifer A. Youngman	Development Editor
Sheila K. Hewitt	Production Editing Supervisor
Keely Moore	Design Manager

ADMINISTRATIVE STAFF

Neil M. Alexander	Publisher
Marjorie M. Pon	Editor, Church School Publications

CREDO CONFIRMATION FOR SMALL CHURCHES: An official resource for The United Methodist Church, approved by the General Board of Discipleship and published by Cokesbury, The United Methodist Publishing House, 201 Eighth Avenue, South, P.O. Box 801, Nashville, TN 37202-0801.

To order copies of this publication, call toll-free 800-672-1789. Call Monday through Friday, 7:00–6:30 Central Time; 5:00–4:30 Pacific Time; Saturday, 9:00–5:00. You may fax your order to 800-445-8189. Telecommunication Device for the Deaf/Telex Telephone: 800-227-4091. Use your Cokesbury account, American Express, Visa, Discover, or MasterCard.

11 12 13 14 15 16 17 18 19 20 — 10 9 8 7 6 5 4 3 2 1

Contents

INTRODUCTION

CHRISTIAN EDUCATION

MENTORING

WORSHIP

SERVICE

RETREATS

UNIT 1 SESSIONS: KNOW YOUR STORY

Credo Contributors

KEVIN ALTON is a United Methodist youth worker, worship leader, writer, husband, father, and friend. In his free time, Kevin enjoys songwriting and recording with his band, Purrington. Kevin has a passion for confirmation, considering it a gift to be present as youth are led through this doorway in their spiritual journey. Kevin lives in the Chattanooga area with his wife, Britta, and their two boys, Grey and Penner.

- *Confess*
- *I Believe (The Creeds)*
- *Prayers, Presence, Gifts, Service, and Worship (PPGSW)*
- *Going Forth*

REV. DEE DEE AZHIKAKATH is an ordained elder in the Desert Southwest Annual Conference and has experience working in churches in Texas, New Jersey, Arizona, and England. She has served on the General Commission on Religion and Race and the General Board of Church and Society and has taught confirmation in rural, multi-church settings; in large, suburban churches; and in campus ministry.

- *Worship*
- *Sacraments*
- *Living a Holy Life*

TIM GOSSETT is a long-time youth ministry and Christian education veteran, having worked as a youth director, a campus ministry assistant, a Christian education director, a writer, an editor, and a member of a camp staff. A graduate of United Theological Seminary, with degrees in Religious Education and Religious Communications, he is the author of several youth ministry books. He blogs about Christian education and youth ministry, from his home in Ames, Iowa.

- *Christian Education and Confirmation*
- *Way of Discipleship*

- *Way of Salvation*
- *Wesleyan Quadrilateral*

REV. KAREN TROGDON KLUEVER is a deacon in the South Carolina Conference, serves as a minister to youth and college students, and has more than 20 years of youth ministry experience. She developed and wrote *Synago*, for student-led, small-group Bible study, and has designed models for confirmation and youth Bible study in her local church. She enjoys planning and leading youth retreats, mission trips, and worship. Karen has undergraduate and graduate degrees in journalism, with a master's in Christian education from Pfeiffer University. She lives in Charlotte, North Carolina.

- *Renounce, Reject, Repent*
- *Accept*

KARA LASSEN OLIVER, while at Vanderbilt Divinity School, took a job at the United Methodist National Youth Ministry Organization (now the Division on Ministries with Young People); and youth ministry has been forever woven into her life and journey. Inspired by the creativity, honesty, and important questions of youth, she moved into youth ministry in a local church in Nashville, Tennessee, and along the way became a writer and editor. Since July 2009, she has been serving with her family as Volunteers in Mission in Malawi.

- *Creation*
- *Sin*
- *Redemption*

MARK RAY, in more than 15 years as a volunteer at Christ Church United Methodist in Louisville, Kentucky, has taught middle-school and high-school Sunday school, led confirmation, and slept on more hard floors and smelly mattresses than he cares to remember. He has authored or contributed to several curriculum and programming resources.

- *Church*
- *Holy Spirit*
- *New Creation*

REV. CHRIS HUGHES is a writer, musician, retreat leader, and United Methodist pastor in Salisbury, North Carolina. For several years, Chris and his wife, Gloria, have led confirmation retreats for the Southeastern Jurisdiction of The United Methodist Church. Chris has written and recorded music for several worship resources and is the author of *The Porpoise-Given Life.*

- *Retreats*

REV. TAYLOR BURTON-EDWARDS is an ordained elder, serving as Director of Worship Resources, with the General Board of Discipleship. He received his Master of Divinity from The Southern Baptist Theological Seminary and his M.A. from Associated Mennonite Biblical Seminary. Taylor and his wife, Grace, an Episcopal priest, have two sons, Jacob and Will.

- *Worship for Confirmands*

LANECIA ROUSE is a beloved, recovering sinner, who delights in music, photography, listening, writing, traveling, friendship, coffee chats with her sister, and kingdom living and loving. She serves in ministry at Belmont UMC in Nashville, Tennessee, where she has shared the journey of faith with some amazing youth, after serving a year in the British Methodist Church, following her Master of Divinity studies at Duke Divinity School.

- *Service and Confirmation*

Review Team

SARAH ARTHUR
Youth Ministry Author and Speaker
Lansing, Michigan

REV. STEPHEN CADY
United Methodist Pastor
Kansas East Annual Conference

BISHOP MINERVA CARCAÑO
United Methodist Bishop
Desert Southwest Annual Conference

REV. TERRY CARTY
Executive Director, Youth Worker Movement
United Methodist Pastor
Tennessee Annual Conference

KIM GEORGE
United Methodist Children's Director
Arlington, Texas

REV. JENNY HALLENBECK
United Methodist Pastor
Dakotas Annual Conference

REV. SUSAN HAY
Director, Youth Ministries
General Board of Discipleship

BISHOP ROBERT HOSHIBATA
United Methodist Bishop
Oregon Idaho Annual Conference

DR. SONDRA MATTHAEI
United Methodist Professor of Christian Religious Education
St. Paul School of Theology,
Kansas City, Missouri

DR. M. DOUGLAS MEEKS
Professor and Chair in Wesleyan Studies and Theology
Vanderbilt Divinity School,
Nashville, Tennessee

BLAIR GILMER MEEKS
United Methodist Author and Liturgy Specialist
Nashville, Tennessee

ERICA MUNOZ
Children, Youth, and Young Adult Coordinator
Greater New Jersey Annual Conference

REV. MIKE RATLIFF
Associate General Secretary, Division on Ministries With Young People
General Board of Discipleship

REV. BRYAN TENER
United Methodist Pastor
Oklahoma Annual Conference

DR. ED TRIMMER
Chair, Department of Religion
Professor of Youth Ministry
Huntingdon College,
Montgomery, Alabama

DEVELOPMENT TEAM AND CONSULTANTS

Development Team

Neal Bowes
Stephanie Hand
Chris Hughes
Karen Kluever
Camille Mattick
J.C. Mitchell
Shelly Petz

Consultants

Sarah Arthur
Ann Cover
Timothy Eberhart
Jacob Fasig
Susan Hay
MaryJane Pierce Norton

The Joy of the Small Church Setting

Welcome to Credo Confirmation for Small Churches. You are about to embark on a sacred journey in the life of your church, and our hope and prayer is that this resource will be your trusted partner along the way. The joy of the small church setting is that the young people have probably grown up together and have a built-in sense of community. They are also probably already plugged in to service roles throughout the church, because the small church needs everyone to do his or her part. Members of small churches are generally close-knit, often include multiple generations of families, and are there because they want to know and be known by other members. So the idea of dedicating some time to grow in faith, service, and community probably comes easily for small church families.

The Credo Confirmation for Small Churches curriculum is designed to meet the specific needs of churches with fewer than 150 members. In other words, this book should speak your language. Because many small churches have confirmation classes about once every 3–4 years, the session plans include activities suitable for a wide age range. In addition, activities have been adapted for groups of 5 or fewer young persons.

In order to create a deeper sense of community, invite mentors to attend each class session. Seek out a few co-teachers or older youth assistants to be part of the group. Try to get your group of confirmands and volunteers to at least 8 people total. This will help your confirmands feel like they're part of something bigger than simply a class that they have to take because they've reached a certain age.

Some smaller churches have partnered with other small United Methodist churches in the area to have joint confirmation classes. If you think that partnering is an option for your church, reach out to see what possibilities might exist for joint classes or retreats. In addition, seek out connections in the district and conference by participating in district and conference confirmation events. Partnering will help make the experience come alive for your group and will help confirmands see themselves as part of a larger community.

Your small church has an opportunity to make a big impact in the lives of your confirmands. Who knows, maybe one of them will be your pastor one day! Do all you can to create a sense of pilgrimage or rite of passage on this journey. Make it something more than their usual experience. Take them on an adventure of discipleship, community, fellowship, and worship.

Blessings as you begin!

Introduction and Core Principles

Before you do anything else, grab a copy of *The United Methodist Hymnal* and turn to page 33. Read the "Baptismal Covenant I," a service that many United Methodist congregations use to confirm young people who have completed the church's confirmation program. The service begins by describing confirmation as a "reaffirmation of our faith," a renewal of "the covenant declared at our baptism," an acknowledgment of "what God is doing for us," and an affirmation of "our commitment to Christ's holy church."

This statement gives a good overview of the goals of any confirmation program. Confirmation is an opportunity for young people to affirm the faith into which they were baptized and, for those who were baptized as infants or small children, to renew the baptismal vows taken for them by their parents or guardians. Confirmation also makes young people aware of how God is and has been at work in their lives, even before they were old enough to realize it. And confirmation affirms a new commitment—a new covenant relationship—between a young person and Christ's body, the church.

CORE PRINCIPLES

The CREDO (CREE-doh) confirmation program is grounded in these three core principles:

- Confirmation is the continuation of one's faith journey (a journey begun at baptism) and the beginning of one's covenant relationship with the church—not an end unto itself.
- Confirmation is more than just a series of classes. Confirmands must be fully engaged in the life of the church through worship, service, small groups, and involvement in other ministries.
- Confirmands should emerge from their confirmation experience prepared for a life of Christian discipleship.

CREDO reinforces the connection between baptism and confirmation. Confirmands will remember their baptism (or, if they have not yet been baptized, anticipate their baptism) and learn about the baptismal vows that they took, that they will take, or that were taken on their behalf. Confirmands will understand confirmation as a way to claim and affirm the work done by the Holy Spirit in their baptism.

EMPHASES

Instruction is an important and essential part of any confirmation program. Through confirmation, young people claim the faith of the church. They must have a familiarity with what Christians (and specifically United Methodist Christians) believe, value, and do. Thus CREDO provides session plans for confirmation classes. But instruction is only one aspect of the confirmation program. The confirmation vows not only hold confirmands accountable to certain beliefs but are also a way of life and a commitment to Christ's body, the church. In addition to learning about their faith, confirmands must also experience their faith and have a sense of how to live as a disciple of Christ in a covenant relationship with the church. They do this by attending and participating in weekly Sunday worship, by working alongside other Christians in service of God and neighbor, by participating in Christian education, by having relationships with other Christians that are grounded in mutual support and accountability, and by being engaged in the ministries of the church.

Christian education

Your confirmation program is an important Christian education ministry, but it is not likely the only education opportunity for young people. And it is impossible (yes, impossible) for a confirmand to learn everything he or she needs to know about the Bible, Christian faith, and Christian living before confirmation Sunday. Christian education is a lifelong endeavor, and young people should make Christian education a habit by participating in educational opportunities such as Sunday school classes, mid-week Bible study groups, and/or youth fellowship gatherings. If it is possible, your confirmands should be involved in at least one other Christian education setting while they are going through the confirmation program.

Mentoring relationships

Mentors should be adults with a mature faith who can set for young confirmands an example of how to grow in faith. Confirmands and their mentors should meet regularly for the duration of the confirmation program. Mentors are not teachers and need not be Bible experts or trained theologians. But they should be available to offer support and encouragement, to talk with confirmands about tough faith questions, and to discuss with confirmands the key teachings of the confirmation program. More comprehensive information on mentoring is available in the "Mentoring and Confirmation" section of this resource and in the book *Credo Confirmation Guide for Parents, Mentors, and Adult Leaders.*

Worship

Often when people talk about "going to church," they are talking about attending worship. While *worship* and *church* are not synonymous, worship is crucial to the life of the church and of each individual congregation. Worship is a way that we tell our story and pass down our beliefs and practices to subsequent generations; it is a way that Christians of all "ages, nations, and races" come together to express their common faith; and it is a way that we say yes to the God who said yes to us through our baptism. Being present each week in worship is an important way in which young people honor the commitment to the church, a commitment they make when they take their confirmation vows. It is important that young people get into the habit of attending worship while they are going through the confirmation program so that they will understand what is expected of them if they take the confirmation vows.

service

Although he was the Son of God and the Messiah, Jesus became a servant (see **Philippians 2:7**). He served others by healing, feeding, and teaching and by washing his disciples' feet. Following Jesus' example of service always has been an important part of Christian discipleship, and those who take the confirmation vows in The United Methodist Church vow to "faithfully participate in [the church's] ministries" by (among other things) their service. While the word *service* may bring to mind images of raking leaves or restoring homes (and while these activities are important), service is about more than just work projects. Young people in the church may serve as acolytes, ushers, or greeters during worship; they may serve God and neighbor by raising money for missions and ministries that meet needs in the community and around the world; they may serve members of the congregation by praying and worshiping with persons who are physically unable to attend Sunday worship; they may serve by helping to lead a vacation Bible school program for younger children; and they may get their hands dirty by participating in the aforementioned work projects. Confirmands must understand that service is an important part of Christian living, that those who are confirmed in The United Methodist Church take a vow of service, and that the service must be performed in a spirit of love for God and neighbor. To get in the habit of serving, confirmands should be expected to complete a certain number of service hours as part of the confirmation program.

retreats

The word *retreat* means to get away or to withdraw. And while retreats give us opportunities to withdraw from our normal routine, they also give us an opportunity to draw closer to God and to our fellow Christians. On retreats, young Christians can experience God and Christian community without the distractions of television, mobile phones, the Internet, schoolwork, and household obligations. CREDO recommends that every confirmand participate in at least one retreat.

sessions

Although CREDO emphasizes that confirmation is more than just a series of classes, confirmation class sessions are nonetheless a critical part of the confirmation experience. The 18 sessions in the CREDO program tell confirmands the story of our faith, teach them about core Christian beliefs and practices, explain to them distinct United Methodist emphases, and help them develop a faith vocabulary. These sessions fall into three units: "Know Your Story," "Confirm Your Faith," and "Live Your Commitment."

CREDO Goals

The underlying goals of CREDO are to prepare confirmands (if they choose) to take the confirmation vows and to live lives of Christian discipleship. More specifically, CREDO aims to:

- Teach confirmands the story of their faith, as contained in the Old and New Testaments and in the history and traditions of Christianity and The United Methodist Church.
- Give confirmands a basic understanding of Christian theology, including the doctrine of the Trinity, creation, sin, and grace.
- Teach confirmands the traditions and doctrinal emphases that make United Methodism unique.
- Foster relationships between confirmands and Christian adults in the congregation who can set an example of how to live as a mature Christian.
- Give confirmands an understanding of the importance of Christian education as a lifelong endeavor, and help confirmands develop a habit of participating in Christian education.
- Give confirmands an understanding of Christian worship as practiced in The United Methodist Church and why worship is an essential part of Christian discipleship.
- Challenge confirmands to serve God and others through the life and ministry of the congregation.
- Give confirmands an opportunity to go on retreats, withdrawing from their normal routine and drawing closer to God and their fellow Christians.
- Teach confirmands about the vows they will have an opportunity to take and the commitments that one makes when one says yes to those vows.

Credo Components

In addition to this book, Credo offers the following print and electronic resources to help you achieve for your small church the goals listed on page 11:

CREDO CONFIRMATION STUDENT JOURNAL

The *Credo Confirmation Student Journal* is not a traditional classroom student book. Instead of providing confirmands pen-and-paper activities to complete in the classroom, it encourages them to develop habits of prayer and devotion. The Student Journal includes a devotional reading and journaling questions related to each confirmation class session. In the days following each class session, confirmands should read that session's devotion and spend time reflecting on and/or writing in response to the journaling questions. Confirmands also should discuss their reflections and writings with their confirmation mentor.

CREDO
achievement
Know your story...
Confirm your faith,
Live your commitment
Confirmation Journal

The Credo Confirmation Student Journal also challenges confirmands to write a credo, or statement of belief, as they go through the confirmation program. After each session, they will complete a sentence that summarizes their belief about what they learned in that session. Taken together, these sentences will be a written affirmation of the confirmands' faith.

CREDO CONFIRMATION GUIDE FOR PARENTS, MENTORS, AND ADULT LEADERS

Confirmation is not just a personal rite. It involves the families of the confirmands and the entire congregation. For many Christians faith formation begins at home. And while the congregation strives to nurture young Christians in the faith, parents and/or guardians provide many of these fledgling disciples day-to-day support. But parents are by no means alone in this effort. Each confirmand should have a confirmation mentor, an adult in the congregation with whom he or she will meet regularly throughout the confirmation process (and possibly beyond). Other adults in the congregation who work with confirmands, such as youth and children's ministers, Sunday school teachers, and music ministers, also play important roles in the confirmands' faith development. And, of course, as those being confirmed stand before the congregation on Confirmation Sunday, the entire congregation vows to "Do all in [its] power to increase *their* faith, confirm *their* hope, and perfect *them* in love" (*The United Methodist Hymnal*, page 43)

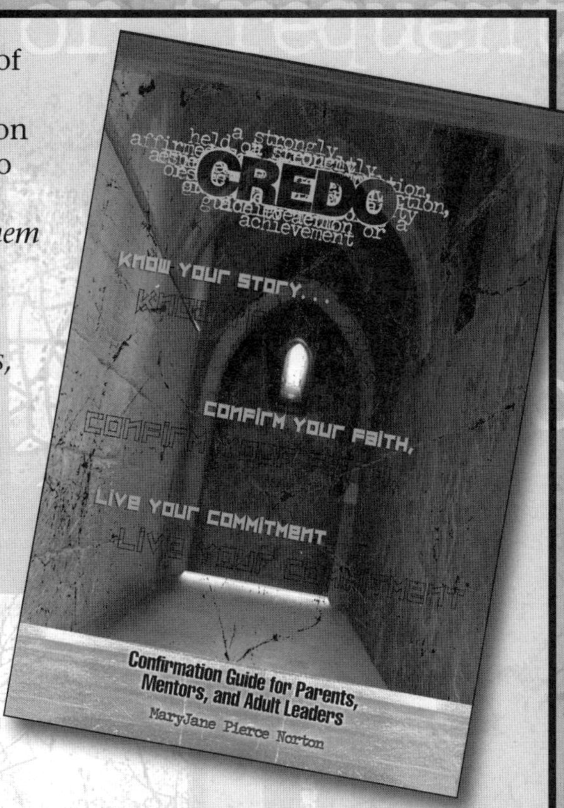

The *Credo Confirmation Guide for Parents, Mentors, and Adult Leaders* gives these adults information about what confirmands are learning and experiencing in their confirmation classes so that they can have meaningful conversations about topics such as grace and redemption and the Wesleyan quadrilateral. The book also provides valuable information about adolescent development as it relates to faith formation.

CREDO ADULT LEADER WEBSITE

www.credoconfirmation.com

The Credo Confirmation website at *www.credoconfirmation.com* has all of the reproducible handouts and additional information and activities related to the sessions and retreats that you will need. Prior to each session, make sure to print out the handouts and have them ready for your session.

The site also provides activities for the confirmands that will reinforce what they have learned in the sessions. Check the site for updates and for information about additional Credo confirmation resources.

Covenant and Expectations

Before your confirmation program begins, establish a confirmation covenant with your confirmands and their parents. A sample covenant is available at *www.credoconfirmation.com.* Be clear about the expectations that confirmands must meet and how these expectations relate to the confirmation vows.

SUGGESTED EXPECTATIONS FOR CONFIRMATION

attend all confirmation classes

While circumstances inevitably will arise that cause some confirmands to miss an occasional class (such as family emergencies), all participants and their parents need to understand that anyone wishing to be confirmed must make confirmation a priority. Be clear to families of confirmands that attendance is not optional. If a confirmand cannot attend a class because of an emergency, work with the confirmand, along with his or her parents and mentor, to make sure he or she gets any information that was missed.

attend worship each sunday

Weekly worship is the most comprehensive way in which a congregation rehearses its faith and is recharged by God. Those wishing to take the confirmation vows and enter into a covenant with the body of Christ and with your congregation need to attend worship for most, if not all, of the Sundays for the duration of the confirmation program. While it is best for the confirmands to worship with the congregation in which they are being confirmed, it is more important that they develop weekly worship habits. If a confirmand splits time between two parents who attend two different churches, it is OK if he or she worships with one congregation one week and with another congregation the next. It also is OK for confirmands who are spending a weekend at the home of a friend or out-of-town family member to attend worship with their hosts. Consider requiring confirmands to attend worship at least three Sundays per month (allowing for exceptions in the case of family emergencies).

meet regularly with a mentor

You can find information on recruiting and training mentors in the "Mentoring and Confirmation" section of this resource. Be sure to adhere to your congregation or annual conference's Safe Sanctuaries standards where mentoring relationships are concerned. Also consider having confirmands and their mentors sit together in worship at least once per month.

Participate in a Christian Education Setting Other Than Confirmation

This may not be possible if your confirmation classes meet during the Sunday school hour and your congregation has no other education opportunities for confirmation-age youth. (If this is the case, you might consider launching a mid-week small group ministry.) If your confirmation classes meet on Sunday afternoon or evening or during the week (and if your congregation offers Sunday school classes for confirmation-age youth), confirmands should get in the habit of attending Sunday school each week. Consider requiring confirmands to attend Sunday school at least three Sundays per month, possibly with the option of substituting a mid-week Bible study.

Fulfill a Service Requirement

Service should be completed through the ministries of the congregation and can include participating in traditional service projects, helping with ministries to homeless and/or hungry persons, assisting with vacation Bible school, or serving as an acolyte or other worship leader. The number of service hours you require will vary depending on the length of your program. But 20 hours over the course of a school year is a good requirement.

Attend a Retreat and the Prayer Lock-In

Getting away from routines and familiar settings provides valuable opportunities for deep spiritual reflection and an intimate connection with God and others. This resource provides a confirmation retreat plan as well as a prayer-focused lock-in. Many United Methodist annual conferences and districts also host confirmation retreats that your group may be able to participate in. Make sure that your confirmation schedule includes either the retreat included here or a conference retreat so that your class gets the benefit of concentrated time away focused on their growing discipleship.

Confirmation Class Sessions and Scope and Sequence

TEACHING OBJECTIVES

CREDO includes lesson plans for 18 confirmation class sessions. These sessions are designed around 3 primary teaching objectives:

- Give confirmands a basic knowledge and understanding of the Christian story, beginning with Creation then the introduction of sin and evil into the world, reaching its climax with redemption through Christ's death and resurrection, and continuing—through the Holy Spirit and the church—into the present day and beyond. The "Know Your Story" unit deals mainly with this objective.
- Teach confirmands about the core beliefs, practices, and emphases of United Methodist Christians. The "Confirm Your Faith" unit deals mainly with this objective.
- Explore with confirmands the vows that they will take if they choose to be confirmed so that they understand the commitment they will be making and the expectations that come with being confirmed as a professing member of The United Methodist Church. The "Live Your Commitment" unit deals mainly with this objective.

SESSION STRUCTURE

Opening Ritual

Each session begins with an opening ritual based on **John 15:1-11.** Before classes begin, work with the confirmands to create a vine or tree trunk. You may do this by drawing or painting the vine or trunk on a wall or a large sheet of paper; or you might create a three-dimensional vine or trunk using wood or other building materials. As much as possible, allow the confirmands to guide the process; encourage them to be creative.

During the sessions in the "Know Your Story" unit, confirmands will add branches to the vine or trunk; during the "Confirm Your Faith" unit, they will add leaves; during the "Live Your Commitment" unit, they will add fruit. They will write on the branches, leaves, and fruit something they have gained from the confirmation experience. Branches may be drawn or painted or may be fashioned from sticks or dowels; leaves and fruit may be drawn or painted, cut from colored paper, or purchased from craft stores. Leaf and fruit patterns abound on the Internet.

ACTIVITIES

Each of the 18 confirmation class session plans includes about 2 hours worth of teaching-and-learning activities. The activities are divided into 3 sections: "What?" "So What?" and "Now What?" The "What?" activities introduce the topic of the session. The "So What?" activities explore why the topic is relevant for United Methodist Christians. The "Now What?" activities look at how confirmands may apply and respond to what they have learned. Additional activities and options are available at *www.credoconfirmation.com.*

CLOSING RITUAL

Each session concludes with a closing prayer in which each participant has the opportunity to say a prayer of thanks for something that he or she has learned or experienced during that session or some other aspect of the confirmation program. The closing ritual ends by using John Wesley's Rule as a benediction:

Do all the good you can,
By all the means you can,
In all the ways you can,
In all the places you can,
At all the times you can,
To all the people you can,
As long as ever you can.

While there is no evidence that this rule originated with John Wesley, it has been a popular saying among United Methodists for many years and is a great summary of how to live our lives in response to Wesley's second General Rule, "Do good."

SCOPE AND SEQUENCE

KNOW YOUR STORY

- **Creation** looks at God the Father and Creator, the implications of our being created in God's image, and the implications of all things being God's handiwork.
- **Sin** explores how God's good Creation was tainted by sin and brokenness and how sin is present in the world today.
- **Redemption** looks at God the Son and Redeemer and how God is always doing the work of redeeming a broken world.
- **Holy Spirit** looks at God the Holy Spirit and Sustainer and the movement of the Holy Spirit through Scripture and the history of the church and into our lives today.
- **Church** tells the story of Christ's body, the church, and discusses what it means to be part of the universal church, The United Methodist Church, and a local congregation
- **New Creation** looks at how individuals and all of creation are and will be made new in Christ.

Confirm Your Faith

- **Way of Discipleship** looks to devotion, worship, compassion, and justice as a road map for Christian living.
- **Way of Salvation** explores the way of salvation in the United Methodist tradition—prevenient grace, justifying grace, and sanctifying grace.
- **Wesleyan Quadrilateral** introduces the four Wesleyan tools of discernment, as identified by Albert Outler—Scripture, tradition, experience, and reason.
- **Worship:** discusses the who, why, how, where, and with whom of worship
- **Sacraments:** takes a close look at baptism and Holy Communion.
- **Living a Holy Life:** explores holiness, sanctification, and Christian perfection.

Live Your Commitment

- **Renounce, Reject, Repent:** Do you renounce the spiritual forces of wickedness, reject the evil powers of this world, and repent of your sin?
- **Accept:** Do you accept the freedom and power God gives you to resist evil, injustice, and oppression in whatever forms they present themselves?
- **Confess:** Do you confess Jesus Christ as your Savior, put your whole trust in his grace, and promise to serve him as your Lord, in union with the church which Christ has opened to people of all ages, nations, and races?
- **I Believe (The Creeds)** focuses on the Apostles' Creed (part of the confirmation vows), the creed the confirmands will have written in their student journals, and assorted other statements of faith.
- **PPGSW:** As members of this congregation, will you faithfully participate in its ministries by your prayers, your presence, your gifts, your service, and your witness?
- **Going Forth:** May the God of all grace, who has called us to eternal glory in Christ, establish you and strengthen you by the power of the Holy Spirit, that you may live in grace and peace.

Confirmation Class Scheduling Options

18 Sessions in 36 Weeks (a School Year)

Each of the 18 sessions includes about 2 hours worth of teaching activities, You may divide each session into two 1-hour classes. A note at the midway point of each session plan tells you where to break if you choose to split the session into 2 classes. Dividing each session gives you the option of doing 1 class per week for 36 weeks. This option works well for groups that do confirmation classes during Sunday school over the course of a school year (which is approximately 36 weeks).

18 Sessions in 18 Weeks

If you prefer to do confirmation during a single season (such as in the fall or in the spring), your classes may meet each week for 18 weeks and for approximately 2 hours per week.

18 Sessions for Sunday School and Youth Group

If your class if made up of the members of your youth group and youth Sunday school class, you may want to break up the 18 sessions into one hour each. The first hour of the session would be taught in Sunday school. The second hour could be taught in part of your youth group time. A note at the midway point of each session plan tells you where to break if you choose to split the session into 2 classes.

6 Sessions per Season for 1 Year

With this model, classes would meet for 6 weeks in the fall, 6 weeks in the winter, and 6 weeks in the spring.

6 Sessions per Retreat

If you choose to take your confirmands out of a traditional classroom setting, you may turn each 6-session unit into a weekend retreat. Resources for putting these retreats together are available on the Credo website.

Christian Education and Confirmation

By Tim Gossett

Expectations for Christian Education

Confirmands should participate in a Christian education setting in addition to confirmation class. This might not be possible if your confirmation classes meet during the Sunday school hour and your congregation has no other education opportunities for confirmation-age youth. (If this is the case, you might consider launching a mid-week Bible study.) If your confirmation classes meet on Sunday afternoon or evening or during the week (and if your congregation offers Sunday school classes for confirmation-age youth), confirmands should get in the habit of attending Sunday school each week. Consider requiring confirmands to attend Sunday school at least three Sundays per month, possibly with the option of substituting a mid-week Bible study.

A comic strip years ago poked fun at the state of Christian education in the life of the church; and sadly, the state is little changed. In the first panel, the pastor stands before the congregation, facing a group of about a dozen young youth and saying to the worshipers, "This morning, we recognize our confirmands. . . ." In the second panel, which flashes forward to a similar scene a few years later, the pastor says, "This morning, we recognize our graduates. . . ." Finally, in the third panel, the pastor looks down and sees before him only two youth, neither of whom he recognizes any longer.

The comic strip's point is unfortunately true of many congregations. Following confirmation, many youth seem to disappear from the life of the church. Perhaps the promises youth make at confirmation are empty ones, as if they had their fingers crossed behind their backs as they took their confirmation vows. But more likely, families, congregations, and the youth themselves misunderstood the purpose of confirmation and its place in the Christian life. Simply put, confirmation is not the end of the faith formation journey but just one stepping stone along a lifelong path. When he or she is confirmed, a young person should be confirming a faith that has been nurtured over time and that will continue to be nurtured throughout that young person's life.

Confirmation and Other Youth Education Ministries

Take some time to map out all of the ways that the youth in your confirmation program are involved in the life of the church, and, particularly, in education ministries (Sunday school, youth fellowship, Bible studies, camps, vacation Bible school, and so forth). List everything you can think of, from the obvious ongoing activities to less obvious ones, such as helping in the nursery, taking a leadership role in the Easter sunrise service, or going on a church-sponsored trip to an amusement park.

If you gave this exercise careful consideration, you probably became aware that your congregation ministers to confirmation-age youth in several ways, even if your church doesn't have a formal youth ministry. All of the adults in the congregation are involved in educating confirmation-age youth, even if they are unaware of the roles that they play. Here are some ways that you can help the congregation understand these roles:

- Introduce the confirmands to the congregation toward the beginning of the confirmation process.
- Add the members of the confirmation class to the prayer lists in your church bulletin or newsletter and/or on the church website.
- Remind your congregation's ministry teams to create youth-friendly events as they do their planning.
- Occasionally mention in a sermon the confirmation mentors and the roles they play.
- Encourage members of the congregation to learn the names of the youth and children sitting near them during worship.
- Post in your church building promotional materials related to confirmation and other youth events.
- Make sure that the adult leaders involved more directly in educating the youth in your church—Sunday school teachers, youth fellowship volunteers, Bible study leaders, youth choir directors, and so on—are communicating with one another. These adult leaders need to be supportive of one another's ministries and should discuss information such as what they're studying or discussing with the youth, important dates, and concerns about the youth.

Christian Education Doesn't Start and End With Confirmation

Education is an essential part of any confirmation program. Confirmands should learn the story of their faith, as told in Scripture and in the history and tradition of the church; they should learn the core doctrines of Christianity and of The United Methodist Church; and they should learn spiritual practices and what it means to live a life of Christian discipleship. But it is unfair to expect young people to learn during confirmation classes everything they need to know about the Bible, the Christian faith, and Christian living. Christian education is a lifetime endeavor, and confirmation is an opportunity to help confirmands develop lifelong learning habits.

One way to help confirmands make a long-term commitment to Christian education is to encourage or require participation in other education ministries as well. If your confirmation class sessions meet during the evening or on Sunday afternoon, you could require or expect the confirmands regularly attend Sunday school. (You would need to make exceptions or provide alternatives for confirmands who split time between their divorced parents.) If your confirmation class sessions meet during the Sunday school hour, you might require participation in youth fellowship or a midweek Bible study.

Regardless of your arrangement, it is important that your congregation see confirmation as part of its larger Christian education ministry. Those involved in planning and teaching children's Sunday school classes should consider how they are preparing children for confirmation. Each person working with youth should try to build on what youth learned in confirmation and should seek opportunities to make connections between what youth are learning in Sunday school or youth group and what they learned during confirmation. Even adult Sunday school classes and Bible studies can revisit the confirmation vows. The church can provide confirmation opportunities for adults as well. After all, there is not designated age for confirmation; and in the United Methodist tradition, confirmation is a repeatable rite.

DEVELOPMENTAL CHARACTERISTICS OF YOUTH

While confirmation may seem to be a unique learning experience that is separate from other formational experiences for youth, it is not. Confirmation leaders, like Sunday school teachers and youth fellowship leaders, benefit from a familiarity with sound educational principles and adolescent development.

Your approach to teaching confirmation should be developed with attention to the characteristics of the group you are teaching. Younger youth (early adolescents) and older youth (middle adolescents) are at different stages of cognitive, physical, and social development. You'll have the best learning environment possible if you tailor your teaching to the needs of your group members. Take a few minutes to reflect on the chart on page 23, noting your own thoughts and observations about the implications of each row for your setting.

Role of a Confirmation Leader

In many congregations, confirmation falls outside of the youth and children's ministry departments. Thus some confirmation leaders—including confirmation mentors—have little engagement with other youth or children's ministries. Training adults involved in confirmation to be ministers and educators of young people is essential to a successful confirmation program. Here are a few things for confirmation leaders to know and discuss:

Leaders do not need to be experts in the Bible nor live a saint-like life, but they should have a passion for growing in their faith and in their knowledge of Scripture. It's entirely OK for a leader to say in response to a question about the Bible, "I don't know the answer to that question. Let's find the answer together." The youth should see in the faith lives of confirmation leaders evidence that they have matured beyond their own confirmation experience have committed themselves to continual spiritual growth.

Great confirmation leaders are great listeners. They pay attention to what confirmands are actually saying (verbally and nonverbally) and aren't inwardly focused on what their next question will be. They understand that they do not have to fill up silence by restating a question or providing the answer but, instead, are willing to wait patiently for youth to think about their answers to questions.

Leaders maintain appropriate boundaries with youth. This includes following appropriate Safe Sanctuaries policies adopted by the congregation, such as never meeting one-on-one with a youth or child in a room without a window or behind a closed door, having a background check done on all adult workers with children and youth, making sure that at least two adults (unrelated to each other) are always present during classes or events, and not driving with only one youth in the car. It also means being sensitive to the emotional boundaries of youth during conversations.

Leaders are not youth with a few extra years, inches, and pounds added on. In other words, adults should not try to be cool or to act like teens in order to try to gain acceptance by youth. Adults should act like adults. That *does not* mean that adults cannot have and display a youthful spirit, a joyous and fun-loving personality, an enjoyment of the things youth like, or a great sense of humor. Instead, it's a recognition that they have accepted a leadership role and will make decisions that keep the youth's best interests at heart.

Developmental Characteristics of Youth

YOUNGER YOUTH (12–14)	OLDER YOUTH (15–17)
Vary widely in growth patterns and sexual maturity, both between and within gender groups	Less range of differences in size and physical maturation
Rapid physical growth means appearance and coordination changes; are easily embarrassed by their bodies	Body image and appeal is of significant concern; eating disorders can develop
Are concerned with justice (fairness) and equality; are beginning to think abstractly, but still think largely in concrete, literal, either-or terms.	Have a greater ability than younger youth to understand moral and ethical complexity; think abstractly
Understand cause and effect, and are growing in their ability to use logic to solve problems	Like to demonstrate their acquired knowledge
Can imagine consequences for their actions	Can see issues from multiple perspectives
Desire to visit places beyond their own community	Desire to understand and visit other countries
Have a greater attention span than they did as children and are ready for in-depth, long-term engaging experiences	Generally have longer attention spans than younger youth, but lose patience quickly with activities they deem pointless
Are developing an interest in the opposite sex and want to engage with and understand each other	Seek emotional and physical intimacy with others
Their peers are their second family, and they greatly desire peer approval	Peers are still important, but service to others, beyond their peer group, is also valued
Are beginning to question authority and family or church values	See adults—including adults in positions of authority—as fallible, yet desire their respect
Prefer coming up with their own ideas and solutions to going along with ready-made ones	Wish to take on leadership roles
Are the center of their own universe	Less self-centered than younger youth; try on multiple roles and ways of being in the world
Strive for independence yet understand they need the help of adults	Are identifying their unique gifts and searching for possible vocations
Desire privacy from parents and other adults	More freely reveal their thoughts and feelings to adults than do younger youth
Are frequently forgetful and prone to making poor decisions	Can be responsible with money, jobs, and so on; but judgment and decision-making skills vary greatly among older youth
Often feel all-knowing, invulnerable, and powerful	Understand better than younger youth the fragility of all life

Leaders need to communicate with the parents or guardians of the youth—not just with the youth themselves. For example, leaders should always copy the parents when sending e-mail or text messages to set up times and places to meet. Information about schedule additions or changes should be sent to the parents and not simply mentioned to the youth.

Aspects of Faith Development

Just as one passes through various phases of physical development, one also passes through different phases of faith development. But there is one significant difference between the two: Whereas physical development largely (but not entirely) is the result of genetics and age and tends to occur at a similar rate in most people, spiritual development depends on God's grace—and how one responds to God's grace—and is different for every person. One can get stuck in a particular phase of faith development or can even revert to a previous stage.

Those who study spiritual growth have described the stages of faith development in different ways. Perhaps the best-known way of identifying faith stages comes from James Fowler, in his book *Stages of Faith: The Psychology of Human Development and the Quest for Meaning*. Another important assessment of phases of spiritual maturity comes from John Westerhoff's *Will Our Children Have Faith?* Both Fowler and Westerhoff offer descriptions of faith development that are very useful in understanding the way one's faith changes over time, but Westerhoff's model is simpler and better suited for Credo. He describes four primary stages of faith development:

1. **Experienced Faith** is common during the younger years of childhood and mainly involves the imitation of actions. For example, a child may pray the Lord's Prayer without grasping the full meaning of all of the words. Because young children are dependent on their families, there is a sense of faith identity that forms related to the family.

2. **Affiliative Faith** is common in older childhood and the early adolescent years. Here the dominant characteristic is belonging to a group, and behavior centers around imitation of the group. The individual identifies with a faith community where he or she feels a sense of belonging and in which his or her beliefs and actions are rooted. You may find that many confirmands—especially at the start of the confirmation journey—display characteristics of affiliative faith.

3. **Searching Faith** becomes more common in late adolescence and is connected with the formation of identity. A youth begins an internal and external dialogue, asking, "Is this what I believe? Why, or why not?" Youth or adults at this stage do not blindly accept what others have said to them, because they need to find certainty for themselves. This stage of faith adds a cognitive dimension to a person's faith journey, and a person going through the stage of Searching Faith begins to integrate head and heart.

   Because Searching Faith is a common faith stage for confirmands, it is important to understand more about it. This questioning stage generally goes one of two ways. Some persons question the tenets of faith, the validity of the Bible, the teachings of the church, or the differences between denominations and faith systems; and they decide they can no longer believe. Youth who make such a decision might drop out of confirmation. Some youth will remain at this stage, becoming adults with an immature faith. Some become vulnerable to cults or decide that they wish to become part of another church group (especially if their friends attend elsewhere). But many—especially those who have a companion on the journey—will successfully grow through this stage and will move on to the final stage.

4. **Owned Faith,** as Westerhoff defines it, is rare until early adulthood. It can come about only as a result of growing through Searching Faith. After wrestling with the question, "Is this what I believe?" one can resolve that question for oneself. Owned faith is a strong, vital faith that one lives by, expresses to others, and would even be willing to die for. Growing into this stage of faith does not mean that one stops having or asking questions but, instead, that one has learned to embrace questions as a means to further and deepen one's spiritual connection with God and others.

CONFIRMATION AND FAMILY LIFE

Youth spend far more time with parents than with confirmation leaders and other adults they know through church. Parents and guardians have a greater influence on the lives of confirmands than the confirmation experience does. Since parents and guardians vary widely in their commitment to the Christian faith, you have no guarantee that additional faith formation happens within the home.

On the bright side, the fact that a parent requires, allows, and/or supports his or her teenager's involvement in confirmation can be his or her entry point into greater participation in the life of the church. Even if parents are not involved in the life of the congregation or have not matured in their faith, the confirmation experience of their adolescent children can spark dialogue within the family about matters of faith. Confirmation also is a time when parents tend to be more open than usual to the church's guidance when it comes to nurturing their children's faith.

Keys to Increase Parent Involvement in Confirmation

- Give parents faith formation resources: devotional guides, family talk sheets, and so forth.
- Encourage families to do a family service project—on their own or with other families—during the confirmation process.
- Offer a parallel confirmation class for the confirmands' parents and guardians.
- Let parents know that at any time they may visit with you about the confirmation program and their teen's experience.
- Encourage parents to pray for their confirmand and the confirmation class as a whole, and give parents an example of how to do this.

CHRISTIAN EDUCATION AND CONFIRMATION

While confirmands learn a great deal in confirmation classes, on confirmation retreats, and through other aspects of your confirmation program, they should emerge from confirmation with the understanding that Confirmation Sunday is not a graduation from Christian education. Christian education is important to a life of Christian discipleship. It provides opportunities for acquiring knowledge, questioning and articulating one's beliefs, and fellowship with Christian friends.

Congregations and confirmation leaders must create a culture in which Christian education is a practice that spans a lifetime. They can do this by making available Sunday school classes and/or other educational opportunities by people of all ages, by giving young children a solid biblical foundation so that they are prepared for confirmation as youth, and by helping youth and adults retain and build on what they learned and experienced in confirmation.

Mentoring and Confirmation

One of the primary goals of any confirmation program is to equip and inspire young people to devote themselves to lives of Christian discipleship. We do this by telling the story of our faith, introducing young people to essential Christian beliefs and practices, inviting young people to enter into a covenant relationship with the church, and making clear what will be expected of them as professing members of The United Methodist Church. But one of the most effective ways to prepare confirmands for a life of discipleship is to foster relationships between the confirmands and adults in the church who are striving to be faithful disciples.

EXPECTATIONS FOR MENTORING RELATIONSHIPS

Confirmands should meet regularly with a mentor. You can find information on recruiting and training mentors in this section of this resource. Be sure to adhere to your congregation or annual conference's Safe Sanctuaries standards where mentoring relationships are concerned. Also consider having confirmands and their mentors sit together in worship at least once each month.

In recent decades, many congregations have made mentoring part of their confirmation program. Generally, program leaders pair each confirmand with an adult from the congregation who is not his or her parent or close relative; or they assign one or more adults to a small group of confirmands. While mentors certainly provide leadership, they usually are not part of the leadership team in charge of teaching confirmation classes or leading retreats. Rather, they lead by walking alongside youth, offering emotional support, being present with the youth during confirmation classes and retreats, and being available to discuss with youth tough questions about faith.

WHOM SHOULD WE RECRUIT AS MENTORS?

Mentors should be persons with a mature faith. This does not mean that they have to be perfect Christians or that they cannot have doubts. It also doesn't mean that they have to be biblical scholars, trained theologians, or pastoral counselors. It does mean that they are committed to growing in faith, are striving to be holy, and can be honest and open about their faith.

Mentors need to love and care for the youth with whom they work, but they need to relate as adults to these youth. Some adults who work with youth fall into the trap of trying to act like youth. But no adult should see ministry with young people as an opportunity to relive his or her teenage years. As John Gooch writes in *Claiming the Name: A Theological and Practical Overview of Confirmation,* "Youth don't need more 'pals.' They need someone who is willing to relate to them as an adult."

Your congregation may already have mentors in place. Many congregations pair children with faith friends when they begin kindergarten or first grade. If children have continued these relationships, it makes sense for faith friends to become confirmation mentors. Ideally, these relationships can continue throughout the adolescent years. John Gooch suggests that every young person should have godparents who are members of the congregation. Traditionally, godparents make a commitment, upon a child's baptism, to nurture that child in faith. In cases where parents name as godparents friends or relatives who live in another state or attend another congregation, Gooch suggests that each young person have a second pair of godparents who are part of the congregation. He says that, if we really take seriously the Baptismal Covenant, it makes sense to have godparents serve as mentors for young people from baptism, through confirmation and adolescence, and into adulthood.

Karen Kluever, a youth pastor and confirmation leader at Woodland United Methodist Church in Rock Hill, South Carolina, pairs each of her confirmands with a "grandfriend," an older adult mentor/Christian friend. Some people feel as though ministry to young people is the domain of twenty- and thirty-somethings. Involving older adults affirms for an older generation that the spiritual formation of youth is a multigenerational endeavor.

You can find additional information on mentoring models at *www.credoconfirmation.com*. Prayerfully consider which arrangement would best facilitate the spiritual growth of and would most honor the spiritual gifts of your confirmands and mentors.

Having youth meet with a single adult mentor raises safety concerns. While you should have complete confidence in the mentors you recruit and have faith that they would not harm a youth with whom they have a mentoring relationship, *Safe Sanctuaries for Youth* (a resource produced by the General Board of Discipleship of The United Methodist Church) warns, "Abusers thrive on secrecy, isolation, and their ability to manipulate their victims." It adds, "When abusers know that they will never have a chance to be alone with potential victims, they quickly lose interest in working with youth" (page 38).

To ensure that an adult mentor will never be alone with youth, require mentors to meet with youth in public places, such as restaurants or in an open space in the church. Also do not allow mentors to drive youth anywhere unless there is another adult in the car. Similar principles apply to mentor-youth conversions by phone, text-message, social-networking sites, and e-mail. Having two adults work as a mentoring team greatly reduces the risk of abuse, especially if those adults are not related. Regardless of your mentoring arrangements, you should screen potential adult mentors by doing a criminal background check. This may seem extreme, but it is one of the most effective ways to prevent abuse. (For more information on safety see the *Credo Confirmation Guide for Parents, Mentors, and Other Adult Leaders* or visit the *Safe Sanctuaries* website at *www.gbod.org/safesanctuaries*.)

Older youth who have been already confirmed also may play a mentoring role. Younger youth benefit greatly from relationships with older adolescents who have continued to grow in faith in the few years since they took their confirmation vows. These former confirmands set a positive example of how to stay faithful to one's relationship with Christ and the church during the teenage years; they also act as a reminder that confirmation is not an end unto itself but is one important step along one's faith journey. Many confirmation programs have involved older youth with great success. (Michael Ratliff, Associate General Secretary of the Division on Ministries With Young People, when he was in local church ministry, referred to his older youth confirmation helpers as "ex-cons.") But older teens should act as mentors in addition to, not in place of, adult mentors.

WHAT SHOULD MENTORS DO?

Simply put, mentors should walk with confirmands on the confirmation journey. Mentors should be visibly present during the confirmation experience, should be familiar with what the confirmands are learning and experiencing, and should stand with confirmands during the rite of confirmation.

Mentors should also be part of the confirmation leadership team, and they should be clear about what is expected of them. You might ask that they attend all of the confirmation class sessions or that they participate in a confirmation retreat. You might ask that they meet weekly or bi-weekly with their confirmand(s) or that they sit with their confirmand(s) each Sunday in worship. Expectations of mentors will vary from congregation to congregation, but it is essential that these expectations are clear and that mentors are thoroughly involved in the confirmation experience.

Mentors need to know that they are not teachers. They likely will learn as much from the youth as the youth learn from them. Instead of imparting knowledge, mentors should show support, invite questions, and be available to listen. They should take seriously all of the doubts, concerns, and struggles of the young person(s) with whom they are in relationship. Mentors should be honest about their faith, without passing judgment; they should be loving, without excusing bad behavior. Most important, they should set for confirmands an example of Christian discipleship.

More information on the role of mentors is available in the *Credo Confirmation Guide for Parents, Mentors, and Adult Leaders*.

HOW DO WE TRAIN MENTORS?

The first step in training mentors is to help them understand the importance of the ministry they are involved in. Confirmation is the affirmation of the faith into which a person was baptized and is a crucial step along a young person's spiritual journey. Agreeing to serve as a confirmation mentor is not a responsibility that one should take lightly.

Gather your mentors and introduce them to the confirmation program. Give each of them a copy of the *Credo Confirmation Guide for Parents, Mentors, and Adult Leaders*. Discuss with them the theology behind confirmation and the place of confirmation in The United Methodist Church. Go over the various components of the CREDO program, and take the mentors through the scope and sequence of the confirmation class sessions found in the book's introduction and on the website. Explain to the mentors their role in the confirmation experience and the expectations that you (and the confirmands and parents) have for them. Address risk management issues, and go over your congregation and/or youth ministry's safety policies. Incorporate a time of worship and devotion into this gathering, praying with mentors and allowing them time to reflect on this ministry to which they have been called. Consider providing dinner for this gathering, and be sure to provide childcare.

Develop a confirmation covenant for the mentors to sign that again explains their role and the expectations you have for them and that also lists dos and don'ts related to safety and boundaries (such as, "If you meet one-on-one with a confirmand, be sure that you are in a public place"). A sample covenant for mentors is available at *www.credoconfirmation.com.*

Throughout the confirmation experience, check in with mentors to see how they are doing, to answer any questions they may have (whether about their role or about theology or Scripture), and to see how you and other adult leaders can help them. Always make sure that mentors know that they are valued and important and that you support them in their ministry.

Resources for Mentors

Each mentor should have a copy of the *Credo Confirmation Guide for Parents Mentors, and Adult Leaders* (ISBN: 9781426706271). This book helps mentors understand their role, provides valuable information about adolescent faith development, and gives summaries and discussion questions for each confirmation class session.

The CREDO website at *www.credoconfirmation.com* has additional resources related to mentors.

Worship and Confirmation

By Taylor Burton-Edwards
Director of Worship Resources
The General Board of Discipleship

Your confirmands likely have thoughts and feelings about worship, whether they grew up worshiping in your congregation, have recently come to your congregation after worshiping elsewhere, or are new to the church altogether. Some who have spent a week at church camp, who attend parochial schools, or who have had the opportunity to worship with several congregations have experienced worship in a wide variety of styles and settings.

One can hope that your confirmands can identify worship experiences or parts of your congregation's worship services that they enjoy and in which they have found a meaningful connection with God. Chances are, some youth will have no problem naming aspects of worship that they find boring or annoying. Maybe the music feels outdated, the prayers don't connect with them, the sermons don't answer the question they've been asking, or the Scripture readings seem either mumbled or overdone. Maybe the youth don't care for the music of the choir or the praise band, or they get frustrated by the lag between when the PowerPoint® slides are supposed to appear and when they actually do.

There are a lot of ways worship can miss its marks. And when worship misses those marks enough, it's easy to tune out or not attend worship at all. But that would be to presume that the point of Christian worship is satisfying the individual worshiper. It's not. It's about God and what God is doing with and through all of us, especially those who—as confirmands—are saying yes in answer to the yes that God said to them in the covenant of baptism.

It is possible that worship hasn't clicked for some of your confirmands because it has felt to them like a series of seemingly irrelevant, disconnected, or even random acts of introspection and group excitement. But there is a deep logic that underlies the basic pattern of Christian worship and informs everything we do there. We see this logic at work in the baptismal covenant that is the basis of our confirmation vows.

THE BAPTISMAL COVENANT AND THE BASIC PATTERN OF CHRISTIAN WORSHIP

The basic pattern of our Christian worship, from the earliest days, can be described as a drama in four acts. In Act I, Entrance, we gather from many places and assemble ourselves as the body of Christ to offer ourselves in praise and thanksgiving to God.

In Act II, Proclamation and Response, we hear Scripture read and proclaimed; and we respond with affirmations of faith and prayers for the church and the world.

In Act III, Thanksgiving and Communion, we present ourselves to God as a living sacrifice, with gifts of bread and cup, and receive them back again as body and blood of Christ.

And in Act IV, Sending Forth, we are sent into the world to live more faithfully as disciples of Jesus. (See *The United Methodist Hymnal,* page 2.)

If that pattern is practiced well, the flow of one act into another comes to "feel right" over time. But we don't worship just to keep the flow going. We don't even worship for the sake of the drama as a whole. Rather, we worship because we know that, through the drama and each of its four acts, we are participating in a living, active reminder of God's yes and our desire to keep saying yes. In other words, through Christian worship, we rehearse God's covenant with us in baptism and find ourselves recharged to live more faithfully into this covenant.

The Entrance act of worship is more than just a beginning, a gathering, or a time to settle down and reconnect with God. It is for us, as it had been in early Christianity, an assembly around the baptismal font. Many United Methodist (and other Christian) congregations have restored the ancient practice of placing the baptismal font near the entrance of the worship space so that persons can see and touch the water and remember their baptism as they enter. Even if the font is not or cannot be placed near the entrance of the worship space, a greeting or some opening words spoken around or near the font reminds us who we are and who we are called to become.

Confirmands, who are considering and/or preparing to say yes to God's yes, need to understand that we become members of Christ's body, the church, upon baptism. Confirmation is a means of affirming and professing our membership.

The Proclamation and Response act is an assembly around the Word of God revealed in Scripture and preaching. This is why, in many churches, worshipers stand for the reading of the Gospel text and/or other Scriptures. In Christian worship, we read Scripture—not just as good advice for our lives but because we believe that Scripture contains "all things necessary to salvation" (Article V of The Articles of Religion of the Methodist Church). Salvation is not simply insurance for the life to come, but is participation and partnership in all the ways that God works to transform the world and deliver God's creation from captivity to sin and death. Those

Expectations for Worship

Confirmands should attend worship each week. Weekly worship is the most comprehensive way in which a congregation rehearses its faith and is recharged by God. Those wishing to take the confirmation vows and enter into a covenant with the body of Christ and with your congregation need to attend worship for most, if not all, of the Sundays for the duration of the confirmation program. While it is best for the confirmands to worship with the congregation in which they are being confirmed, it is more important that they develop weekly worship habits. If a confirmand splits time between two parents who attend two different churches, it is OK if he or she worships with one congregation one week and with another congregation the next. It also is OK for confirmands who are spending a weekend at the home of a friend or out-of-town family member to attend worship with their hosts. Consider requiring confirmands to attend worship at least three Sundays per month (allow for exceptions in the case of family emergencies).

who say yes to God's yes seek guidance, correction, and support from Scripture and the proclamation of the gospel so that we may "work out [our] own salvation" (**Philippians 2:12**) and live more faithfully into the covenant we've made with God and the church.

Thanksgiving and Communion is an assembly around the Lord's Table. When we pray for the Holy Spirit to be poured out on us and on the gifts of the bread and the cup that we offer, we are asking not only to be in communion with Christ but also that in receiving his body and blood "we may be for the world the body of Christ redeemed by his blood" (*The United Methodist Hymnal,* page 10). Confirmands need to understand that Holy Communion is more than just a "holy moment." Holy Communion is a reaffirmation of our pledge to take Christ into the world, which we do in worship's final act, Sending Forth.

But the relationship between Christian worship and saying yes to God's yes goes even deeper. The vows that we say yes to are remembered and rehearsed in Sunday worship.

THE CONTENT OF THE COVENANT IN CHRISTIAN WORSHIP

- **Do you renounce the spiritual forces of wickedness, reject the evil powers of this world and repent of your sin?**

This vow is, in effect, an act of treason against every authority on earth, except that of God in Jesus Christ. Renunciation is an active and intentional breaking of allegiance. Rejection means not recognizing the claim of another to have authority over you. Repentance means changing one's whole mindset, one's whole consciousness. The question about repentance isn't simply about feeling sorry for specific things we have done or left undone. Repentance means that we turn and pledge to keep turning away from all we had thought or done that sprang from any allegiance to evil or any claim it made or may ever again try to make on our lives.

When we gather around the font and remember our baptism during the Entrance, the first act of worship, we also remember where our allegiances lie and that we are offered the "mind of Christ" (**1 Corinthians 2:16; Philippians 2:5**) instead of the "wisdom of the world" (**1 Corinthians 1:18-25**). When we assemble around the font, whether literally or imaginatively, we continually remind ourselves that we have renounced and will continue to renounce, reject, and repent of any allegiance, claim or action that does not align with the way of Jesus, our one Lord. For "there is one body and one Spirit, just as you were called to one hope of your calling, one Lord, one faith, one baptism" (**Ephesians 4:4-5**).

- **Do you accept the freedom and power God gives you to resist evil, injustice and oppression in whatever forms they present themselves?**

It is one thing to renounce evil; it is quite another to stand against and dismantle evil wherever it appears. When we say yes to God's yes, we are pulled into the struggle against evil. This is why worship includes Scripture reading and preaching. Scripture and preaching are the most explicit ways in worship that we are made more aware of our failures and limitations in resisting evil, reminded to re-claim our strengths and gifts, and empowered to exercise the freedom and power God gives us to better resist evil in the days ahead.

- **Do you confess Jesus Christ as your Savior, put your whole trust in his grace, and promise to serve him as your Lord, in union with the church which Christ has opened to people of all ages, nations and races?**

The confessions "Jesus Christ is Lord" and "Jesus Christ is Savior" were also acts of treason during the first several centuries of Christian history within the Roman Empire. The titles "Lord" and "Savior" belonged specifically to the Emperor and to no one else. By using such names for Christ, the early Christians not only negated the claim that Caesar was Lord or Savior, but they also redefined the terms *lord* and *savior*. While affirming that Christ rules over all, Christians understand Christ's rule to be the rule of God's kingdom and of love and justice.

At its most basic, Christian worship rehearses us in the first three parts of this vow. We confess that Jesus is Lord and Savior and "put our whole trust in his grace" throughout every "act" of Christian worship—in greetings, songs, hymns, the reading of Scripture, sermons, confessions of faith and sin, acts of pardon, prayers, sacraments (both baptism and Holy Communion), benedictions, and sending forth.

But Christian worship also should rehearse us in the last part of the vow. When we gather as congregations on Sunday morning, we do not (and must not!) gather as separate "generational" or "ethnic" or "cultural" groups. Doing so would violate our baptismal covenant. This does not mean that such groups may not gather for all sorts of purposes, also involving worship, at other times and places. But for Sunday worship, we are called to gather together across generations, across ethnic and cultural lines, and across the many other barriers that divide us. By gathering in such a way, we bear witness to our intention to live our lives in the world "in union with the whole church which Christ has opened to people of all ages, nations and races."

- **According to the grace given you, will you remain faithful members of Christ's holy church and serve as Christ's representatives in the world?**

In worship, we remember that God has claimed us in baptism. We listen to Scripture and preaching to better learn how to be faithful members of Christ's holy church. We confess our faith, pray for the church and the world, confess our sins, receive God's pardon, and offer one another the peace of Christ as those who have desire to grow in faithfulness. We gather around the Lord's Table to offer our gifts and ourselves as a living sacrifice to God.

All of this prepares us for the final act, the Sending Forth, where we affirm our call to "serve as Christ's representatives in the world." In the prayer of thanksgiving following Holy Communion, we ask God to "send us now into the world in the strength of your Spirit to give ourselves to others" (*The United Methodist Hymnal,* page 11). And in the dismissal and sending, we are sent forth specifically in the name and as representatives of our Triune God, blessed and reminded of God's presence with us as we go.

SUNDAY WORSHIP AS NECESSARY BUT INSUFFICIENT

Confirmands need to understand that worship is necessary and completely relevant to who we are as Christians. Sunday worship is the most comprehensive way in which a congregation rehearses its faith and is recharged by God.

Sunday worship is a necessary part of Christian discipleship. But it is not sufficient. Nor is it meant to be. Sunday worship summarizes and deeply expresses our call to discipleship, but it does not substitute for our living out that call in our daily lives. To do that, we must do what Jesus himself told his disciples: "If any want to become my followers, let them deny themselves and take up their cross daily and follow me" (**Luke 9:23**). This means that worship is not just something we do with the congregation on Sunday. Worship is something we do every day, albeit in ways that are different than the ways we worship on Sunday. Connecting with God through daily prayer, Scripture reading, devotional reading, and conversation with Christian friends also are important ways that we worship.

Introduce confirmands to some of the resources that are available for daily worship and reflection, including "An Order for Morning Praise and Prayer" and "An Order for Evening Praise and Prayer," in *The United Methodist Hymnal* (pages 876 and 878, respectively) and *Devo'Zine,* the daily devotional magazine for youth published by The Upper Room.

But confirmands also need to understand that worship is not the only thing we do as Christians. The baptismal covenant should influence all aspects of our lives, and it helps to have a small group of Christian friends who meet regularly and hold one another accountable to the vows they have taken. Covenant Discipleship groups, which confirmands learn about in the "Way of Discipleship" session, are one way in which United Methodists have come together in small groups to offer one another support and accountability.

Confirmands, who are considering saying yes to God's yes, should be expected to worship with the congregation every Sunday. (Although we must also understand that, due to illness or divided families, this is not always possible.) They also should get in the habit of worshiping throughout the week though prayer, reflection, and Scripture reading. Such practices of worship should become for them what God intends them to be—a means of grace by which the Holy Spirit works to transform them more and more fully into the image of Christ.

CONFIRMATION SUNDAY WORSHIP SERVICE

The entire congregation needs to understand how important confirmation is to the life of the church. The confirmation Sunday worship service is an opportunity to lift up the ministry of confirmation while also creating a memorable experience for those being confirmed. Young people celebrate all sorts of milestones—earning the Eagle Scout rank or Girl Scout Gold Award, being inducted into National Honor Society, winning an athletic competition, or graduating from high school—with memorable ceremonies and rituals. The rite of confirmation should be at least as meaningful and memorable as these other important adolescent moments. The confirmation Sunday worship service should make clear the importance of confirmation in the life of the congregation and of those being confirmed.

Here are some things to keep in mind as you plan your confirmation Sunday worship service:

- **Confirm during your regular Sunday worship service.** Confirmation, by its nature, involves the entire community of faith. Thus it is important that the whole congregation participate. Sunday afternoon or weeknight confirmation services for parents and families cut out the rest of the congregation and deny church members the opportunity to vow to "nurture one another in the Christian faith and life and include [those being confirmed] in [their] care" (*The United Methodist Hymnal,* page 35).

- **Include the entire Baptismal Covenant I in your confirmation service.** *The Book of Discipline* says, "Becoming a professing member requires the answer of faith of the baptized person made visible in a service of profession of Christian faith and confirmation using the vows of the Baptismal Covenant." The vows of confirmation listed in the *Discipline* are the basis of Baptismal Covenant I (which begins on page 33 of *The United Methodist Hymnal*) and of the sessions in the "Live Your Commitment" unit of this confirmation program. Thus all of the vows in the Baptismal Covenant I service are essential to the rite of confirmation and the responsibilities of a professing member of The United Methodist Church.

  The rest of the service also is essential. The "Thanksgiving Over the Water" puts the covenant of baptism in the context of our faith story (from the waters of creation to Jesus' command to baptize and make disciples of all nations), invokes the Holy Spirit, and reminds us that confirmation is an act of God's grace for which we should be thankful. The reciting of the Apostle's Creed allows the congregation to affirm the faith of the church into which the confirmands are being confirmed.

- **Include in the service parents, mentors, and other members of the congregation involved in confirmation.** While the pastor has the responsibility of organizing confirmation classes and while the youth minister, the children's minister, and/or a dedicated volunteer may act as a confirmation teacher or director, an effective confirmation program requires the time and effort of many church members, including parents, mentors, siblings and other family members, Sunday school teachers, retreat leaders, children's or youth choir directors, and so on. All of these people can participate in the confirmation rite by standing with the confirmands and by laying hands on persons being confirmed. You might also invite mentors to say some words on behalf of the confirmands they've worked with, letting the congregation know how these young people have grown in faith through the confirmation process.

- **Incorporate your vine and stoles into the service.** The opening ritual for the confirmation class sessions involves creating a vine, or tree, inspired by **John 15:1-9.** At the beginning of each session, confirmands will add branches, leaves, or fruit to this vine. There are several ways that you can create this vine: Your group could paint a vine as a mural on the wall of your meeting space; you could draw or paint a vine on a large sheet of paper, posterboard, or butcher paper; or you

Suggested Hymns for Confirmation Service

From *The United Methodist Hymnal:*

- On Eagle's Wings (143)
- Seek Ye First (405)
- The Church's One Foundation (545 and 546)
- We Are the Church (558)
- Pass It On (572)
- This Little Light of Mine (585)
- Here I Am, Lord (593)

From *The Faith We Sing:*

- I Have Decided to Follow Jesus (2129)
- Cry of My Heart (2165)

From *Zion Still Sings:*

- Thy Way, O Lord (159)
- I'm Determined" (175)

could build a three-dimensional tree using wood, dowel rods, and craft materials. If your tree or vine can be moved into your worship space, have it on display during the confirmation worship service. Consider reading aloud some of the words and phrases that the confirmands wrote on the branches, leaves, and fruit.

As part of "Credo: Retreat to Advance," each of the confirmands creates a stole to represent their call to be a Christian disciple and a minister of the gospel. Place these stoles around each confirmand's neck as he or she is confirmed.

Mission and Service and Confirmation

By Lanecia Rouse

> "Teacher, which commandment in the law is the greatest?" He said to him, " 'You shall love the Lord your God with all your heart, and with all your soul, and with all your mind.' This is the greatest and first commandment. And a second is like it: 'You shall love your neighbor as yourself.' On these two commandments hang all the law and the prophets."
>
> —**Matthew 22:36-40** (NRSV)

Do all the good you can,
By all the means you can,
In all the ways you can,
In all the places you can,
At all the times you can,
To all he people you can,
As long as ever you can.

—commonly attributed
to John Wesley

Our Heritage: A People Called [United] Methodist

Throughout our history, we United Methodists—and those of our predecessor denominations—have understood ourselves as a people called to love God with our whole hearts, souls, and minds and to love our neighbor as we love ourselves, in response to the two greatest commandments (**Matthew 22:34-40**). Participating in God's work of healing, hope, and radical love is essential to being faithful to these commandments and is a central part of the United Methodist tradition.

While John Wesley affirmed that salvation comes entirely through God's grace, he often preached about the importance of means of grace, practices through which we more fully experience God's grace. These means of grace include praying, reading Scripture, and taking Holy Communion; but they also include doing acts of mercy and justice. Wesley, as well as other leaders throughout our United Methodist history, taught that we Christians should live our lives with regard for the humanity and well-being of all persons.

Expectations for Service

Confirmands should fulfill a service requirement. Service should be completed through the ministries of the congregation and may include participating in traditional service projects, helping with ministries to homeless and/or hungry persons, assisting with vacation Bible school, or serving as an acolyte or other worship leader. The number of service hours you require will vary, depending on the length of your program. But 20 hours over the course of a school year is a good requirement.

Mission and Service: A Way of Life

Throughout Scripture, we encounter stories of people whom God calls to offer hope to the hopeless, freedom for those who are oppressed, sight to those who are blind, food for the hungry, water for those who thirst, comfort for those who mourn, shelter for the homeless, and clothing for those who are naked. Jesus began his earthly ministry by reading from the **Book of Isaiah:** "The Spirit of the Lord is upon me, because he has anointed me to bring good news to the poor. He has sent me to proclaim release to the captives and recovery of sight to the blind, to let the oppressed go free, to proclaim the year of the Lord's favor" (**Luke 4:18-19**). Later Jesus teaches that when we feed the hungry, give water to the thirsty, clothe the naked, take care of the sick, and visit the imprisoned, we are feeding, clothing, caring for, and visiting Jesus himself (**Matthew 25:31-40**).

Serving others in a spirit of Christ's love is essential to living a life of Christian discipleship. In and through mission and service, young people bear witness to Christ's presence, offer their gifts to join in doing the work of God's kingdom, and learn to love while also receiving love. Confirmation is a great opportunity to help young people better understand Christ's call to live missional lives. As we are called to participate in this particular stage of their faith journey, we have a responsibility to prayerfully discern ways for confirmands to offer their gifts in love of and service to their neighbors—both inside and outside the church. God uses mission and service experiences to do incredible things through the lives of those who are offering themselves in service and those who are receiving the gift of embodied love. (And often in these experiences, the lines between giver and recipient quickly become blurred.)

Serving: Being Present

Helping young people claim their identities as children of God and disciples of Christ is central to the confirmation process. And engaging the youth in mission and service opportunities is crucial to teaching young people what it means to be Christian disciples. Few confirmands have the opportunity to embark on a missional journey to Haiti or Burkina Faso to work alongside people who are suffering from poverty or malnutrition or dehydration. But they nonetheless can participate in meaningful mission and service experiences that will draw them closer to God and neighbor. Whether these experiences involve singing or playing music at a local retirement home, serving warm meals to persons without a home, or helping lead vacation Bible school programs for younger children, the experiences should help young people:

—understand the importance of community and our need to be in relationship with other persons;
—discover new passions and callings or affirm existing passions and callings;
—form relationships with persons from various walks of life;
—strengthen relationships with persons they know who are joining them in service;
—encounter Christ in new ways as they seek to be the presence of Christ to others;
—be agents of change as they step out in faith with God; and
—love others as Christ first loved us.

Mission and service experiences allow young people to participate in the healing and restoration of those who are wounded, suffering, and broken; understand the Gospel in new ways; and experience everyday resurrections. The confirmation journey is an ideal time for young people to connect with God and their neighbors through mission and service.

Service-Learning: Reflection and Growth

While it is great for young people to get their hands dirty in service to others, confirmands are most likely to make mission and service a way of life if they have an opportunity to reflect on the work they have done. What did they learn about the need they sought to address? What did they learn about the people they served and worked with? How did they serve Jesus by reaching out to persons in need (**Matthew 25:31-40**)? How did they experience God's kingdom on earth (**Luke 17:20-21**)?

Service-learning adds another dimension to service by giving those who serve an opportunity to reflect on their service experience. While service involves meeting a need, service-learning also involves understanding the need and considering its sources. While service is an act of giving to those whom we serve, service-learning is also an act of receiving from those we serve. While service is about doing something for others, service-learning also is about being in relationship with others. As you engage your confirmands in mission and service, make sure that they have time to reflect on their work before, after, and during the project. Challenge them not only to help persons in need but to strive to understand and be in relationship with persons in need. And help confirmands understand service as an act of faith and a way of showing our love for both God and neighbor.

Discernment: Being Open

Because mission and service experiences are so important to the spiritual formation of young people, those of us who connect confirmands to these experiences have a responsibility to practice prayerful discernment when choosing and/or creating mission and service opportunities. Raking leaves on a Saturday in the fall or working at a soup kitchen once a year are not the only ways that young people can be in mission. When we take time to be in prayer about how God is calling us to join in loving and serving the world, we often find the Spirit taking us to places we might not ordinarily go to be with people we otherwise might not choose to be with. And we might find that these experiences require more than a few hours each year.

As you discern, consider and pray about the following questions:

- How is God calling your confirmands, at this time in their life, to give and receive God's love?
- What gifts do your confirmands have to offer, either as individuals or as a group?
- What are some of the needs of your local, national, and global community?
- Specifically, who, within a five-mile radius of your church building, needs to experience Christ's transforming love?
- How might God use your confirmands' gifts to respond to some of the needs you have identified? How can you confirmands be instruments of God's love to persons who need to experience this love?

In response to **Matthew 25:31-40,** say a prayer asking Christ to show you where he is hungry, naked, orphaned, lonely, thirsty, imprisoned, sick, or oppressed and to point you to ways that your group can provide Jesus with food, clothing, family, community, water, health, or freedom.

You may discover that God is calling your group to offer a creativity camp for children in your neighborhood who are eager to offer something beautiful to the world. You may discover that God is calling your confirmands to serve meals to a group of homeless persons once a month, joining in table fellowship with strangers, and developing relationships over time. You may discover that your confirmands' gifts and passions are suited for eradicating hunger or ending child slavery by standing up to the forces that perpetuate these injustices. The young people in your confirmation group could then become teachers and agents of change in your community. Who knows what opportunities God may be creating or leading you toward? As you prayerfully ask and pray about these questions, prepare to be divinely surprised.

As you discern, learn about and be aware of ways in which people are already working to meet the needs you have identified. People and organizations who are already actively responding to these needs have valuable knowledge and experience and likely have already worked through the logistical challenges of starting a mission and service ministry. Instead of starting from scratch, look for ways to assist and partner with these groups. While joining those who are already in the field is a good tactic for anyone involved in mission or service, it is very important for those who identify as United Methodist Christians. The United Methodist Church is a connectional church. Within the connection, countless congregations, annual conferences, boards and agencies, and church-sponsored organizations are hard at work healing a variety of wounds in their communities and throughout the world. Each of these efforts is an opportunity to strengthen the connection by bringing more people together around a common calling and purpose.

Logistics: Being Prepared

An important part of preparing mission and service experiences, is making sure that you have adult leaders in place who can care for and support the young people as they serve. As you use discernment to select mission and service opportunities for your confirmands, also use discernment in selecting adult leaders. Do not simply enlist anyone who is available; but seek adults who have gifts, passions, and knowledge that will help the young people learn and grow from the mission or service experience. We have a responsibility to do all that we can to create an environment where confirmands can encounter "the abiding love of God and fellowship within the community of faith" (*Safe Sanctuaries for Youth,* page 8).

The United Methodist Church encourages all congregations to have a Safe Sanctuaries policy in place to reduce the risk of abuse of the young people whom God has called us to love. If you partner with organizations that provide mission and service opportunities for youth, make sure that these organizations have similar policies and protections in place.

As the first Christians went out into the world, they usually had a friend by their side. When working with young people, it is best to have by your side a friend who can see what you might not see, hear what you might not hear, and hold you accountable to the goals and expectations you have for your ministry.

It is also important to invite the parents of your confirmands and other members of the congregation to join the group in mission or service. Make sure that you meet with parents at least once in advance of any mission or service project. Provide parents with logistical information (where you will serve; why you have chosen to serve in this particular way; what the confirmands will be doing; what safety precautions you have taken; costs and fundraising strategies; food, lodging, and transportation details; and all of the calendar dates related to the project).

Give the parents any permission slips, medical release forms, and/or insurance and health forms; and let parents know of ways that they can be in prayer for the group. Parents are entrusting their children to your care. One of the responsibilities that goes along with this privilege is making sure that parents have the information they need to support and share in the mission or service experience.

Like the confirmands' parents, the congregation also has entrusted to you the lives of the young people of the church. Therefore, you also have a responsibility to let the congregation know what the confirmands are doing and how members of the church may support their young people in mission and service. Keep the congregation informed by making announcements during worship and by posting updates on the church's website, blog, or social-networking webpage.

Enlist members of the congregation to be prayer partners for each person (confirmand and adult leader) who is participating. Before the mission or service project, prepare (with the confirmands' help) a short presentation to let Sunday school classes and small groups know what the confirmands will be doing. Following the projects, have the confirmands prepare a short presentation for these classes and groups, telling about what they did and learned from their mission or service experience. Young people are eager to be creative; and many are gifted in using various forms of media to tell their story. In addition, their presentation will be a blessing to the congregation.

Discipleship: Taking God's Love Into the World

As disciples of Christ, regardless of our age, we are called to love and serve God and neighbor. Every day, we have opportunities to offer God's transforming and redeeming love to those who are desperately in need of being loved. Confirmands need to understand that mission and service are essential to who we are as followers of Christ. May you discover great joy and grace as you empower, equip, and encourage your confirmands to live a life of mission and service grounded in the life, ministry, and resurrection of Christ.

Credo Retreats Introduction

retreat to advance

Retreat in order to advance? Sounds like a contradiction. In military terms, we equate *retreat* with *defeat*. But in spiritual growth terms, we retreat to advance; we move away to draw close; we withdraw to be drawn in. Retreats help us be still in a world that is constantly "on." Rather than being a way to escape from life, retreats help us move forward in life with a deeper sense of peace, purpose, and partnership with God and others in the family of faith. Rather than being an end in themselves, retreats are an opportunity to begin again, to go back into the world and advance the cause of Christ.

expectations for retreats and confirmation

Confirmands should attend at least one retreat. Getting away from routines and familiar settings provides valuable opportunities for deep spiritual reflection and an intimate connection with God and others. Choose to lead the following retreat or prayer lock-in (see pages 45–59 and 60–66), or search one of the many United Methodist annual conferences and districts that host confirmation retreats for a retreat that your group may participate in.

Why should you do retreats as a part of the confirmation process? Retreats literally help us get away so that we can get close—close to God, close to our confirmation friends and leaders, and close to our sense of being. Retreats can be of various lengths and in a variety of locations; but they should be long enough and far enough away, either in miles or in change of surroundings, for participants to really "get away" so that they can "move toward." Retreats allow us to move

—away from distractions, such as cell phones, videogames, television—toward a focus on God's presence and movement in our lives; toward being still and knowing God.

—away from voices that constantly seek to hold our attention, define us, and shape our worldview and values—toward the voice of God discerned in prayer and worship, and as revealed in the Bible, in creation, and in the life of Jesus.

—away from familiar surroundings, patterns, routines, and habits (ways of acting and reacting) that keep us from seeing new possibilities, thinking new thoughts, and acting in new ways (Look at Kenda Dean and Ron Foster's description of rhythm breaking, *The Godbearing Life: The Art of Soul Tending for Youth Ministry,* Upper Room Books, Nashville, 1998, 117–118.)—toward the establishment of new spiritual habits, devotional practices, and ways of responding to people after the example of Christ.

Moving Toward One Another

Retreats are great ways for young people to experience Christian community. *Community*, in this sense, goes beyond the simple designation of people who happen to live in the same town. "Christian community" is unique for several reasons. First, Jesus Christ is at the center of this community. He is the heart and soul of the group—not only of the individuals in the group. Christian community is a gift bestowed by the Holy Spirit—a gift of deep connection, relationship, shared identity, and common calling. Community is about being known and knowing others more deeply.

Common experiences of worship, devotion, and service in the name of Christ bind people together as a community of disciples. Most of the time, we gather in a Christ-centered community in weekly spurts of worship, in small groups such as Sunday school classes or youth groups, and for the occasional service project. Retreats, with their unique content, removed setting, and concentrated time frames, help us come to a deeper sense of connection, belonging, and identity as disciples of Christ in a Christian community.

Retreating's Greatest Hits

Some elements are common to many spiritual-growth retreats because they get to the heart of the matter, blending content and application, experience and reflection, heart and head, intention and commitment:

- **Candles/Fire/Flame:** Candles—whether in a circle, in a procession, or on an altar—create a sense of peace, awe, and wonder and amplify our awareness of the presence of Christ among us. Bonfires provide a unique setting for worship, witness, and fellowship.
- **Circles:** Gathering into circles gives us a unique look at our faith community. As we worship, we witness to one another across and around the circle, in sharp contrast to the rows in which we often sit for worship. Circles symbolize both the eternity of God and the unity of our group in Christ.
- **Worship:** All of our retreats should include times for worship. Worship may include songs and prayers, Bible reading and reflection, witness, and prayer. Worship, in its fullness, offers something for the head (some thought or perspective that makes us think), something for the heart (some story, witness, or song that touches us in a place too deep for words), and something for the hands (something tangible that engages the senses and amplifies the message of the service).
- **Sacramentals:** Sacramentals are rituals that include prayers and symbolic elements that look and feel a lot like the sacraments of Holy Communion and baptism but are not. These can involve the use of stones, water, oil, or

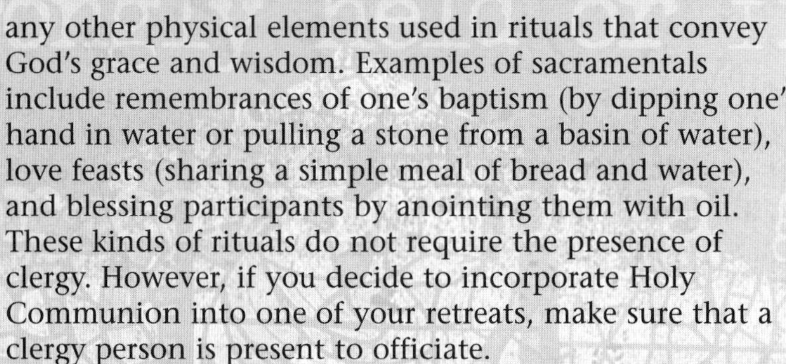

any other physical elements used in rituals that convey God's grace and wisdom. Examples of sacramentals include remembrances of one's baptism (by dipping one's hand in water or pulling a stone from a basin of water), love feasts (sharing a simple meal of bread and water), and blessing participants by anointing them with oil. These kinds of rituals do not require the presence of clergy. However, if you decide to incorporate Holy Communion into one of your retreats, make sure that a clergy person is present to officiate.

- **Opportunities for public witness and commitment:** Young people need the opportunity to bear public witness to their faith in a safe, trustworthy, sacred space. Retreats should include a designated place or a devoted object that will help participants speak from their hearts. A designated chair, a tree stump, or a sturdy box would work. Some groups use a special walking stick, a candle, or an object that has meaning for the group, such as a shell or a handmade cross passed to each speaker, in turn. Depending on the maturity of the group, participants should be given the opportunity for deeper levels of self-disclosure, confession, repentance, and commitment. Anything from simply talking about a favorite part of the retreat to asking for prayer or expressing a new or deeper commitment to Christ should be encouraged.

Connecting Dots and Cultivating Ah-Ha Moments

The Credo confirmation sessions are divided into three units: "Know Your Story," "Confirm Your Faith," and "Live Your Commitment." The included retreat and day of prayer are designed to supplement, not to replace, the content covered in the sessions.

"Retreat to Advance" begins with group-building experiences and includes the exploration of call, identity, and ministry. The retreat could be held as a kick-off for confirmation, a mid-program burst of community, or as a closing act.

"Day of Prayer" gives confirmands a taste of several practices and experiences of prayer.

Retreats give your group the chance to live out the values of Christian community and United Methodism and help confirmands connect some dots in their understanding of what it means to be the church. Be sure to work a retreat into your confirmation schedule to give the students time away and the brain/heart space to listen for God call and to experience God's embrace.

CREDO: Retreat to Advance

INTRODUCTION

The chief task of adolescence may well be identity formation, asking and answering the question, "Who am I?" Unless they are intentional about this task, people become "whatever" people. That is, they become whatever they have been paying the most attention to—whatever has captured their imagination—often with little or no critical reflection or conscious thought.

Many voices call out to youth, inviting them, challenging them, even threatening them to believe and behave in particular ways. These voices promise acceptance, value, belonging, and success if youth listen and none of these things if they don't listen. Young adolescents are becoming more intentional about which voices they will listen to, give credence to, trust, and follow. The purpose of this retreat is to move participants toward a deeper relationship with Jesus Christ and others in the community of faith called the Church.

The confirmation journey is, in large measure, an exercise in choosing the voices we listen to. When Adam explained to God that he was hiding because he was naked, God asked, "Who told you that you were naked?" (**Genesis 3:11**). A follow-up question might be, "And why did you trust him or her?" This retreat will help confirmands sort out the voices and tune in to the voice of God as heard in Scripture; in the life and tradition of the Church; in the counsel of their trusted mentors, teachers, and role models; and in the experiences of their lives.

A well-known bank, quantum physicists, and the prophets and rabbis of the Bible all agree, "The right relationship is everything." Only in relationship do we have being and identity. Other related questions include, "Who am I in relationship with others?" and "Who am I in relationship with God?" and "Who am I in relationship with Jesus, through the Church?" and "What is my role as a Christian in this world?"

SUPPLIES

You may be able to gather many of these materials in a scavenger hunt of the church resources closet or classrooms. Ask participants whether they have any of these items. Be creative and substitute materials as needed.

- ❑ copies of the following items from the website:
  —Morning Watch 1
  —Morning Watch 2
  —Jesus and Me
  —John Wesley's Covenant Prayer
- ❑ Credo Confirmation Student Journals or notebooks
- ❑ recreation equipment and games for free time
- ❑ low table such as an end table or a plant stand
- ❑ large, white candle (to be the Christ candle)
- ❑ a lighter or matches
- ❑ nametags
- ❑ balloons, 9-inch rounds of assorted colors, one balloon for each person (with a few extras in case of popping)
- ❑ markerboard and/or large sheets of paper and broad-tip marker
- ❑ assorted markers, pens, and pencils
- ❑ permanent markers
- ❑ assorted fabric paints and brushes (Fabric paints in squeeze bottles are easier to use for writing on fabric, while the brush-on kind can be easier to use in large areas.)
- ❑ assorted tempera paints and brushes, fabric paint pens, fabric pencils
- ❑ long strips of fabric for stoles: medium-weight, white twill or heavy broadcloth (with sizing) cut into 5-by-52 to 5-by-60 strips (one for each participant, plus a few extras)
- ❑ sheets of construction paper, cut in half
- ❑ paper, several sheets per person
- ❑ tape, masking and transparent (no specific activity but may come in handy)
- ❑ paper lunch bags, one for each person
- ❑ index cards or slips of paper—any useful size and color—number of persons in the group times the number of persons in the group (For instance, if there are 6 members in the group, multiply 6 by 6—equals 36. If there are 10 people in the group, multiply 10 by 10—equals 100 index cards.)
- ❑ sheets of 2-by-4 labels—number of persons in the group times the number of persons in the group (The same number labels as the number of index cards, above.)
- ❑ optional: *The United Methodist Book of Worship*
- ❑ copies of *The United Methodist Hymnal*
- ❑ songbooks and/or lyric sheets (Be mindful of copyright laws.)
- ❑ musical accompaniment: guitar or other instruments
- ❑ food for all of the meals
- ❑ eating and serving utensils
- ❑ cups
- ❑ plates and bowls
- ❑ napkins
- ❑ ordained clergyperson
- ❑ Communion elements (bread and grape juice, consecrated by an elder of the church)
- ❑ chalice or other common cup
- ❑ plate for the Communion bread
- ❑ linen napkins for the Communion elements
- ❑ free-standing cross, candles, colored fabric, and other items to create the altar setting
- ❑ Communion elements and altar ware for Holy Communion

FRIDAY PM

Plan to eat along the way to the retreat site, or prepare and eat the evening meal once you arrive at your retreat site. Upon arrival, settle into your rooms. Then set up your meeting space, including a worship center or an altar table, and prepare materials for the first session.

optional supplies
- ❑ food
- ❑ eating and serving utensils
- ❑ cups
- ❑ plates
- ❑ napkins

preparation: Plan when, where, and what the group will eat.

SESSION 1: BE YOU (2 HOURS)

group covenant

(15 minutes)

Call everyone together, and open with prayer and a couple songs.

Review your group's covenant or any expectations for members of the retreat community. Or have the group develop a community covenant, spelling out behavioral expectations, which all members of the retreat community will sign.

supplies
- ❑ group covenant
- ❑ copies of *The United Methodist Hymnal*
- ❑ musical accompaniment
- ❑ songbooks or lyric sheets
- ❑ optional: marker and markerboard if the group will create a community covenant at the retreat site

Mailbags

(10 minutes)

Give each participant a paper lunch bag, and invite him or her to write his or her name on it and decorate it. These bags will become their mailbags for the weekend. Encourage the confirmands and adult volunteers to write encouraging and thoughtful messages on index cards or slips of paper and drop them into one another's bags throughout the weekend. (Pay close attention to mailbags that seem to be getting few notes, and tap some of the more mature confirmands to write notes to put in them.) Of course, all of the adult leaders will need to write to each of the confirmands.

supplies
- ❑ paper lunch bags
- ❑ assorted markers, pens, and pencils
- ❑ index cards (See Supplies, on page 46.)

balloon exercise

(15 minutes)

Give each participant a balloon. Instruct the participants to blow up their balloon and tie the end closed. Tell them to hold the balloon by the tied, knotted end. (Some participants will find it challenging to blow up the balloon and/or tie the end in a knot. Be ready to help. And some participants will find it difficult to hold their balloon still until everyone finishes.)

This activity has two "rounds," but don't let the group know that.

Round 1: Create a box on the floor using tape that is large enough so that all of the participants can stand comfortably within it. Tell the participants that when you say, "Go," they

supplies
- ❑ balloons, 9-inch rounds of assorted colors, one balloon for each person (with a few extras in case of popping)

are to toss their balloon into the air toward the middle of the box. Tell them that the goal of the group is to keep as many balloons in the air as possible by tapping them with their hands or head. They are not allowed to pick up balloons that hit the floor, nor are they allowed to touch balloons that go outside the box. Tell participants to be careful not to pop any balloons that fall to the floor. Instruct them that when you shout, "Stop!" they should let all of the balloons drop to the floor.

A few minutes into the game, the group will settle into a pattern; and the participants will have reached their ability to keep a certain number of balloons in the air. When the group has reached this point, shout, "Stop!" and have the participants let the balloons drop to the floor. Ask the participants to leave the balloons where they land, instead of retrieving them.

Ask:

- How might this balloon game represent the people of the church? (You might hear answers such as, "We are all different sizes," or "We have to work together to keep everyone 'up.' " that confirmands might reflect about balloons [people] who need more or less attention or care. They may notice that some people focus on only the balloons in the air, while others seem to care more about the ones that drop to the floor. Let the ideas flow for a while; and if necessary, prompt some replies.)
- How would you change the game to make it a better representation of our Christian community?

Round 2: Have participants retrieve any balloons that went out of bounds. Have everyone pick up a balloon from the floor. Make sure that every participant has a balloon for this round. Blow up new balloons to replace any that have popped.

Change the rules, according to the confirmands' ideas. For example: "In this round, the task is still to keep as many balloons in the air as you can. But this time, you are allowed to retrieve balloons from the floor or outside the box then bounce them back into the air with the others."

After a few minutes, tell the participants to stop and allow the balloons to fall to the floor as in the first round. Then ask:

- Now how might this game represent our group or how we want our group to be?

Spend some time discussing and reflecting on caring for one another, reaching out to those who go astray, and the nature of Christian community.

Be sure to keep the balloons, since they will be used again in the closing worship.

Two-Minute Autobiography

(20 minutes)

Regather everyone for more community building. Invite each person to tell his or her life story in two minutes or less. Allow each person to speak when he or she is ready.

Names and Nicknames

(15 minutes)

Invite each confirmands, and each adult who is present, to talk about the meaning or story behind his or her name.. Is he or she named for a particular person? Is there some significance behind the meaning of his or her name? Also ask each person whether he or she has a nickname. Is there a story behind his or her nickname? (Be sure to clarify that you are talking about nicknames that participants claim and are known by, not derogatory names.)

Closing Worship: Who Am I?

(30 minutes)

Scatter the balloons from the first activity on or around the altar table. Have the participants sit on the floor around the table. Hand out nametags and pens. Have each person write his or her name on the nametag and place the tag on the altar. Light the Christ candle.

Say something like: "We're here to build community on this confirmation journey. We're also here to get away from our day-to-day lives and listen for God's call. Sometimes in the busyness of our days we can lose the ability to hear God's voice. We can get so wrapped up in our daily events that we lose our focus on God's will for our lives. We can become so eager to be popular or be liked that we lose the identity God gave us and called 'good.' So we're here this weekend to be together, to search the Scriptures, to pray, to create, to retreat from the world so that we can advance from this place with a renewed dedication to Christ and to our walk with him.

Pray aloud: "Let's pray: Creator and ever-creating God, you dreamed us into being and called us to abundant life here on your earth. You long for us to know you and to recognize that we are always known by you. Would you send your Spirit among us this weekend as we make space to hear your voice? Would you create in us a new heart and give us fresh vision of who we are in you? Thank you for your grace, your mercy, your love. We give this time, our attention, our very lives to grow in that grace, mercy, and love this weekend. Amen."

Invite the youth to speak aloud what they hope to get out of the weekend. Encourage them to expect to meet God.

Sing some favorite songs together and then join together in the Lord's Prayer.

Supplies

- ❑ low table such as an end table or a plant stand
- ❑ large, white candle (to be the Christ candle)
- ❑ Bible
- ❑ a lighter or matches
- ❑ leftover balloons from the "Balloon Exercise"
- ❑ nametags
- ❑ pens
- ❑ copies of *The United Methodist Hymnal,* song-books, or lyric sheets
- ❑ musical accompaniment

Preparation: Create a worship space by placing a low table in a spot where all of the participants can sit on the floor around it. Place the candle and the Bible in the center of the altar table.

supplies
- ❑ items for free-time options

preparation: Gather items that will allow participants several options for a period of free time before lights out. Some options might include playing table games, writing notes for mailbags, and preparing materials for the next day's activities and sessions.

Free Time

Let the participants know the available options for a period of free time before lights out. Some might choose time alone, while others might choose to be together.

SATURDAY AM

supplies
- ❑ food for breakfast
- ❑ eating and serving utensils
- ❑ cups
- ❑ plates and bowls
- ❑ napkins
- ❑ Bibles
- ❑ copies of the "Morning Watch 1" worksheets
- ❑ pens or pencils

preparation: Make copies of "Morning Watch 1" worksheet, from the website.

Morning Watch

(35 minutes)

Gather the group together before or after breakfast, and explain the purpose of Morning Watch. Morning Watch is a time for quiet reflection and solitude. Invite everyone to find a quiet place apart from the group. If a pair of friends choose to go to Morning Watch together, they should refrain from talking to each other.

Instruct the confirmands to take their Bibles, their "Morning Watch 1" worksheets, and pens or pencils with them so that they can look up the complete passages and write or draw their responses to the questions on the sheet. Give the confirmands 30 minutes to complete the exercise, then call the group together for the morning session or breakfast.

SESSION 2: BE WITH JESUS

Jesus and Me?

(50 minutes)

Sing some favorite songs together as you transition from Morning Watch to group time. Choose songs that focus on the love of Christ. Then pray, or invite a young person to lead the group in prayer.

Hand out copies of the "Jesus and Me?" worksheet, from the website. Instruct the participants to complete the column on the worksheet pertaining to their relationships with friends. Give them a few minutes to work, then invite them to talk about their answers.

Then have the participants return to the worksheet to complete the column pertaining to their relationship with Jesus. If youth have questions about how some of the situations apply to their relationship with Jesus, explain that "time alone" could be time spent in personal prayer or devotional reading; "time with others" could be time spent in worship or Christian fellowship. Again, give everyone a few minutes to work; then have the participants talk about their answers.

When they've had plenty of time to discuss, lead the group in John Wesley's Covenant Prayer (below and available on the website).

Covenant Prayer
(From John Wesley's Covenant Service, 1780)

I am no longer my own, but thine.
Put me to what thou wilt, rank me with whom thou wilt.
Put me to doing, put me to suffering.
Let me be employed by thee or laid aside for thee,
  exalted for thee or brought low for thee.
Let me be full, let me be empty.
Let me have all things, let me have nothing.
I freely and heartily yield all things to thy pleasure and disposal.
And now, O glorious and blessed God,
  Father, Son, and Holy Spirit,
    thou art mine, and I am thine.
So be it.
And the covenant which I have made on earth,
  let it be ratified in heaven.
Amen.

Call attention to the phrase "thou art mine, and I am thine." Then ask:

- How do you know that you are Christ's and that Christ is yours?

SUPPLIES
- ❑ copies of the "Jesus and Me?" handout
- ❑ copies of John Wesley's Covenant Prayer, at left or from the website
- ❑ pens or pencils

PREPARATION: Make copies of the "Jesus and Me" handout, from the website. Also make copies of John Wesley's Covenant Prayer, at left or from the website.

THEOTOKOS

(30 minutes)

Now that youth have spent some time thinking about their relationship with Jesus Christ, transition to thinking about what that means for them and how they live out their chosen-ness.

Invite a volunteer to read aloud **Isaiah 43:1-3.**

Say: "The prophet Isaiah reminds us that God claims us, saying, 'You are mine.' "

Ask:

- What is something that is yours that you don't want anyone else to mess with?
- To what lengths will you go to protect this thing?

Ask a volunteer to read aloud **John 15:16.**

Say: "Jesus said, 'You did not choose me but I chose you.' Jesus' teaching in this verse ties into baptism in our United Methodist tradition. We believe that baptism is a sacrament through which God claims us. Those who were baptized as infants were not able to choose *to be* baptized or *not to be* baptized. Baptism is also a ritual through which the church claims us. However, in confirmation, we accept for ourselves the responsibilities of being part of the body of Christ, the church."

SUPPLIES
- ❑ Bibles

NOTE: Participants will add the word *Theotokos* to their stole later in the retreat.

Ask the participants whether they recall any people in Scripture whom God called for a particular purpose. As needed, introduce some of the following examples:

- Noah (**Genesis 6:11-22**)
- Moses (**Exodus 3:1-12**)
- Gideon (**Judges 6:11-24**)
- David (**1 Samuel 16:1-13**)
- Jeremiah (**Jeremiah 1:4-11**)
- The woman at the well (**John 4:1-42**)

Then review these two biblical "call" stories, and ask the related questions:

- **1 Samuel 3:1-9:** What can we know about Samuel's age in this story? What is the relationship between Eli and Samuel? How did Samuel learn to hear and respond to God's call?
- **Luke 1:26-38:** How did Mary hear God's call? How did she respond? Did Mary have a choice? What was Mary's calling?

Say: "Some Christian traditions give Mary the Greek title *Theotokos,* which means 'God-bearer'—one who brings God into the world. Mary was called to bring God into the world in a very special way, by giving birth to Jesus Christ. But all of us have a responsibility to bring God into the world."

Ask:

- How are you called to bring God into your world
- In other words, how can people around you see God in you?

Job Descriptions

(30 minutes)

Have the group brainstorm a list of things that would be included in the job description of a minister. What does a minister, pastor, or priest do? Record these items on a markerboard.

Supplies

- ❑ Bibles
- ❑ markerboard
- ❑ marker

Ask:

- What on this list are we, as Christians, *not* called to do?

If participants question whether all Christians are called to preach, teach, or visit the sick, remind them that not all preaching comes from a pulpit in a church and that not all teaching happens in a classroom. Remind the participants that Jesus instructs us, in Scripture, to visit the sick and imprisoned. As necessary, refer to Scriptures such as **Matthew 25:31-40; 28:18-20;** and **Acts 1:8.**

Ask a volunteer to read aloud **John 14:12.** Then have the group brainstorm a list of the "works" that Jesus does. Record their responses on a markerboard.

Say: "Jesus tells us that, as his followers, we will do all of these things as well as even greater things. We are blessed to be partners in Christ's ongoing mission."

Ask a second volunteer to read aloud **1 Peter 2:9-10.** Then ask:

- Who is the "you" whom Peter refers to (as in "You are a chosen race")? (*The early Christians in Peter's original audience and us, Christ's followers today.*)

Say: "If you are a minister, raise your hand."

Tell the group that every person should raise his or her hand. Refer to the Scriptures, above, as needed.

SATURDAY AFTERNOON

Lunch and Free Time

After lunch, give the group some free time. Also set aside some time in the late afternoon for some organized recreation. Plan about an hour's worth of fast-paced cooperative, community-building games. (Since one of the objectives of this retreat is to model Christian community, select games that emphasize cooperation rather than competition.) Links to websites and books containing such games are available at the website. Remind the participants to check their mailbags.

You may choose to take a free-time break sometime during the stole-making project or to lead organized group games just to break up the day.

supplies

- ❑ food for lunch
- ❑ eating and serving utensils
- ❑ cups
- ❑ plates and bowls
- ❑ napkins
- ❑ items for free time

preparation: Be sure that writing supplies are near the mailbags. Put out items for free time.

SATURDAY LATE AFTERNOON

SESSION 3: LET CHRIST GUIDE

Say: "while many people think of a minister as an ordained clergy person, everyone who takes the vows of confirmation is a minister. This afternoon we will make stoles similar to those worn by clergy persons and other church leaders. Stoles signify the yoke worn around the neck of oxen by which oxen are guided. Jesus says to us, "Take my yoke upon you" (**Matthew 11:29**); and, "My yoke is easy, and my burden is light" (**Matthew 11:30**). Wearing a stole symbolizes being tethered to Jesus and allowing Jesus to take the lead.

SUPPLIES
- ❑ long strips of fabric for stoles (See Supplies on page 46.)
- ❑ permanent markers
- ❑ fabric paints and brushes

STOLE MAKING, ROUND 1

(30 minutes)

Give each person a long strip of fabric that will become a stole. Set out assorted permanent markers and fabric paints, but instruct the participants to leave the materials alone until you give them instructions.

Ask:

- What is a stole? (Allow confirmands an opportunity to answer the question before allowing the adults to have a chance to answer.)

Say: "In United Methodism, ordained clergy are traditionally the only ones who wear stoles in worship. But we, like many other Christians, believe that all of Christ's followers are called to be ministers--remember, we are God-bearers to the world. So each of us will make a stole to represent our call to ministry."

Instruct the participants to lay their stole fabric on the table, with both ends, side by side, nearest them and the bend (the part that will go around their neck) farther away from them. Be sure that the stoles are not twisted, that what will be the front of each stole is facing up.

Ask participants to place their left hand on the part of the stole that is closest to their left hand. (This will be on their right side when they are wearing their stole.) Confirmands will start here, working up from the bottom, following these instructions:

1. On the lower right end, one hand-width (about 4 inches) from the bottom, write the name you prefer to be called.
2. Somewhere on this same side of the stole, above your name, write three positive adjectives that describe you.
3. Also on this side of the stole, still toward the bottom, draw a symbol to represent yourself. This could be a symbol related to an activity or interest that you're passionate about or something that you're known for among your friends and family.

Give everyone plenty of time to work, then invite each person to present what he or she wrote or drew.

STOLE MAKING, ROUND 2

(30 minutes)

SUPPLIES
- ❑ participants' stoles
- ❑ permanent markers
- ❑ fabric paints and brushes

Instruct participants to resume work on the same side of their stole (the side that will be on their right side when they are wearing the stole).

4. Ask them write and/or draw above their work from Round 1 the various roles they play in their life. Examples include, but are not limited to, the following:

- son/daughter
- musician
- environmental steward
- student
- gamer
- Scout
- athlete
- friend
- tutor

5. Then instruct the participants to write the word *Christian* above all of the roles they have listed. Explain that "Christian" is their name above all names, the name that defines and shapes how they live out all of the other roles that they play.

After all of the participants have had a chance to write and/or draw all of the roles they play (including Christian), ask them to take a break from working on the stole to reflect on what they have done so far. Invite them to pick one of the roles they have listed on their stole to pair it with the word *Christian,* using *Christian* as an adjective (for example: "Christian friend." Have each person name his or her word pair. It's OK to have duplicates.

Then ask:

- How does being a Christian—a disciple of Jesus—make a difference in the various roles you play?

STOLE MAKING, ROUND 3

(30 minutes)

SUPPLIES
- ❑ Bibles
- ❑ participants' stoles
- ❑ permanent markers
- ❑ fabric paints and brushes

Ask volunteers to read aloud each of the following Scriptures about who God says we are:

- **Psalm 8**
- **Psalm 139:1-18**
- **Isaiah 43:1-3**
- **Romans 8:14-17**
- **1 Timothy 4:12**

6. Instruct the participants to move farther up the stole on the same side and to record words, phrases, and verses about who God says we are (from the Scriptures above). Examples include, but aren't limited to, the following:

- wonderfully made
- mine
- saints
- sinners

Give the participants an opportunity to talk about the words, phrases, and verses they included on their stoles.

Supplies
- ❑ participants' stoles
- ❑ permanent markers
- ❑ fabric paints and brushes

Stole Making, Round 4

30 minutes)

During this round, confirmands will start to work on the right side (which will be the left side when being worn).

Again, instruct the participants to lay their stole fabric on the table, with both ends, side by side, nearest them and the bend (the part that will go around their neck) farther away from them. Be sure that the stoles are not twisted, that what will be the front of each stole is facing up.

7. Tell the participants to add to their stoles symbols, words, and short phrases for the three persons of the Trinity: God the Father, Jesus, and the Holy Spirit. (For example, the word *Creator* might represent God the Father, a cross might represent Christ, and a dove might represent the Holy Spirit.)
8. Invite the participants also to add other faith words and symbols that have meaning to them. Give participants an opportunity to talk about the words, phrases, and symbols they chose and why they chose them.
9. Then ask the confirmands to think of someone who has been a role model them in their walk with God--someone who has been a God-bearer for them. Instruct each person to add to his or her stole a name or symbol for a Christian role model in his or her life.

Supplies
- ❑ participants' stoles
- ❑ permanent markers
- ❑ fabric paints and brushes

Stole Making, Round 5

(30 minutes)

Invite each participant to return to add to what will be the left side of his or her stole (above those things that he or she added in Round 4).

10. Add the word *Theotokos,* as a reminder of our calling to bring God into the world (See "Theotokos," above.)
11. Have the participants trace one of their hands and label the thumb and finger outlines with the letters *P, P, G, S, W* (for *prayers, presence, gifts, service,* and *witness*) so that one letter is on each of the five fingers.
12. Ask the participants to add one or more of these Scripture citations:
    - **1 Peter 2:9-10** ("You are a chosen race, a royal priesthood.")
    - **John 14:12** ("The one who believes in me will also do the works that I do and, in fact, will do greater works than these.")
    - **1 Timothy 4:12** ("Let no one despise your youth, but set the believers an example in speech and conduct, in love, in faith, in purity.")
    - Additional favorite Scriptures or inspirational quotations
13. Invite the participants to sign one another's stoles in the remaining space.

EVENING MEAL

After the meal, give the group some free time if time is available. Remind the everyone to check mailbags.

SUPPLIES
- ❑ food for the meal
- ❑ eating and serving utensils
- ❑ cups
- ❑ plates and bowls
- ❑ napkins

SATURDAY PM

CLOSING WORSHIP AND RECEIVING OF STOLES

(30 minutes)

SUPPLIES
- ❑ completed stoles
- ❑ copies of *The United Methodist Hymnal*
- ❑ songbooks or lyric sheets
- ❑ musical accompaniment

Gather for closing worship, and make sure that each person brings his or her stole. The youth should not put on the stoles.

Begin by having the group sing familiar songs and by offering prayers of thanksgiving for your time together and prayers of intercession for those in need.

Invite any clergy who are present to put on the stoles that signify their roles as ordained ministers.

Then invite the adult participants to come forward and to hand their stoles to a clergyperson (or to the person leading the retreat if a clergyperson is not present). The clergyperson should place the stoles around each adult's shoulders, saying these words (or something similar):

> God bless you in your ministry of confirmation
> as part of our shared ministry in the priesthood
> of all believers and the ministry of all Christians.

Encourage the confirmands to watch and pray silently as each adults receive his or her stole.

After all of the adults have received their stole, instruct them to make a circle, leaving plenty of space between themselves for confirmands to join the circle as they receive their stoles.

Invite each confirmand to hand his or her stole to one of the adults. The adults should place the stoles around the confirmands' shoulders, saying this blessing:

> God bless you in your confirmation journey
> and your unfolding ministry as part of the
> priesthood of all believers. I love you and will
> be with you every step of the way.

Adults may add blessings and comments specific to each confirmand, as appropriate.

As confirmands receive their stoles and blessings, remind them to join the circle. When everyone has joined the circle, encourage all of the participants to look around at "the church."

Then have everyone sing a song of commitment such as "I Have Decided to Follow Jesus" (2129, *The Faith We Sing*) or "A Charge to Keep I Have" (413, *The United Methodist Hymnal*).

NOTE: Although we traditionally attribute this saying to John Wesley, there is no evidence that Wesley ever actually said it. Still, Wesley's Rule has been a popular saying among United Methodists for decades and serves as a great summary of how to live our lives in response to Wesley's second General Rule, "Do good."

Benediction

(5 minutes)

Gather the confirmands into a circle. Go around the circle and allow each person to offer a prayer thanking God for your time together and all that the group has learned and experienced and asking for God's guidance as you go forth. Close this prayer time by saying aloud and in unison the benediction, John Wesley's Rule. (Write this benediction on a markerboard or print out the poster from the website.)

Do all the good you can,
  By all the means you can,
  In all the ways you can,
In all the places you can,
At all the times you can,
To all the people you can,
As long as ever you can.

SUPPLIES
- ❑ items for free time

Free Time

Offer several options for a period of free time before lights out. These options could include table games, writing notes for mailbags, and preparing materials for the next day's activities and sessions.

SUPPLIES
- ❑ food for breakfast
- ❑ eating and serving utensils
- ❑ cups
- ❑ plates and bowls
- ❑ napkins
- ❑ Bibles
- ❑ copies of the "Morning Watch 2" worksheets
- ❑ pens or pencils

PREPARATION: Make copies of "Morning Watch 2" worksheets, from the website.

SUNDAY AM

Morning Watch

(35 minutes)

Gather the group together before breakfast (or after) and hand out copies of the "Morning Watch 2" worksheet. Remind the group to take their Bibles and find a place for solitude and quiet reflection. Allow the participants 30 minutes to complete the exercise then gather for the morning session or breakfast.

Affirmation Posters

(20 minutes)

Give each person a sheet of labels (such as those used in computer printers) and a half-sheet of construction paper. Instruct the participants to write on a separate label an affirming message for each person in the retreat community.

When everyone is finished writing messages, instruct the participants to write their names at the top of their half-sheets of construction paper. Then have everyone pass his or her construction paper to the person to his or her right. Instruct everyone to place on the construction paper the label with the affirming message for the person whose half-sheet

he or she is now holding. Then have everyone pass that paper to the person on the right. Continue until the half-sheets return to their owners. Each person's paper should include an affirming message from every person in the community. These posters will be treasured reminders of this retreat.

SUPPLIES
- ❑ sheets of labels
- ❑ sheets of construction paper, cut in half
- ❑ pens

COMMUNION

(30 minutes)

SUPPLIES
- ❑ Bibles
- ❑ ordained clergyperson (See "Preparation," below.)
- ❑ Communion elements and altar ware for Holy Communion
- ❑ chalice or other common cup
- ❑ plate for the Communion bread
- ❑ linen napkins for the Communion elements
- ❑ copies of *The United Methodist Hymnal*
- ❑ songbooks or lyric sheets
- ❑ musical accompaniment

PREPARATION: An ordained clergyperson will be needed to consecrate the Communion elements. If possible, this clergyperson should be present; if not, he or she may consecrate the elements beforehand.

Close this retreat with a service of Holy Communion. Use "A Service of Word and Table II" (page 12, *The United Methodist Hymnal*). Ordained clergy will need to consecrate the Communion elements. If possible, this clergy person should be present; if not, he or she can consecrate the elements beforehand. If a clergy person is unavailable, substitute a service that doesn't involve Communion, such as "The Love Feast" service (pages 581–584 of *The United Methodist Book of Worship*).

Make sure that ordained clergy is present to administer the sacrament if you have not had the Communion elements consecrated beforehand.

Begin with your group's favorite worship songs. Use **Matthew 16:13-17** ("Who do you say that I am?") as your Scripture text for worship.

After the Scripture reading, invite the group to participate in the reading. Read the Scripture once; then go around to each person and say his or her name, followed by the question, "Who do you say that he is?" If a participant feels led, he or she may speak a response such as "He is the Son of God." or "He's my savior." Or he or she may choose to speak a prayer for more belief, such as "I believe; help my unbelief."

Songs related to Holy Communion might include the following:

- "Time Now to Gather" (2265, *The Faith We Sing*)
- "Taste and See" (2267, *The Faith We Sing*)
- "Be Present at Our Table, Lord" (621, *The United Methodist Hymnal*)
- "Let Us Break Bread Together" (618, *The United Methodist Hymnal*)

Toward the end of The Great Thanksgiving, before The Lord's Prayer, invite the participants to give thanks for those who have helped them on their faith journey.

Conclude with a benediction addressed to the participants, telling them to go forth as members of Christ's holy church, loved by God, and called to do the work of God's kingdom.

Credo:
Day of Prayer

INTRODUCTION

Those who take the confirmation vows make a commitment to, among other things, uphold the church with their prayers. As members of the body of Christ, we have a responsibility to be *pray-ers*—people who pray silently and aloud, alone and with others, and with our very lives. Jesus' disciples said to him, "Teach us how to pray." So prayer must be something that we can learn to do or learn to do better. This retreat will introduce confirmands to a variety of prayer forms and will help them develop the holy habits of prayer and meditation.

You may do your Day of Prayer as a day apart—a one-day experience held within your sanctuary, at the home of a church member who has some property large enough to do some walking around, at another church nearby, or at a retreat center. Or you may choose to do a lock-in-style event that is focused on rest and prayer—sort of the opposite of what a normal youth lock-in is!

It will be important to get away from phones and the temptation to split your attention between the retreat and routine responsibilities. If you don't do a Day of Prayer, you might still choose to use some of these prayer practices in a retreat or in confirmation classes.

SUPPLIES

- ❑ Bibles
- ❑ paper
- ❑ chairs
- ❑ pens, pencils, markers, and/or crayons
- ❑ copies of "The Lord's Prayer Reverse Paraphrase" handout, from the website
- ❑ copies of *The United Methodist Hymnal*
- ❑ songbooks or lyric sheets (Be mindful of copyright laws.)
- ❑ musical accompaniment: guitar or other instruments
- ❑ stopwatch or watch that displays seconds
- ❑ worship center/altar space
- ❑ healthful snacks and drinks (preferably water) for appropriate breaks
- ❑ Optional: food for a light noon meal that might be served after "A Silent Walk" or at any time that fits within the flow of the retreat. Have on hand breakfast foods if you plan an overnight stay.

opening song

(10 minutes)

Begin with a song about prayer. Make this song a theme song for the entire retreat. Options include:

- "Teach Me How to Pray," by Chris Hughes (more information at *credoconfirmation.com*)
- "Lord, Listen to Your Children Praying" (156, *Zion Still Sings,* and 2193, *The Faith We Sing*)
- "O Lord, Hear My Prayer" (2200, *The Faith We Sing*)
- "Take Time to Be Holy" (395, *The United Methodist Hymnal*)

Following the opening song, say: "Today we will experience and practice many kinds of prayer, including silent prayers, group prayers, and prayers that involve trying out various postures. In general, this retreat is an exercise in paying attention—paying attention to the presence of God and the movement of the Holy Spirit. Let go of any distractions, such as school or other things that are going on this weekend, and be fully present."

supplies

- ❑ copies of *The United Methodist Hymnal,* songbooks, or lyric sheets
- ❑ musical accompaniment: guitar or other instruments

breath prayers

(30–40 minutes)

Invite the participants to sit in chairs and to get in a comfortable sitting position, with both feet on the floor and their back against the back of the chair.

Say: "We're going to spend a few moments becoming aware of our breath."

Instruct the participants to close their eyes and to breathe in their regular rhythm, counting slowly to themselves as they breathe in and as they breathe out. (For example, someone might count "one, two, three" as he or she breathes in and "one, two, three, four" as he or she breathes out.)

After a few moments, ask the participants to slowly open their eyes. Ask:

- How many counts did it take you to breathe in? to breathe out?

Then say: "Now I want you to breathe on my count. You'll inhale four counts, pause, then exhale four counts."

Instruct the participants to close their eyes, take a deep cleansing breath, then exhale. Have them breathe on your count, inhaling for four counts, pausing, then exhaling for four counts. Repeat this cycle several times.

Then invite the participants to open their eyes.

Say: "Now I want you to find your own deep breathing rhythm."

supplies

- ❑ chairs (enough for each participant to sit in one)

Tell the participants to once again close their eyes and to pay attention to how many counts it takes for them to fully fill their lungs and how many counts it takes for them to exhale completely. Instruct participants to control their breathing so that they inhale and exhale in the same number of counts (with a pause in between).

After everyone has had time to fall into a good rhythm, gently call the participants' attention back to you. Then invite them to open their eyes.

Say: "Praying to the rhythm of your breathing is an ancient devotional practice. One common Christian breath prayer is 'Lord Jesus Christ, have mercy on me.' We can pray the first part, 'Lord Jesus Christ,' as we inhale and the second part, 'have mercy on me,' as we exhale. If you breathe deeply and slowly, with a long count, you may be able to say the entire prayer as you inhale and again as you exhale."

Ask the participants to again take a cleansing breath. Invite them to repeat this simple breath prayer—"Lord Jesus Christ, have mercy on me"—in rhythm with their breathing. After they have prayed this way for a while, gently invite their attention back to you.

Explain that they may lengthen the basic prayer for longer or deeper breathing patterns. They might choose to pray, "Lord Jesus Christ, Son of God, have mercy on me, a sinner." Or they might choose to pray a different prayer, reciting the names of the people they love and whom Jesus calls them to love. For example: "Lord Jesus, I love you. Heavenly Father, I love you. Holy Spirit, I love you. Mom and Dad, I love you. Hungry persons in my community, I love you. Persons suffering from AIDS or Malaria, I love you."

After this time of prayer, invite the participants to take the first of several prayer walks. Tell them to walk around outside (or inside if the weather is bad), saying a breath prayer. Tell participants to stay together on this walk and to remain silent. Have the participants spend about 15 minutes walking.

ACTS prayers

(15–20 minutes)

Call the participants back together, and have them gather into a circle. Discuss their experience with breath prayer, asking questions such as:

- What did you like most about this type of prayer?
- What was most challenging about this type of prayer?
- How did you experience God through this type of prayer?

Then say: "We're going to learn a different style of prayer called an 'ACTS prayer.' "

Explain the ACTS prayer pattern:

A—Adoration: prayers of praise and expressions of love and worship

C—Confession: owning up to what we have done or said that is against God's will for us (sins of commission) or to what we have left undone, things we could have done or ought to have done that would have been right and good and faithful (sins of omission)

T—Thanksgiving: things, persons, and experiences for which we are thankful

S—Supplication: prayers of need, especially for other people (Such prayers are also known as intercessory prayers.)

Explain that the prayers they will pray that follow the ACTS pattern will be one-word or one-short-phrase prayers. Tell everyone to bow his or her head. Then go around the circle and give each person an opportunity to offer a one-word or one-phrase prayer of adoration. Tell the participants to offer a single word or phrase describing the qualities and characteristics of God the Father, Christ, and/or the Holy Spirit. These might include *Creator, holy, wonderful, great, loving, Counselor, Comforter.*

Assure the participants that it is OK to repeat words. After going around the circle, begin again by asking everyone to offer a one-word or one-phrase prayer of confession. These might include words such as *anger, greed, laziness, disrespect, neglect.*

Go around a third time, this time having everyone offer a prayer of thanksgiving ("for food," "for family," "for the church," and so forth).

Finally, invite everyone to offer a prayer of supplication ("persons who are hungry," "cancer patients," "war," and so forth).

Be Still and Know God

(20 minutes)

Supplies

- ❑ stopwatch or watch that displays seconds

Take a short break, then gather everyone back together.

Say: "Learning to be still is an important skill for disciples of Christ to master. Many of us are not accustomed to being still, but stillness can be a gift. As **Psalm 46** says, 'Be still and know that I am God' (verse 10)."

Challenge the participants to be completely silent for one minute. Then experiment with silence for increasingly longer periods of time (such as 2 minutes and 5 minutes). Ask the group to be aware of the sounds they hear when everyone is silent. As you enter into longer periods of silence, invite the participants to try different prayer postures. Here are some positions to try:

- palms open in front of you, instead of hands folded
- looking up, instead of looking down
- lying on your back on the floor
- praying on your knees
- praying with your face in your hands
- praying prostrate on the floor with your arms out to your side, your body in the shape of the cross

After each period of silence, ask questions such as:

- What was challenging about remaining silent for this period of time?
- How did you experience God in the silence?
- What prayer posture did you try? What did you like or dislike about this posture?

Supplies
- ❑ Bibles
- ❑ stopwatch or watch that displays seconds

A Silent Walk

(25–40 minutes)

Invite the participants to go on a second prayer walk. Have them walk and pray for at least 15 minutes, with the goal of praying for 30 minutes. (The dynamics of your group and the layout and location of your retreat space will play a part in determining how long the prayer walk will last.) Be clear about boundaries.

Before sending everyone off, ask volunteers to read aloud **Luke 24:13-35** (the walk to Emmaus). Talk with the group about how the two disciples were walking together when a person whom they did not recognize came to join them. Of course, the disciples would realize that the person walking alongside them was Jesus, now resurrected.

Say: "As you walk together in silence, keep your hearts open for the presence of Christ with you. Keep your eyes open for anything that reminds you of Christ or his teaching or his body, the church."

Depending on your retreat setting, you might also ask everyone to bring back from the walk an object that serves as a metaphor for God the Father, Jesus, the Holy Spirit, or the Church. Examples might include a rock (like Peter's faith, upon which Jesus built his church) or a branch (which reminds us that Jesus is the vine and we are the branches).

After the allotted time has passed, gather everyone back together and discuss the experience of silently walking and being mindful of Christ's presence.

The Lord's Prayer

(20–25 minutes)

Gather the group together in a worship space. Have the group sing one of the songs mentioned in the first activity, "Opening Song" or a musical version of The Lord's Prayer (such as 2278, in *The Faith We Sing*). Then say The Lord's Prayer together.

Hand out copies of "The Lord's Prayer Reverse Paraphrase" handout, from *credoconfirmation.com*. Explain to the participants that, for each line of The Lord's Prayer, they will write a reverse paraphrase of that line—a paraphrase that gives the line the opposite meaning. For example, "Our Father, who art in heaven, hallowed be thy name," might become, "I don't need a heavenly father, and I'm going to cuss like a sailor."

Give the participants plenty of time to work, then invite volunteers to read aloud their reverse paraphrases. Ask:

- How, do you think, did this exercise give the prayer, or certain lines, new meaning?
- How, do you think, is God like a good and loving parent?
- What, do you think, does it mean when something is "holy" or "hallowed"?
- What, do you think, does it mean for God's will to be done on earth as in heaven?
- How, do you think, can you fully depend on God to provide your daily needs?
- What does it mean to you that God, through Christ, forgives your sins?
- Why, do you think, is it important that we also forgive those who sin against us? How can God give us the strength to forgive even when doing so is difficult?
- What are some of the temptations you face? How does God help you avoid or deal with temptation?
- How does God deliver us from evil?

Invite the participants to reflect on what they need to be forgiven for and whom they need to forgive.

Then ask a volunteer to read aloud The Lord's Prayer as it appears in **Matthew 6:9-13.**

Offertory Preparation, Repentance, and Dedication

(40 minutes)

Tell the participants that they will have 30 minutes to prepare an offering for the closing worship service (the next activity). This preparation should be done in silence.

Say: "Your offering will fall into one of two categories. One category is a *dedication offering*. A dedication offering is a personal gift, talent, or goal that you want to give to God. As you offer it, you are dedicating it to God's glory.

"The second category is a *repentance offering*. Is there something in your life that is keeping you from loving God with all your heart, mind, soul, and strength? Has something come between you and God? Is it hurting your other relationships? A repentance offering might be an unhealthful habit, a grudge

Supplies
- ❑ Bible
- ❑ lyric sheets
- ❑ copies of *The United Methodist Hymnal*, songbooks, or lyric sheets
- ❑ musical accompaniment: guitar or other instruments
- ❑ copies of "The Lord's Prayer Reverse Paraphrase" handout, from the website
- ❑ pens or pencils

Preparation: Make copies of "The Lord's Prayer: Reverse Paraphrase" handout, from the website.

supplies
- ❑ Bibles
- ❑ paper
- ❑ pens, pencils, markers, and/or crayons

note: Do not expect or encourage confirmands to leave items behind, but if some decide that what they have offered has become a distraction and has kept them from focusing on their relationships with God and others, allow them to leave the item in your care. Give the item to the confirmands' parents along with an explanation of why it was left behind.

that you hold, or something you have become obsessed with. As you offer it, you are asking God to help you turn away from it and turn back toward God."

Tell the participants that they should be prepared to bring some tangible representation of the offering. Dedications might include, for example, a cell phone (if excessive texting or gossiping is keeping them from God), a guitar pick (if music is one of their gifts), a piece of jewelry or an electronic device (if they feel as though they obsess too much about material things), a poem (if writing is one of their gifts). Point out that paper and writing utensils are available if they need them. Some participants may ask whether they will get their offerings back. The answer is yes, unless they choose to leave them behind. (See the note in the margin.)

Tell the participants that you will invite them to bring their offerings to the altar table. They will have the opportunity, but are not required, to tell the group about what they are bringing and why.

Closing Worship

(20 minutes)

supplies
- ❑ worship center/altar space
- ❑ Bible
- ❑ lyric sheets
- ❑ musical accompaniment
- ❑ dedication and repentance offerings

preparation: Assemble the worship center/altar space.

Gather the group into a circle for a round of prayers. One person (you as a leader or one of the other participants) will start by offering a spoken prayer about whatever is in his or her heart. When the first person finishes, he or she will gently squeeze the hand of the person on his or her right. This person then will offer a spoken prayer. Continue around the circle. If a participant is not comfortable praying aloud, he or she may simply squeeze the hand of the person on his or her right.

After this time of prayer, have the group sing some familiar worship songs, including songs about prayer (see "Opening Song," page 61). If you have chosen a theme song for this retreat, include that song as well. As the participants sing, invite them to get into prayer postures that are helpful to them.

Following the singing, invite participants to bring their dedication and repentance offerings to the altar table. Allow each person to talk about his or her offering and why he or she brought it. Take time to pray (silently and/or aloud) for each person who comes.

Finally, with hands stretched out over the offering table, offer closing prayers of thanksgiving, hope, and dedication.

Offer a benediction, and invite the participants to retrieve their offerings (if they choose to; see the margin note above) and to exchange signs of God's love and peace.

Creation

INTRODUCTION

The Credo Confirmation program includes 18 lessons divided into three units: "Know Your Story," "Confirm Your Faith," and "Live Your Commitment." The first unit, "Know Your Story," gives confirmands an overview of their faith story as found in the pages of Scripture and in the history and tradition of the church. The second unit, "Confirm Your Faith," teaches confirmands about the essential beliefs, doctrines, and values that we—as United Methodist Christians—hold and about how these beliefs, doctrines, and values are rooted in our story. The third unit, "Live Your Commitment," teaches confirmands how Christians can and should live in response to who we are and what we believe.

The "Know Your Story" unit begins (as it should) with God's creation of the heavens and the earth. The accounts of Creation in the opening chapters of Genesis teach us that God created all things, created humankind in God's image, and declared all of Creation good. All of these truths have implications for who we are as God's beloved creations and how we live in relationship with others, with God, and with the rest of Creation.

In the first two chapters of Genesis, we not only see the different aspects of Creation—light, darkness, water, land, life, and so forth—but we also learn about God. We learn that God is creative and is responsible for crafting the entire universe. We learn that God is pleased with this creation, that God considers it special. We learn that God created one creature—humankind—in God's own likeness and that God expects human beings to live in relationship with one another. The lessons that we learn in these accounts of Creation appear over and again throughout the Christian story and have implications for how we live our daily lives.

Hear the Creation Story Again for the First Time

In this session, confirmands will learn the story of Creation, a story that they may have learned as children. Those who are familiar with the story likely learned what things God created on each of the six days and about the one tree in the garden from which the first humans were not allowed to eat. Confirmation gives youth the opportunity to go deeper—to

read the text for themselves and to discern what God is saying through Scripture. As young people mature in faith, the Creation accounts in Genesis are about much more than the day on which God created the moon and stars or the names of the rivers surrounding Eden. These Scriptures teach us about God and ourselves and our relationship with God. They illustrate God's love and creativity and remind us that, as beings created in God's image, we too have the capacity to love and to create.

The opening chapters of Genesis also teach us that we have a responsibility to be good stewards of all that God has created. Stewardship of creation has become a popular subject in the church in recent years as Christians have become increasingly concerned about the state of the natural world. While caring for the environment is an important part of what we're called to do as God's children, stewardship of creation is much more that just being eco-friendly. It involves how we use all that God has entrusted to us. This includes our gifts, our relationships with others, our time, our ability to love, and all of the other resources God has provided for us.

God the Creator

Our faith story starts with Creation, and Creation starts with God. This session teaches (or reminds) confirmands that we serve a triune God: one God in three persons. Later sessions in this unit will look at Christ—God the Son, or Redeemer—and the Holy Spirit—God the Sustainer. But since this session is about Creation, it will focus on God the Father, or Creator.

As you discuss God with the young people in your confirmation group, be sure to anchor the discussion in concepts that are concrete. The idea of a triune God can be difficult for a young person to grasp. (For that matter, the Trinity can be a difficult concept for seminary-educated adults to grasp.) When you introduce each person of the Trinity, talk about specific characteristics of that person and specific ways in which that person interacts with humanity and creation. Instead of trying to explain who God the Creator is, look at what God does and how we experience God in the world around us.

SUPPLIES AND PREPARATION

BASIC SUPPLIES

❑ Bibles of various translations ❑ markerboard or large sheets of paper ❑ markers ❑ pens or pencils	❑ clear tape and/or glue ❑ masking tape ❑ index cards or paper cut about the same size (3-by-5 or 4-by-6) ❑ sheets of posterboard	❑ paper (Use paper that has already been used on one side as much as possible, depending on the activity.) ❑ scissors

ACTIVITY	PREPARATION	OTHER SUPPLIES
WHAT?		
Opening Ritual	Create a "vine." Write the opening meditation—which is adapted from 1 Chronicles 16:8, 12, 15, 23—on a markerboard; or project the meditation, using the slide on the website.	❑ vine that will be added to each session ❑ vine branches (1 for each student)
SO WHAT? PART 1		
Order of Creation	Make a copy of "Order of Creation" on the website. Cut the strips apart, and put each set in a separate envelope.	❑ 2 envelopes ❑ strips of paper cut from "Order of Creation"
The Days of Creation	Gather supplies.	❑ 6 sheets of posterboard or 15–24 feet of large paper from a roll (such as butcher, mural, or kraft paper)
Names of God	Gather supplies.	❑ Bible dictionaries ❑ concordances ❑ hymnals
SO WHAT? PART 2		
First Person	Gather supplies.	
Created in God's Image	Gather supplies.	
Created to Be Caretakers	Gather copies of the "Preamble to the Social Principles," or make copies of the handout from the website.	❑ copies of the "Preamble to the Social Principles"
NOW WHAT?		
Stewards for a Day	Gather supplies.	❑ mural or posters from the "Days of Creation" activity ❑ note cards
Closing Ritual	Write the benediction, "John Wesley's Rule," on a markerboard; or print out the poster from the website.	

WHAT?

SUPPLIES
- ❑ vine that will be added to each session
- ❑ vine branches (1 for each student)
- ❑ markers or pens

PREPARATION: Create a "vine." Write the opening meditation—which is adapted from 1 Chronicles 16:8, 12, 15, 23—on a markerboard; or project the meditation, using the slide on the website.

OPENING RITUAL

(10 minutes)

Each session in CREDO CONFIRMATION begins with an opening ritual inspired by **John 15:1-9** ("I am the vine, you are the branches"—verse 5*a*). Prior to the first session, you will need to create a "vine." Draw a tree trunk on a large sheet of paper, paint a trunk on a wall in your meeting space, construct a vine or tree out of wood. Be creative, and involve the confirmands as much as possible. Also prior to the first session, you will need one "branch" for each confirmand (see below).

During the six sessions of first unit, "Know Your Story," the confirmands will add branches to the vine or trunk. During the second unit, "Confirm Your Faith," the confirmands will add leaves to the branches. And during the final unit, "Live Your Commitment," the confirmands will add fruit to the branches ("Those who abide in me and I in them bear much fruit"—**John 15:5*b***). Be creative in how you represent the branches, leaves, and fruit that grow from the vine or trunk.

As the confirmands arrive for the first session, give each person a branch or a way to make one. Invite each person to write on his or her branch something that he or she has gained from the time he or she has spent in the church so far. This might include knowledge gained from a Sunday school teacher, the love and support of an older member of the congregation, the friendship of fellow Christian young people, a relationship with God. Instruct the confirmands to attach their branches to the vine.

Say: "Jesus teaches, 'Just as the branch cannot bear fruit by itself unless it abides in the vine, neither can you unless you abide in me' (**John 15:4*b***). When we, the branches, abide in Christ, the vine, we are drawn into God's ongoing story. This story involves several people who are rooted in Christ and who have branched out into the world, touching people with God's love and grace."

When all of the confirmands have arrived, invite each person to talk briefly about what he or she wrote on his or her branch. Then invite the youth to read aloud the opening meditation (included on the website in the "Opening Meditations" handout), which is adapted from **1 Chronicles 16:8, 12, 15, 23:**

> Give thanks to the LORD,
>   and make God's deeds known among the peoples.
> Remember the wonderful works that God has done;
>   remember God's covenant forever.
> Sing to the LORD, all the earth.
>   Tell of God's salvation every day.

SO WHAT? PART 1

Order of Creation

(15 minutes)

Give each student one of the two sets of slips cut from "Order of Creation" on the website. Give the youth 3 minutes to put the activities of Creation in order, without referring to the Bible. (Make sure that both sets of slips are assigned.)

After 3 minutes, ask each youth to tape his or her slips, in the agreed upon order, on a wall. Then ask volunteers to read aloud **Genesis 1:1–2:4*a*** and **2:4*b*-25** to check the their accuracy.

supplies
- ❑ envelopes
- ❑ strips of paper cut from "Order of Creation" (one for each student)
- ❑ tape

preparation: Make a copy of "Order of Creation" on the website. Cut the strips apart, and put each set in a separate envelope. Make a set for each student.

The Days of Creation

(20 minutes)

Before students arrive, place on the floor the sheets of posterboard or a long sheet of paper divided into six equal sections. Label the six sheets of posterboard or sections "Day 1," "Day 2," "Day 3," and so on. Set a Bible and several markers at each section or posterboard.

Assign one or more day and its (or their) corresponding board(s) to each youth and have the youth read their Scripture(s) from the list below.

Day 1: Genesis 1:1-5

Day 2: Genesis 1:6-8

Day 3: Genesis 1:9-13

Day 4: Genesis 1:14-19

Day 5: Genesis 1:20-23

Day 6: Genesis 1:24-31

Instruct the youth to draw their assigned day of Creation exactly as it is described in their assigned verses from the first chapter of **Genesis.** Ask the youth to try to forget the picture Bibles they may have used as children or the posters that may have hung in their Sunday school classrooms. The youth are to pay attention to exactly what the Bible says.

Give the confirmands about 10 minutes to work. Then invite them to examine each section of the story.

Ask:

- What looks familiar to you?
- What did you read, hear, or see during this activity that you had not thought about or heard before?

supplies
- ❑ Bibles
- ❑ 6 sheets of posterboard or 15–24 feet of large paper from a roll (such as butcher, mural, or kraft paper)
- ❑ markers

SUPPLIES
- ❑ Bibles
- ❑ Bible dictionaries
- ❑ Bible concordances
- ❑ hymnals

NAMES OF GOD

(15 minutes)

Say: "The Bible is the work of many people and communities over many years, each of whom came to know God in a unique way and each of whom chose names for God that described their relationship with God and their understanding of God's action in the world."

Provide Bibles, Bible dictionaries, Bible concordances, and hymnals. Challenge the class to search through Scripture, using the tools provided, to identify as many names for God as possible. Give the confirmands a few minutes to work, offering guidance where needed. Then ask:

- What do each of these names tell us about who God is and what God desires for Creation?

NOTE: If you choose to divide this session into two one-hour classes, break here.

SO WHAT? PART 2

SUPPLIES
- ❑ markerboard or paper
- ❑ markers or pens

FIRST PERSON

(15 minutes)

Say: "As Christians, we believe in the Trinity: one God who is three persons."

Ask:

- Who are the three persons of the Trinity?

Say: "We often refer to the persons of the Trinity as God the Father, Jesus Christ the Son, and the Holy Spirit. But it can be helpful to refer to the persons of the Trinity by some of the key roles they play. While all three persons play several roles and always work together, we're going to focus on three key roles in this unit: Creator, Redeemer, and Sustainer. In the Scriptures we read from Genesis, we see God in the role of Creator."

Lift up The United Methodist Church's teaching on God the Creator, from "The Confession of Faith of the Evangelical United Brethren Church, Article I—God," which is found in *The Book of Discipline of The United Methodist Church* (and printed below). Explain that the Evangelical United Brethren Church was one of two denominations that merged in 1968 to form The United Methodist Church.

As you read aloud the following paragraph, ask the confirmands to pay attention to the words used to describe God:

> We believe in the one true, holy, and living God, Eternal Spirit, who is Creator, Sovereign, and Preserver of all things visible and invisible. He is infinite in power, wisdom, justice, goodness and love, and rules with gracious regard for the well-being and salvation of [humankind], to the glory of his name.

Ask:

- What words does this statement use to describe who God is and what God does?

Record these words on a markerboard or sheet of paper.

Say: "The Scriptures from Genesis and the statement from our *Book of Discipline* show us that God loves all that God created and cares about the 'well-being and salvation' of all people."

Created in God's Image

(30 minutes)

Supplies
- ❑ Bibles
- ❑ paper
- ❑ pens or pencils

Say: "**Genesis 1:27** says that God created us in God's image. This doesn't necessarily mean that we physically look like God but means that we share many of God's characteristics."

Ask:

- What is something you have worked hard to create? (*works of art, projects they have built or put together with their parents, a website they have constructed, and so forth*)
- How do you feel about these creations? What have you done to protect or preserve them?

Say: "Like God, we have the ability to create and to care for our creations. Creativity is one important way in which we bear God's image."

Look at the other characteristics of God that the confirmands listed during the previous activity. Discuss each characteristic, and talk about whether it is also true of human beings (or is potentially true of human beings).

Then say: "Since we are created in God's image, as we learn more about who God is, we learn more about who we are and whom God calls us to be."

Ask volunteers to read aloud each of the following Scriptures. Discuss with the class how each passage describes God.

- **Matthew 20:1-16** (*like a generous boss*)
- **Luke 15:8-10** (*like a rejoicing woman*)
- **Luke 15:11-32** (*like a forgiving father*)
- **John 10:1-18** (*like a shepherd*)
- **John 13:3-5, 12-16** (*like a servant*)

Ask:

- What do these Scriptures tell us about who God is?
- What do they tell us about who God wants us to be?

Created to Be Caretakers

(15–20 minutes)

Give the youth copies of the "Preamble to the Social Principles" handout. Ask a volunteer to read aloud the preamble.

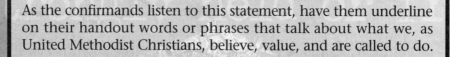

SUPPLIES
- ❑ copies of the "Preamble to the Social Principles"

PREPARATION: Gather copies of the "Preamble to the Social Principles," or make copies of the handout from the website.

NOTE: The Preamble to the Social Principles is from *The Book of Discipline of The United Methodist Church,* paragraph 160.

As the confirmands listen to this statement, have them underline on their handout words or phrases that talk about what we, as United Methodist Christians, believe, value, and are called to do.

Preamble to the Social Principles
We, the people called United Methodists, affirm our faith in God our Creator and Father, in Jesus Christ our Savior, and in the Holy Spirit, our Guide and Guard.

We acknowledge our complete dependence upon God in birth, in life, in death, and in life eternal. Secure in God's love, we affirm the goodness of life and confess our many sins against God's will for us as we find it in Jesus Christ. We have not always been faithful stewards of all that has been committed to us by God the Creator. We have been reluctant followers of Jesus Christ in his mission to bring all persons into a community of love. Though called by the Holy Spirit to become new creatures in Christ, we have resisted the further call to become the people of God in our dealings with each other and the earth on which we live.

Grateful for God's forgiving love, in which we live and by which we are judged, and affirming our belief in the inestimable worth of each individual, we renew our commitment to become faithful witnesses to the gospel, not alone to the ends of the earth, but also to the depths of our common life and work.

Let the students ask questions about any parts of the statement that didn't make sense to them. Invite volunteers to tell what words and phrases they underlined. Be sure to discuss concepts such as being "faithful stewards of all that has been committed to us" (managing and caring for all that God has given us) and being called to "become new creatures in Christ" (living as people claimed, loved, and called by God.)

Ask:

- What does this statement say about creation?
- What does this statement say about our Creator?
- According to this statement, what responsibilities do we have as God's children and as caretakers of God's creation?

Remind the confirmands of **Genesis 1:28,** in which God gives humankind dominion over the earth, and **Genesis 2:15,** in which God tells Adam to till and keep the garden.

Say: "Often when Christians talk about caring for Creation or being good stewards of Creation, we are referring to caring for the environment. This is important, because the natural world is part of God's beloved creation. But being a steward of creation is about more than just living an eco-friendly lifestyle. We also have to use our gifts and talents to honor God, to show people God's love, and to let people know the good news about what God has done through Jesus Christ."

NOW WHAT?

Stewards for a Day

Have the confirmands take another look at the mural or posters that they created as part of the "Days of Creation" activity. As you focus on each of the 6 days, challenge the youth to think of ways that they could be good stewards of that aspect of Creation. For example, the vegetation created on the third day could be used to feed those who are hungry or to prepare a meal that would bring people together in fellowship; since the sun and moon created on the fourth day define our sleep/wake cycles and is how we measure time, the youth could talk about making wise and faithful use of time. Have the youth write these examples of stewardship on note cards and clip them to the appropriate poster or section of the mural.

Say: "God declared all of creation 'good,' and we have talked about many ways that we can care for God's good creation. In coming sessions, we'll look at how sin and death entered the picture and how God—through Christ and the Holy Spirit—is hard at work healing and redeeming creation."

Supplies
- ❑ mural or posters from the "Days of Creation" activity
- ❑ pens or pencils
- ❑ note cards
- ❑ paper clips

Closing Ritual

(10 minutes)

Gather the confirmands into a circle. Lead them in prayer, giving thanks to God for your time together and all that the group has learned and experienced. Then go around the circle, inviting each one to pray aloud one word or phrase that describes something he or she learned during today's confirmation class. This could include something they learned during this session.

After everyone has shared, say a brief closing prayer. Then invite the confirmands to say aloud and in unison the following benediction, called "John Wesley's Rule":

Do all the good you can,
By all the means you can,
In all the ways you can,
In all the places you can,
At all the times you can,
To all the people you can,
As long as ever you can.

Note: Although we traditionally attribute this saying to John Wesley, there is no evidence that Wesley ever actually said it. Still, Wesley's Rule has been a popular saying among United Methodists for decades and serves as a great summary of how to live our lives in response to Wesley's second General Rule, "Do good."

Supplies
- ❑ markerboard
- ❑ marker

Preparation: Write the benediction, "John Wesley's Rule," on a markerboard; or print out the poster from the website.

Note: Before you dismiss, instruct the confirmands to read, reflect on, and journal about the material in the "Creation" section of the *Credo Confirmation Student Journal* before your next session. Also encourage them to do the activities related to "Creation" on the confirmand website at *www.credoconfirmation.com.*

Sin

INTRODUCTION

The previous session told the story of Creation. God created the heavens and the earth and declared all of Creation good. Scripture tells of the creation of the first humans and of how God called these persons to be caretakers of an idyllic garden. The Bible begins with paradise, with God, with humankind, and with all of creation living in right relationship.

This session tells the story of how things went wrong.

Like the accounts of Creation, the story of the first sin and its consequences is likely familiar to confirmands who grew up in the church. They know that in the middle of the garden is the tree from which Adam and Eve are forbidden to eat, that a serpent tempts Eve to take a bite of the forbidden fruit, and that Adam decides to do likewise. The students know that, after Adam and Eve sinned, they realized that they were naked and they felt shame for the first time. And the confirmands may be familiar with the punishments that God handed down. Again, confirmation gives the students an opportunity to go deeper and to consider not only the consequences of sin for Adam and Eve but also how sin affects our relationships with God, with one another, and with all of Creation.

Many confirmands will have had the misfortune of experiencing a broken or damaged relationship. Some may come from families torn apart by divorce; some may have been hurt or let down by an adult whom they trusted and respected; many have had fights with close friends. While those of us who work with students never want them to experience the heartache of broken or damaged relationships, these experiences give young people a sense of the pain and destruction caused by sin.

"ALL HAVE SINNED AND FALL SHORT OF THE GLORY OF GOD"

Any discussion of sin must take into account the fact that all persons are sinners. As Paul writes, "[All] have sinned and fall short of the glory of God" (**Romans 3:23**). This session affirms that no one can avoid the temptation to sin; but it also affirms that sin excludes no one from God's grace or the possibility of redemption and reconciliation. Too often, young people feel that they do not measure up to the moral and ethical standards of the church or that the church is full of hypocrites, who say one thing on Sundays and live by a different set of rules other days of the week. In reality, the church is full of sinners trying to live faithfully each day, failing miserably some days and succeeding in inspiring ways other days.

Young people may take comfort in knowing that the great heroes of our faith were all guilty of sin; but God, nonetheless, continued to work in their lives. Sarah laughed upon hearing of God's promises; Moses murdered an Egyptian slave master; David committed adultery; Peter denied Jesus; Paul persecuted Christians. John Wesley, the founder of Methodism, barred the girl he was in love with from Holy Communion after she married a romantic rival. God loves us and uses us despite our sin.

Grace to Fix a Broken World

Young people also need to recognize all of the ways in which sin is at work in the world. Sin not only affects individuals who make poor decisions and damage their relationships with other people, but it also infects entire institutions, cultures, and nations. Such corporate sin is responsible for horrors such as poverty, racism, and genocide. Sometimes we participate in corporate sin without even being aware that we are. In the United Methodist tradition, we address corporate sin through documents such as our Social Principles and *Book of Resolutions*. As a church, we strive to be aware of and to reject all forms of sin and injustice.

While all sin, personal and corporate, disrupts our relationship with God, no sin removes us from God's presence. In the United Methodist tradition, we affirm that God's grace surrounds us. Sin does not have the last word; love does. Again, to quote Paul, "God proves his love for us in that while we still were sinners Christ died for us" (**Romans 5:8**).

This session teaches confirmands about sin and brokenness; but it also points them to the following session, in which they will learn about redemption and reconciliation.

SUPPLIES AND PREPARATION

BASIC SUPPLIES

❑ Bibles of various translations ❑ markerboard or large sheets of paper ❑ markers ❑ pens or pencils	❑ clear tape and/or glue ❑ masking tape ❑ index cards or paper cut about the same size (3-by-5 or 4-by-6) ❑ sheets of posterboard	❑ paper (Use paper that has already been used on one side as much as possible, depending on the activity.) ❑ scissors

ACTIVITY	PREPARATION	OTHER SUPPLIES
WHAT?		
Opening Ritual	Write the opening meditation—which is adapted from 1 Chronicles 16:8, 12, 15, 23—on a markerboard; or project the meditation, using the slide on the website.	❑ vine from previous session ❑ vine branches (1 for each student)
SO WHAT? PART 1		
Back to the Beginning	Hang in your meeting space "The Days of Creation" mural or posterboards from the previous session.	❑ mural from "The Days of Creation" in the Creation session
Who Sinned?	Make copies of the "Who Sinned?" worksheet.	❑ 2 bells ❑ copies of the "Who Sinned?" worksheet
Corporate Sin	Select from the most current Social Principles of The United Methodist Church and/or *The Book of Resolutions of The United Methodist Church* a few statements and/or resolutions that address collective sin. These might involve racism, sexism, hunger, poverty, or poor environmental stewardship.	❑ a copy (or copies) of the Social Principles of The United Methodist Church and/or *The Book of Resolutions of The United Methodist Church* ❑ a globe ❑ an adhesive bandage for each person ❑ optional: newspapers, news magazines, and/or computers with Internet access
SO WHAT? PART 2		
Reconcile? No Way!	Gather supplies.	
Where There's Sin, There's Grace	Gather supplies. Make sure that any cracked mirrors don't have sharp edges.	❑ mirrors and cracked mirrors
NOW WHAT?		
Sin Is Real	Make copies of the "Sin Is Real" handout.	❑ copies of the "Sin Is Real" handout
Closing Ritual	Write the benediction, "John Wesley's Rule," on a markerboard; or print out the poster from the website.	

WHAT?

opening ritual

(10 minutes)

As confirmands arrive, point them to the confirmation vine begun in the "Creation" session (page 70); and give each person a branch. Invite the confirmands to reflect on the previous session and to write on their branch something they learned or experienced during that session. Ask the confirmands to attach their branch to the vine. Remind the youth that this vine and its branches represent God's story, a story that they are a part of.

When all of the confirmands have arrived, invite each person to talk briefly about what he or she wrote on his or her branch. Then invite the youth to read aloud the opening meditation, which is adapted from **1 Chronicles 16:8, 12, 15, 23:**

> Give thanks to the LORD,
> and make God's deeds known among the peoples.
> Remember the wonderful works that God has done;
> remember God's covenant forever.
> Sing to the LORD, all the earth.
> Tell of God's salvation every day.

supplies
- ❑ vine from previous session
- ❑ vine branches (1 for each student)
- ❑ markers or pens

preparation: Have on hand supplies for the youth to add branches to the vine. Write the opening meditation—which is adapted from 1 Chronicles 16:8, 12, 15, 23—on a markerboard; or project the meditation, using the slide on the website.

note: Take time before you get started to talk with the confirmands about what they read and wrote in the "Creation" section of their *Credo Confirmation Student Journal.*

SO WHAT? PART 1

back to the beginning

(20 minutes)

Ask volunteers to talk briefly about what they learned about Creation from the previous session. Then review the mural or posters they created.

Ask the youth to turn in their Bible to **Genesis 3.** Ask volunteers to read aloud the Scripture, each person reading one verse at a time until the passage is complete.

Say: "This Scripture tells the story of sin entering God's Creation. Sin is our brokenness, our separation from God, our fractured world, and our need of healing."

Ask:

- Who sinned in this Scripture? What was sinful?
- What happened as a result of these sins? What relationships were hurt?

Say: "In the last session we learned that God created all things and declared all of Creation 'good.' But when sin enters the story, God's good Creation is damaged."

Refer the confirmands to the mural or posters they created during the previous session. Then ask:

supplies
- ❑ Bibles
- ❑ mural from "The Days of Creation" in the Creation session
- ❑ paper
- ❑ color pencils or markers

preparation: Hang in your meeting space "The Days of Creation" mural or posterboards from the previous session.

- How has sin damaged some of the things pictured in our mural? (If youth struggle with this question, suggest specific sins including *hatred, pollution, violence, greed,* and *apathy*.)

Hand out paper and markers or colored pencils; and ask the confirmands to illustrate, by drawing or writing, one way in which sin has damaged some part of Creation. Encourage the confirmands to think not only about physical damage but also emotional and spiritual damage and damage done to relationships. Give everyone plenty of time to work, then invite the confirmands to present their illustrations and writings and to explain how sin has damaged Creation.

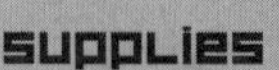

- ❑ Bibles
- ❑ 2 bells
- ❑ copies of the "Who Sinned?" worksheet

preparation: Make copies of the "Who Sinned?" worksheet.

who sinned?

(15 minutes)

Say: "We all sin. No matter how good or bad we think we are, or how good or bad we think other people are, every person sins."

Distribute copies of the "Who Sinned?" worksheet from the website. Ask the confirmands to complete the worksheet by reading the assigned Scriptures and identifying the "sinner" in each one.

Give the students plenty of time to work, then talk about the sinners in each Scripture and about how these persons sinned. (The sinners include: *1. The serpent, Eve, Adam; 2. Cain; 3. Jacob, Rebekah; 4. Rachel, Jacob; 5. Moses, the Egyptian slavemaster; 6. David; 7. Judas; 8. Peter; 9. Ananias, Sapphira; 10. Simon the magician.* The confirmands might find additional examples of sinners in these Scriptures.)

Point out that these are only a few of the many sinners we read about in Scripture. Then ask:

- Which of these sinners are best known for the sins they committed?
- Which of these sinners are better known for faithful and heroic acts?
- What relationships were hurt because of these sinful acts?
- How could these broken relationships be restored?

To show an example of how one broken relationship from these Scriptures—Peter's relationship with Jesus—was restored, ask a volunteer to read aloud **John 21:15-20.**

corporate sin

(25 minutes)

Say: "We looked at several examples from Scripture in which individuals committed sins against other people and against God. But sin isn't always an individual act. Groups of people—communities and even nations—also can be guilty of sins."

Have the confirmands turn to the table of contents in their Bible. Point out that the books of **Isaiah** through **Malachi** are the books of the prophets.

Say: "God spoke through these Old Testament prophets to hold accountable the nations of Israel and Judah—as well as their neighbors—for worshiping idols, forging alliances with wicked nations, and oppressing the poor."

To give the students an example, ask a volunteer to read aloud **Amos 5:21-27,** in which God scolds the nation of Israel for idolatry and injustice.

Ask the confirmands whether they are familiar with the story of Jonah. Invite a volunteer to retell the story from memory. As needed, provide corrections and clarifications and help fill in gaps. Then ask a second volunteer to read aloud **Jonah 3,** in which God sends the prophet Jonah to Nineveh to hold the entire city accountable for its wickedness. (Thanks to Jonah, all of the people of Nineveh repent; and God spares the city.)

Have the students return to the table of contents. Point out the New Testament epistles, **Romans** through **Jude.**

Say: "Many of these epistles, or letters, were written not to individuals but to churches. The apostle Paul, who wrote several of these letters, often held entire Christian communities accountable for their behavior or lack of understanding."

To give the students an example, ask a volunteer to read aloud **1 Corinthians 1:10,** in which Paul urges the Christians in Corinth to erase any divisions that have hurt the community.

Explain that, in the United Methodist tradition, we have a history of focusing on both personal and collective sins. We challenge individuals to be disciplined and to avoid doing harm. ("Do no harm" is the first of John Wesley's General Rules.) We also hold the church and the communities and nations in which we live to a standard of justice and righteousness.

Read aloud or summarize these statements and/or resolutions for the confirmands. If you have on hand several copies of the Social Principles pamphlet and/or *The Book of Resolutions,* give the students a few minutes to scan these resources to get a broader sense of the church's social witness.

After the students have looked at several examples of collective sin, from Scripture and from church tradition, challenge the confirmands to work as a group to come up with examples of collective sin in the world today. (These might include *failing to respond to poverty, hunger, and dehydration; working to end slavery and genocide in some parts of the world; and being poor stewards of the earth's resources.*) You might choose to provide current newspapers and news magazines to help the confirmands come up with ideas. If your building and equipment allow you to do so, you might also have the students look for ideas on the Internet.

supplies

- ❑ Bibles
- ❑ a copy (or copies) of the Social Principles of The United Methodist Church and/or *The Book of Resolutions of The United Methodist Church*
- ❑ a globe
- ❑ an adhesive bandage for each person
- ❑ optional: newspapers, news magazines, and/or computers with Internet access

preparation: Select from the most current Social Principles of The United Methodist Church and/or *The Book of Resolutions of The United Methodist Church* a few statements and/or resolutions that address collective sin. These might involve racism, sexism, hunger, poverty, or poor environmental stewardship.

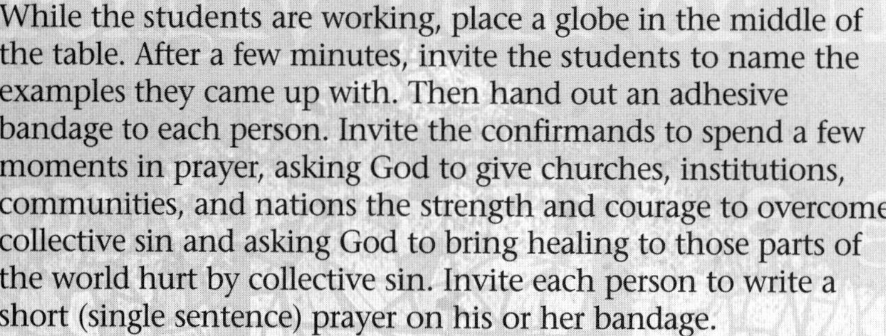

While the students are working, place a globe in the middle of the table. After a few minutes, invite the students to name the examples they came up with. Then hand out an adhesive bandage to each person. Invite the confirmands to spend a few moments in prayer, asking God to give churches, institutions, communities, and nations the strength and courage to overcome collective sin and asking God to bring healing to those parts of the world hurt by collective sin. Invite each person to write a short (single sentence) prayer on his or her bandage.

Gather the students into a circle. Close the activity by passing the globe around the circle, allowing each person to place his or her bandage on the globe and to pray aloud. When all of the students have added their bandages, place the globe back in the center of the circle. Then pray together the Lord's Prayer.

NOTE: If you choose to divide this session into two one-hour classes, break here.

SO WHAT? PART 2

RECONCILE? NO WAY!

(15 minutes)

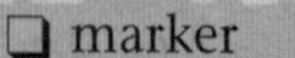

SUPPLIES
- ❑ Bibles
- ❑ scrap paper
- ❑ markerboard
- ❑ marker

Ask the confirmands whether they are familiar with the word *reconciliation*. If they are, invite them to define it. (One possible definition is "the act of resolving disputes or mending differences.")

Say: "Reconciliation is a way in which we heal the divisions caused by sin."

Then ask volunteers to read aloud **Isaiah 11:1-9.** Have the students name the improbable reconciliations described in the passage (such as the wolf living with the lamb or the cow and the bear grazing together).

Then give the students 5 minutes to list as many current-day, unthinkable reconciliations as they can think of. These may be serious (such as nations or cultures that have been at war for years), or silly (such as cartoon heroes and villains), or anything in between. List these on a markerboard or on paper.

Talk with the group about the examples that the confirmands came up with. For each one, ask:

- What are the differences that these two individuals (or groups of people) cannot reconcile?
- How is sin responsible for these differences?
- How might some of these differences be reconciled? (For some of your examples, answering this question may be very difficult. Acknowledge that, from a human perspective, resolving some of these differences might seem impossible but that all things are possible through God's grace.)

Where There's Sin, There's Grace

(20 minutes)

Remind the group that, during the previous session, you discussed being created in God's image and reflected on God's love, goodness, and generosity.

Say: "Sin corrupts and distorts God's image in us."

Pass around a mirror; and ask the youth to look at their reflection as they think of the gifts and abilities they have that reflect God's image. Then pass around the cracked mirror, and ask the students to reflect on how sin (in the form of poor choices and broken relationships) has distorted that "perfect image of God."

Hand out sheets of paper and Bibles. Then ask three volunteers to read aloud the parable of the prodigal son from **Luke 15:11-24.** (The parable also is known as the parable of the father and two sons, but this activity focuses on the prodigal son.) The first volunteer should read aloud verses 11-12; the second, 13-19; and the third, 20-24. Pause after each reading, and invite the youth to draw a picture of the prodigal son's image from that part of the story. (For example, they might draw a face that shows the son's emotions or a more elaborate picture that illustrates his attitude and behavior.)

After the reading, invite volunteers to present their drawings and to explain how they portrayed the prodigal son in the various parts of the story.

Ask:

- How did the younger son sin?
- How did his sin hurt his relationships with his father and brother? (You might also discuss how the elder brother sinned and how that had a negative effect on these relationships as well.)
- How did the younger son expect his father to respond when he returned home?
- How did the father in this story respond when his younger son returned home?

Say: "The father in this story responds to his son with grace. This does not mean that he excuses his son for running off and squandering his inheritance. What it means is that the father forgives his son and seeks to restore his relationship with him. This story illustrates the grace that God offers each of us. We all sin and stray from God; but God is always eager and ready to welcome us back."

Tell the youth that grace is an important part of the Christian story and is particularly important in the United Methodist tradition. In the second unit, your class will take a more detailed and thorough look at grace.

Supplies
- ❑ Bibles
- ❑ a mirror and a cracked mirror
- ❑ paper
- ❑ markers or color pencils

Note: Make sure that that any cracked mirrors don't have sharp edges.

NOW WHAT?

SUPPLIES
- ❑ Bibles
- ❑ copies of the "Sin Is Real" handout

PREPARATION: Make copies of the "Sin Is Real" handout, from the website.

SIN IS REAL

(15 minutes)

Make copies of the "Sin Is Real" handout, from the website. Or in the interest of saving paper, copy onto a markerboard the quotations below. Have the confirmands look over the quotations and then discuss what each one has to say about sin.

> "Sin is not hurtful because it is forbidden, but it is forbidden because it is hurtful."—Benjamin Franklin
>
> "Pleasure is the bait of sin."—Plato
>
> "A sin takes on a new and real terror when there seems a chance that it is going to be found out."—Mark Twain
>
> "He that falls into sin is a man; that grieves at it, is a saint; that boasts of it, is a devil."—Thomas Fuller
>
> "Sin with the multitude, and your responsibility and guilt are as great and as truly personal, as if you alone had done the wrong."—Tryon Edwards
>
> "Not to be ashamed of sin is to sin double."—German proverb

Ask:

- What have you learned today about sin?
- How has this session made you aware of sins that you had overlooked or had not been aware of?
- What can you do this week to eliminate sin in your life?

SUPPLIES
- ❑ markerboard
- ❑ marker

PREPARATION: Write the benediction, "John Wesley's Rule," on a markerboard; or print out the poster from the website.

NOTE: Before you dismiss, instruct the confirmands to read, reflect on, and journal about the material in the "Sin" section of the *Credo Confirmation Student Journal* before your next session. Also encourage them to do the activities related to "Sin," on the confirmand website.

CLOSING RITUAL

(10 minutes)

Gather everyone into a circle. Lead a prayer, giving thanks to God for all that the group has learned and experienced. Go around the circle, inviting each person to pray aloud a word or phrase that describes a learning from the past week.

After every person has had a chance to contribute, say a brief closing prayer. Then invite the confirmands to say aloud the benediction, called "John Wesley's Rule":

Do all the good you can,
By all the means you can,
In all the ways you can,
In all the places you can,
At all the times you can,
To all the people you can,
As long as ever you can.

Redemption

INTRODUCTION

So far, we've seen God create the heavens and earth and declare all of Creation good; we've seen God create humankind in God's image; we've seen humankind give in to temptation; and we've seen sin and death distort and disrupt God's perfect Creation.

But God does not let sin and death have the last word. From the moment that sin entered into creation, God has been working to redeem and restore the world. In the first session we learned about one person of the Trinity: God the Father, or Creator. God's ultimate act of redemption involves another person: Jesus Christ—God the Son, or Redeemer. *The Book of Discipline of The United Methodist Church* says:

> In God's self-revelation, Jesus Christ, we see the splendor of our true humanity. Even our sin, with its destructive consequences for all creation, does not alter God's intention for us—holiness and happiness of heart. Nor does it diminish our accountability for the way we live (¶ 101).

God, in the person of Jesus, became fully human and died on the cross. His death was "the perfect and sufficient sacrifice for the sins of the whole world, redeeming [humanity] from all sin" (*Discipline,* ¶ 103, Article VIII). Then, through his resurrection, Christ defeated death, giving us hope that one day we will experience resurrection and live eternally with God.

LIFTING OUR EYES TO THE HILLS

Redemption is another concept that can be difficult for younger youth to comprehend. First, the idea of being redeemed from sin is a lot for anyone to understand. Second, many young people feel invincible and are not aware of the immediacy of their need for redemption. Often, they see redemption as more of a faraway reckoning than part of their daily walk with God.

A helpful way to prepare to teach young people the hard-to-understand concept of redemption is to read from **Psalms 120–134,** the Pilgrim Psalms or Psalms of Ascent. These are songs of pilgrims journeying to Jerusalem to celebrate religious festivals. While reading these psalms, one can imagine the ancient pilgrims joining one another on their way up the Temple mount, singing together.

Christian discipleship is a similar journey: It is a pilgrimage of regeneration and redemption. We need to get in the habit, with each step we take along our journey, of lifting our "eyes to the hills," from where our help will come (**Psalm 121:1**). We must "wait for the LORD . . . more than those who watch for the morning" . . . because with God "is great power to redeem" (**Psalm 130:5-7**). Redemption is an opportunity to spend eternity in God's presence starting now.

The Good News of Redemption

In human societies, the legal repercussions for breaking the rules can be strident and unyielding. Many youth may attend schools that have "zero tolerance" policies toward certain behaviors. Thus, it might be difficult for young people to believe that they can truly be forgiven for and redeemed of bad decisions and sinful choices. A single bad decision, an act of being in the wrong place at the wrong time, a brief lapse of judgment, or succumbing to temptation can have dire consequences for young people today. Shame and fear can cause youth to bear their sins and burdens quietly and in isolation.

The message of redemption should be delivered with gentleness and joy. It is the essence of the "good news" that Jesus spoke of. Because of Christ's life, death, and resurrection, we are free to live without the burden of sins. **First Peter 2:24** says, "[Jesus] himself bore our sins in his body on the cross, so that, free from sins, we might live for righteousness." Jesus saves us from sin but saves us for a life lived in service to God and others.

SUPPLIES AND PREPARATION

BASIC SUPPLIES		
❑ Bibles of various translations ❑ markerboard or large sheets of paper ❑ markers ❑ pens or pencils	❑ clear tape and/or glue ❑ masking tape ❑ index cards or paper cut about the same size (3-by-5 or 4-by-6) ❑ sheets of posterboard	❑ paper (Use paper that has already been used on one side as much as possible, depending on the activity.) ❑ scissors

ACTIVITY	PREPARATION	OTHER SUPPLIES
WHAT?		
Opening Ritual	Write the opening meditation—which is adapted from 1 Chronicles 16:8, 12, 15, 23—on a markerboard; or project the meditation, using the slide on the website.	❑ vine from previous sessions ❑ vine branches (1 for each student)
SO WHAT? PART 1		
Returning Home	Place the baseball bats across a starting line for a dizzying relay race. Place the bases at the opposite end of the room.	❑ several baseball bats ❑ several baseball bases (Frisbees© or paper plates can serve the purpose.)
Re-re-redemption		
Counterintuitive	Use painter's tape or a roll of receipt paper to make a vertical line on a wall from the floor to the ceiling of your meeting space. Use a marker to mark the line in 6-inch increments.	❑ painter's tape or a long sheet of roll paper
Stories of Redemption	Make copies of the handout "Stories of Redemption," on the website.	❑ copies of the handout "Stories of Redemption"
SO WHAT? PART 2		
Bear Witness	Invite a guest speaker to come in to tell his or her story of redemption.	❑ guest speaker
Our Redeemer	Gather 4 or 5 damaged items that could be repaired, such as a chair or small table with a broken leg, ripped clothes, or a broken toy that could be fixed with glue or screws.	❑ broken items that could be repaired
Redemption in the United Methodist Tradition	Gather supplies.	❑ *Book of Discipline*
NOW WHAT?		
Prayer of Confession	Gather supplies	❑ *UM Hymnals* or *Books of Worship*
Closing Ritual	Write the benediction, "John Wesley's Rule," on a markerboard; or print out the poster from the website.	

SUPPLIES
- ❑ vine from previous sessions
- ❑ vine branches (1 for each student)
- ❑ markers or pens

PREPARATION: Have on hand supplies for the youth to add branches to the vine. Write the opening meditation—which is adapted from 1 Chronicles 16:8, 12, 15, 23—on a markerboard; or project the meditation, using the slide on the website.

NOTE: Take time before you get started to talk with the confirmands about what they read and wrote in the "Sin" section of their *Credo Confirmation Student Journals.*

SUPPLIES
- ❑ carpet or cardboard squares (at least 2, but not more than the number of participants)
- ❑ masking tape

WHAT?

OPENING RITUAL

(10 minutes)

As confirmands arrive, point them to the confirmation vine and give each person a branch. Invite the confirmands to reflect on the previous session and to write on their branch something they learned or experienced during that session. Ask the confirmands to attach their branch to the vine. Remind the youth that this vine and its branches represent God's story, a story that they are a part of.

When all of the confirmands have arrived, invite each person to talk briefly about what he or she wrote on his or her branch. Then invite the youth to read aloud the opening meditation, which is adapted from **1 Chronicles 16:8, 12, 15, 23:**

> Give thanks to the LORD,
> and make God's deeds known among the peoples.
> Remember the wonderful works that God has done;
> remember God's covenant forever.
> Sing to the LORD, all the earth.
> Tell of God's salvation every day.

SO WHAT? PART 1

RETURNING HOME

(15 minutes)

Use masking tape to mark a starting line at one end of your meeting space and a finish line at the other end. Hand the students the carpet or cardboard squares (at least two but no more than the number of participants). Challenge the youth to get from the starting line to the finish line then back to the starting line without anyone in the group touching the floor in between. They will do this by stepping on the carpet or cardboard squares. There are a couple rules that make this game even more challenging:

- Carpet or cardboard squares may not be left unattended. If no member of the group is standing on a square, one of them should immediately pick up that square. If no one does, the group is no longer allowed to use that square.
- If a member of the group steps on the floor, he or she must return to the starting line. The rest of the group must go back to retrieve this person.

After the game, say: "In this activity, you journeyed away from home then found your way back. In the previous session, we learned about sin and how sin separates us from God and disrupts our relationships with God and others. In other words, we learned about ways in which we wander away from home. In this session, we'll learn about redemption—the way in which God overcomes our sin, restores relationships, and welcomes us back home."

re-re-redemption

(20 minutes)

supplies

- ❑ Bibles
- ❑ markerboard or paper
- ❑ marker or pen

Ask the confirmands to name as many words as they can that start with "re-" (such as *redo* and *reconnect*). Record these words on a markerboard or paper. If no one named the word *redemption,* add this word to the list.

Ask:

- How would you define the word *redemption*?
- Where have you heard the word *redemption* before? (They may have redeemed tickets for prizes at a redemption center at a fair or arcade or they may have heard *redemption* used to describe someone who has overcome a past mistake in judgment.)

Say: "In biblical times, redemption was often associated with slavery."

Ask a volunteer to read aloud **Leviticus 25:47-49.** Explain that, in many ancient cultures, selling oneself into slavery was a way to pay off a debt. Redemption meant paying off one's debt—or having one's debt paid off by someone else—and being released.

Then ask a volunteer to read aloud **Romans 7:14-20.** Ask:

- What does it mean to be a slave to sin? How does sin keep people from being free?

Ask another volunteer to read aloud **Romans 8:1-8.** Ask:

- How can we be freed from slavery to sin?

Write and then read aloud the following definition of *redemption*:

> *Redemption:* the state of being redeemed; deliverance from sin through the life, death, and resurrection of Christ

counterintuitive

(10–15 minutes)

Ask the confirmands to line up in front of the wall with the prepared vertical line. (See the sidebar on page 90 for instructions.) Challenge them to see how high they can reach on the wall. Tell them that they may jump, but they are not allowed to bend their knees. Give them a couple minutes to think about ways that they might be able to reach higher. Then allow each person to try. Record the heights that each person reaches.

supplies
- ❑ painter's tape or a long sheet of roll paper such as calculator or receipt paper
- ❑ marker
- ❑ markerboard

preparation: Use painter's tape or a roll of receipt paper to make a vertical line on a wall from the floor to the ceiling of your meeting space. Use a marker to mark the line in 6-inch increments.

note: If one or more of your confirmands is unable to jump, select one person to demonstrate the difference between jumping with straight legs and jumping by bending his or her knees.

supplies
- ❑ Bibles
- ❑ copies of the handout "Stories of Redemption"
- ❑ pens or pencils

preparation: Make copies of the handout "Stories of Redemption," on the website.

Then allow each person to try a second time. This time they may bend their knees. Again, record the heights that each person reaches. Most likely, all of the youth will have reached higher by bending their knees than by keeping their knees straight.

Say: "We all know that a person can jump higher by bending his or her knees. But doesn't seem odd that, to go higher, we must first go lower?"

Ask the students to name other counterintuitive actions. (For example, people often prune (cut back) branches of trees so that the trees will grow more.)

Say: "The Bible is full of counterintuitive stories and events. In fact, the greatest of all biblical stories, the story of our redemption, is about the ultimate counterintuitive act. In order for Jesus to become the Savior of humankind and to give us eternal life, he first had to die."

Stories of Redemption

(20 minutes)

Say: "Let's look at some of the counterintuitive moments in the story of our faith."

Distribute copies of the "Stories of Redemption" handout, from the website. Assign each Scripture on the handout to a different youth. You may need to assign more than one Scripture to each person to make sure that all of the passages are accounted for.

The Scriptures are:

Exodus 2:1-10 (Moses' mother, Pharaoh's daughter)
Daniel 3:8-30 (Shadrach, Meshach, and Abednego)
Matthew 5:38-48 (Jesus' teaching on retaliation and enemies)
John 4:7-30 (The woman at the well)
Mark 14:32-42 (Jesus in the garden)
Luke 23:26-43 (Jesus on the cross)

For each Scripture, talk about how the person or persons in the story act in a way that is counterintuitive and what happens as a result.

Say: "These stories of redemption involve people making difficult and unexpected decisions, but many of these stories also involve people putting themselves at great risk. Healing the wounds caused by sin can be difficult and even painful, but the rewards of new life and renewed relationships are worth the risk."

SO WHAT? PART 2

bear witness

(20 minutes)

Invite a guest speaker to come in and tell his or her story of redemption. This could be a person from your congregation who has a powerful testimony of God's grace and salvation. It could be a young adult who has turned his or her life around or an elderly adult who has found peace and rest in God. Ask this person to speak for about 15 minutes, then allow a few minutes for questions.

Have the speaker consider some of the following questions as he or she prepares:

- When and why were you in need of redemption?
- How have you been redeemed by God's grace?
- How has God continued to work in your life?

NOTE: If you choose to divide this session into two one-hour classes, break here.

SUPPLIES
- ❑ Bibles
- ❑ guest speaker

PREPARATION: Invite a guest speaker to come in to tell his or her story of redemption.

our redeemer

(10–15 minutes)

Say: "In the first session, we learned about Creation and talked about God the Father, our Creator. As Christians, we believe in the Trinity—one God who is three persons. God the Father is the person of the Trinity who acts as our Creator. Today we'll look at another person of the Trinity, Jesus Christ, who acts as our Redeemer."

Read aloud **Romans 3:23:** "All have sinned and fall short of the glory of God."

Say: "As we learned in the previous session, we all are sinners. And because we are all sinners, we all need redemption."

Ask the youth whether they are familiar with the verse **John 3:16.** Invite volunteers to read aloud this verse, if possible from several translations.

Say: "**John 3:16** is one of the Bible's best known verses because it reminds us, in one sentence, of the salvation we have in Christ. The following verse, **John 3:17,** while not as well known, is equally important."

Ask a volunteer to read aloud **John 3:17.**

Say: "These two verses together demonstrate that, despite our sin, God doesn't give up on us. God wants to redeem each of us and all of creation; and God sent Jesus Christ to make that possible."

Present to the confirmands some of the broken items that you gathered beforehand. For each item, ask:

SUPPLIES
- ❑ Bibles of various translations
- ❑ 4 or 5 damaged items

PREPARATION: Gather 4 or 5 damaged items that could be repaired, such as a chair or small table with a broken leg, ripped clothes, or a broken toy that could be fixed with glue or screws.

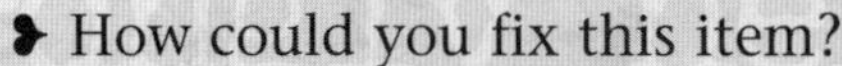

- How could you fix this item?
- When we fix this item, will it be as good as it was before it was broken? Will it be better than it was before it was broken?

Then ask:

- How does God, through Christ, "fix" us?

To answer this question, have the youth read these Scriptures:

- **Romans 5:6-9:** Paul says, "We have been justified by [Christ's] blood" (verse 9). This likely alludes to the ancient Jewish practice of making blood sacrifices to atone for sins. See **Leviticus 4:1–5:13** for information on making sacrifices to atone for sins. ("To atone" means to make amends or make things right.)
- **Romans 5:12-15, 18-19:** Paul says that, since human beings brought sin into the world, a human being—Jesus—must make atonement for the sins of humankind and put human beings back into a right relationships with God.
- **Romans 6:1-11:** Paul says that Christ, through his death, destroyed the power of sin. Through Christ's resurrection, Christ destroyed the power of death. Paul says that we are baptized into Christ's death so that we can share in Christ's resurrection.
- **Philippians 2:5-11:** This ancient Christian hymn praises Jesus' humility and sacrifice. Although he was God in human form, "he humbled himself and became obedient to the point of death—even death on a cross" (verse 8).
- **1 Peter 2:24:** Not only did Jesus save us from our sins by dying on the cross, but Jesus also saved us *for* a life of righteousness.

After each Scripture, ask:

- What does this Scripture tell us about Christ, how Christ is our redeemer, and how Christ atones, or makes amends, for our sins? (You might need to assist in this discussion, using the notes next to each Scripture reference, above.)
- What questions does this Scripture raise for you about how Christ saves us from sin? What is unclear to you about this Scripture?

Say: "As Christians, we believe that Jesus, through his death and resurrection, atoned for our sins and made us right with God. Because of what Jesus has done, we can look forward to living eternally with God."

Additional resources on the subject of atonement, and on different Christian understandings of atonement, are available on the website.

redemption in the united methodist tradition

(5–10 minutes)

Ask a volunteer to read aloud "Article VIII—Reconciliation Through Christ" from "The Confession of Faith of the Evangelical United Brethren Church" under "Our Doctrinal Standards and General Rules" in *The Book of Discipline of The United Methodist Church.* This statement also is available below and at the website. Explain that the Evangelical United Brethren Church was one of two denominations that merged in 1968 to form The United Methodist Church. (The other was the Methodist Church.)

> We believe God was in Christ reconciling the world to himself. The offering Christ freely made on the cross is the perfect and sufficient sacrifice for the sins of the whole world, redeeming man from all sin, so that no other satisfaction is required.

Say: "This statement affirms that Christ is our redeemer and that Christ is capable of atoning for the sins of the entire world."

Allow the confirmands to ask questions, and help them understand the language used in this statement.

Then ask:

- What does it mean that Christ's sacrifice is "perfect and sufficient"?
- How can this statement give us hope and comfort when we struggle with sin?

supplies

- ❑ *The Book of Discipline*

NOW WHAT?

prayer of confession

(15–20 minutes)

Hand out copies of *The United Methodist Hymnal* or *The United Methodist Book of Worship*. Take a minute or two to point out the Table of Contents and to make the confirmands aware of all that is available in these books. Show the youth how they can find hymns, prayers, and liturgies for a variety of occasions and related to a variety of topics. (If you're using hymnals, also point out the various indexes in the back.)

Say: "We know that Jesus, our Redeemer, makes atonement for our sins. But this doesn't mean that we should just go ahead and sin because Jesus has us covered. Instead, we should see redemption as an opportunity to start fresh and to live the life that God desires for us."

supplies

- ❑ *United Methodist Hymnals* or *Books of Worship*
- ❑ paper
- ❑ pens or pencils

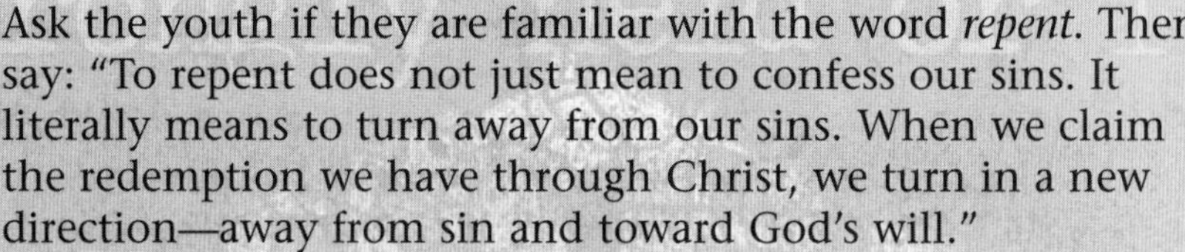

NOTE: Before you dismiss, instruct the confirmands to read, reflect on, and journal about the material in the "Redemption" section of the *Credo Confirmation Student Journal* before your next session. Also encourage them to do the activities related to "Redemption" on the confirmand website.

Ask the youth if they are familiar with the word *repent*. Then say: "To repent does not just mean to confess our sins. It literally means to turn away from our sins. When we claim the redemption we have through Christ, we turn in a new direction—away from sin and toward God's will."

Ask each youth to find a prayer of repentance or a hymn about redemption in the hymnal or *Book of Worship*. Allow each person to name the hymn or prayer he or she chose and to talk about why he or she chose it. (If you have a large group of youth, you might have them complete this part of the activity in small groups.)

Then have the confirmands write an original prayer or song on the subject of redemption. Give the youth plenty of time to work, then allow them to present its prayer or song. Let those who wish to pass to do so.

SUPPLIES
- ❑ markerboard
- ❑ marker

PREPARATION: Write the benediction, "John Wesley's Rule," on a markerboard; or print out the poster from the website.

CLOSING RITUAL

(10 minutes)

Gather the confirmands into a circle. Lead the youth in prayer, giving thanks to God for your time together and all that the group has learned and experienced. Then go around the circle, inviting each person to pray aloud one word or phrase that describes something he or she learned during the past week of confirmation.

After every person has had a chance to contribute a word or phrase, say a brief closing prayer. Then invite the confirmands to say aloud and in unison the benediction, "John Wesley's Rule."

Holy Spirit

INTRODUCTION

Of the three Persons of the Trinity, the Holy Spirit tends to be the hardest for us to understand. We understand God the Father, the Creator, because we encounter this person of the Trinity in the Creation narratives, during conversations with Abraham and Moses, in Israel's deliverance from slavery and exile, and elsewhere in Scripture. We understand Christ because he became fully human as Jesus. He "emptied himself" and "humbled himself" to be "born in human likeness" (**Philippians 2:7, 8**). Jesus experienced all of the suffering and temptation that come with being human.

But the Holy Spirit? The Spirit is much more difficult to relate to. This Person of the Trinity is as hard to hold on to as the wind, which is one image people often use to describe the indescribable. The connection between the wind and the Holy Spirit goes back to the original biblical manuscripts, which were written in Hebrew (much of the Old Testament) and Greek (the entire New Testament). The Hebrew and Greek words for "Spirit," *ruach* and *pneuma* respectively, also mean "wind" and "breath."

Perhaps because the Spirit is so hard to grasp, both literally and figuratively, we tend to give it short shrift, trotting it out at Pentecost and then tucking it away for the rest of the year. (If the Spirit were a person, instead of a Person, it might develop an inferiority complex.)

When we do pay attention to the Holy Spirit, we make a couple of mistakes. First, we focus exclusively on the Pentecost story as if all the Spirit ever did was energize Peter and his companions on a single day two millennia ago (not that it wasn't an amazing accomplishment!). Second, we often reduce the Spirit to a churchy version of the human conscience.

Limiting the Spirit's Scope

To understand the Spirit's role in Scripture, we have to start at the beginning—literally. The Spirit was active in Creation: "Now the earth was formless and empty, darkness was over the surface of the deep, and the Spirit of God was hovering over the waters" (**Genesis 1:2,** NIV). Throughout the Old Testament, leaders such as Moses, Joshua, David, and Solomon receive wisdom and power from the Spirit.

Fast-forward to the New Testament. There Mary becomes pregnant through the Spirit (**Matthew 1:18**), John predicts that Jesus will baptize with the Spirit (**Mark 1:8**), and the Spirit descends on Jesus at his baptism (**Luke 3:21-22**). And all that happens before Jesus' ministry even begins.

At the end of his earthly ministry, Jesus promises his disciples that "the Advocate, the Holy Spirit, whom the Father will send in my name, will teach you everything, and remind you of all that I have said to you" (**John 14:26**). Following his resurrection, Jesus sends his disciples into Jerusalem to wait until they "have been clothed with power from on high" (**Luke 24:49**), a power that comes in the form of "a sound like the rush of a violent wind" and "tongues, as of fire" (**Acts 2:2-3**). The rest, as they say, is church history.

Limiting the Spirit's Power

One mistake we often make with regard to the Spirit is equating this person of the Trinity with the conscience or with the proverbial cartoon angel who hovers over one shoulder, giving us sound advice and arguing with the cartoon devil who sits on the other side of our head.

There's a nugget of truth to this image: In **John 14:26,** Jesus himself calls the Holy Spirit the Advocate (some translations say "Counselor"). Jesus tells his disciples that the Advocate "will teach you everything, and remind you of all that I have said to you." The Spirit plays the angel-on-the-shoulder role, advising us and helping us make tough decisions. But the Holy Spirit is so much more. Focusing only on a single characteristic of the Spirit is as short-sighted as describing the church as a building where people meet together once a week.

The Holy Spirit counsels us; but it also empowers us (**Acts 4:31**), comforts us (**Acts 9:31**), blesses us with spiritual gifts (**1 Corinthians 12:1-11**), fills our hearts with love (**Romans 5:5**), and prays for us in "sighs too deep for words" when we don't know the words to pray (**Romans 8:26**).

The Spirit in the Lives of Young People

Trained theologians struggle to describe and define the Holy Spirit; so young people, especially, will have trouble grasping the concept of the Spirit. To help confirmands better appreciate this person of the Trinity, we need to emphasize all of the roles that the Holy Spirit plays. Some young people will see the Spirit most clearly as an advocate or counselor who provides comfort and advice during difficult times. Some will see the Spirit as the source of their gifts and abilities. Others will know the Spirit best as a giver of strength and courage. A young person might relate to one of these expressions of the Holy Spirit now and might relate to others as he or she grows in faith.

SUPPLIES AND PREPARATION

BASIC SUPPLIES		
❑ Bibles of various translations ❑ markerboard or large sheets of paper ❑ markers ❑ pens or pencils	❑ clear tape and/or glue ❑ masking tape ❑ index cards or paper cut about the same size (3-by-5 or 4-by-6) ❑ sheets of posterboard	❑ paper (Use paper that has already been used on one side as much as possible, depending on the activity.) ❑ scissors

ACTIVITY	PREPARATION	OTHER SUPPLIES
WHAT?		
Opening Ritual	Write the opening meditation—which is adapted from 1 Chronicles 16:8, 12, 15, 23—on a markerboard; or project the meditation, using the slide on the website.	❑ vine from previous sessions ❑ vine branches (1 for each student)
The Spirit in Scripture	Gather supplies.	❑ optional: Bible with pronunciations in it or an audio Bible and equipment to play it on
SO WHAT? PART 1		
Burning, Breathing, Blowing	Tie streamers to the grill of the fan so that, when the fan is turned on, they flutter in the breeze.	❑ candle ❑ small electric fan ❑ streamers of plastic or crepe paper
Blow, Blow, Blow Your Boat	Make copies of the "Origami Sailboat" handout, on the website.	❑ squares of paper ❑ "Origami Sailboat" instructions ❑ small electric fan
The Spirit Moving in You	Be prepared to tell the youth an example from your own life about the Spirit nudging you. (See the activity.)	
SO WHAT? PART 2		
The Spirit Moving in John Wesley	Make copies of the "Spirit Moving in John Wesley" worksheet and narrative, on the website. Optional: Try out the Mentos® rocket to see how it works.	❑ "Spirit Moving in John Wesley" worksheet and narrative ❑ optional: Mentos®, two-liter bottle of diet cola, towels for cleanup, and a basin
Listening for the Spirit	Locate an empty room, and use masking tape to mark on the floor a line parallel to one wall. (Or use a rope to mark a line outside.) Cut out shapes from pieces of colored paper so that you have one shape for every two participants. Scatter these shapes on the floor.	❑ cutouts of shapes from colored paper ❑ masking tape (or a rope if the activity will be done outdoors) ❑ blindfolds (one per pair of youth)
The Spirit on the Move	Make a copy of the "Spirit Movement" cards, on the website, and cut the cards apart.	❑ "Spirit Movement" cards
NOW WHAT?		
Closing Ritual	Write the benediction, "John Wesley's Rule," on a markerboard; or print out the poster on the website.	

WHAT?

supplies
- ❑ vine from previous sessions
- ❑ vine branches (1 for each student)
- ❑ markers or pens

preparation: Have on hand supplies for the youth to add branches to the vine. Write the opening meditation—which is adapted from 1 Chronicles 16:8, 12, 15, 23—on a markerboard; or project the meditation, using the slide on the website.

note: Take time before you get started to talk with the confirmands about what they read and wrote in the "Redemption" section of their *Credo Confirmation Student Journals*.

opening ritual

(10 minutes)

As confirmands arrive, point them to the confirmation vine and give each person a branch. Invite the confirmands to reflect on the previous session and to write on their branch something they learned or experienced during that session. Ask the confirmands to attach their branch to the vine. Remind the youth that this vine and its branches represent God's story, a story that they are a part of.

When all of the confirmands have arrived, invite each person to talk briefly about what he or she wrote on his or her branch. Then invite the youth to read aloud the opening meditation, which is adapted from **1 Chronicles 16:8, 12, 15, 23:**

> Give thanks to the LORD,
> and make God's deeds known among the peoples.
> Remember the wonderful works that God has done;
> remember God's covenant forever.
> Sing to the LORD, all the earth.
> Tell of God's salvation every day.

supplies
- ❑ Bibles
- ❑ scratch paper (preferably paper that has been used on one side already)
- ❑ pens or pencils
- ❑ markerboard or paper
- ❑ marker
- ❑ optional: Bible with pronunciations in it or an audio Bible and equipment to play it on

the spirit in scripture

(20 minutes)

Ask for volunteers to summarize what they learned during the first session, "Creation," about the doctrine of the Trinity.

Say: "During our first session, we looked at the Trinity, focusing on God, the Father and Creator. Then in the previous session, we discussed Jesus Christ, the Son and Redeemer. In this session, we'll take a look at the Holy Spirit."

Ask volunteers to read each of the Scriptures below. For each one, discuss what the passage says about the Holy Spirit. Work together to create a one-sentence summary of each passage. Record these summaries on a markerboard or on paper.

- **Genesis 1:1-5** (The Spirit is present at Creation.)
- **Matthew 3:13-17** (The Spirit descends on Jesus at his baptism.)
- **John 14:25-27** (The Spirit is our teacher and advocate.)
- **Romans 5:1-5** (The Spirit fills our hearts with love.)
- **Romans 8:26-27** (The Spirit intercedes and prays for us.)
- **1 Corinthians 12:1-11** (The Spirit blesses us with spiritual gifts.)

Ask:

- What very important Scripture about the Holy Spirit did we not cover? Allow the youth to guess the Bible passage you're talking about. (***Acts 2:1-21,*** *the Pentecost story*)

Read **Acts 2:1-21** aloud. (Given the difficult names in this passage, it's better not to ask a student to read it aloud.) If possible, read from a Bible that offers pronunciation helps for difficult names or use an audio Bible.

Ask the confirmands to listen carefully to the Scripture for anything that the passage says about who the Holy Spirit is and what the Holy Spirit does. Ask the youth to name these things aloud. List their responses on a markerboard.

Say: "Nowadays, we celebrate Pentecost—the day on which the Holy Spirit descended on Jesus' disciples—as the birthday of the church. Some congregations even serve birthday cake on Pentecost Sunday."

SO WHAT? PART 1

burning, breathing, blowing

(10 minutes)

Say: "Scripture helps us understand who the Holy Spirit is and what the Spirit does by comparing the Holy Spirit with things that we are more familiar with."

Light the candle, and explain that fire is an image people often use to describe the Spirit. This image comes from the Pentecost story. Then extinguish the flame.

Say: "The books in the Bible were originally written in Hebrew and Greek. The Hebrew word for *spirit—ruach* (ROO-ah)—and the Greek word for *spirit—pneuma* (NOO-muh)—also mean 'wind' and 'breath.' "

Invite the confirmands to breathe gently on the backs of their hands.

Say: "The Holy Spirit is the breath of God that fills us with life. We see this image of the Spirit in **Genesis 2:7,** when God breathes life into Adam's nostrils."

Then turn on a small fan that has streamers tied to its grill.

Point out the fan, and say: "The Holy Spirit, like the wind, is invisible but powerful, moving things around as it wills."

Then invite a youth to read aloud **John 3:8:** "The wind blows where it chooses, and you hear the sound of it, but you do not know where it comes from or where it goes. So it is with everyone who is born of the Spirit."

supplies

- ❑ Bible
- ❑ candle
- ❑ matches or a lighter to light the candle
- ❑ small electric fan
- ❑ streamers of plastic or crepe paper

preparation: Tie streamers to the grill of the fan so that, when the fan is turned on, they flutter in the breeze.

Ask:

- How do these images (fire, breath, and wind) help you better understand who the Holy Spirit is and how the Holy Spirit works?
- Which of these images (fire, breath, and wind) best fits your understanding of the Holy Spirit?

Say: "None of these images fully describes or explains the Holy Spirit, but each image gives us a better idea of how the Spirit works in the world."

SUPPLIES
- ❏ squares of paper
- ❏ copies of the "Origami Sailboat" instructions
- ❏ small electric fan

PREPARATION: Choose the instructions on the website, on the websites that are linked there, or your own. Make copies of the instructions, and be sure that you can make the boat.

NOTE: Since people have various learning styles, the best instructions for this activity are the ones that you can follow and help the students follow. That way, you'll be better able to help any youth who need assistance.

Blow, Blow, Blow Your Boat

(10 minutes)

Hand out copies of the Origami Sailboat instructions of your choice. (See the website for options.) Give the students about five minutes to create sailboats, following the instructions. Help students as needed.

Give the confirmands plenty of time to create their boats; then invite them to race their boats across the length of the table, powering them with the wind of the fan used in the previous activity. Don't worry about who wins, just watch how the wind carries the boats across the table.

PREPARATION: Be prepared to tell the youth an example from your own life about the Spirit nudging you.

The Spirit Moving in You

(10 minutes)

Ask:

- When traveling by sailboat or hot-air balloon, what determines your course? (*the wind*)
- What role does the captain or operator of these vehicles play? (*understanding and cooperating with the wind, not fighting against it*)
- Does the wind sometimes take the boat or balloon where the captain or owner doesn't want to go? (*yes*)
- How is the Holy Spirit similar to the wind? (*The Spirit guides our path; it sometimes pushes us in directions we don't feel comfortable going; it's easier to go with the Spirit or wind than to go against it; and so on.*)

NOTE: If you choose to divide this session into two one-hour classes, break here.

Then ask the confirmands whether they have ever felt pulled, perhaps by the Spirit, to do something that they didn't really want to do. This might be anything from being nice to an annoying sibling to reaching out to someone at school whom everybody else ignores or abuses.

Be prepared to tell the youth an example from your own life, perhaps about the Spirit nudging you into a line of work that you hadn't previously considered, pushing you to sacrifice something that you enjoyed but knew that you could do without, instructing you to make changes in the way you budget your time and/or money.

SO WHAT? PART 2

THE SPIRIT MOVING IN JOHN WESLEY

(20 minutes)

Tell the confirmands that you will tell them a story about how the Holy Spirit touched the life of John Wesley, a founder of the Methodist movement, but that you're going to let them help tell the story in the style of Mad Libs™.

Give each student a copy of the "Spirit Moving in John Wesley" worksheet, from the website. Let the youth shout out suggestions as you fill in the worksheet. Then read aloud "The Spirit Moving in John Wesley Narrative," from the website, filling in the blanks with their suggested words.

Finally, read aloud the story, using the correct words.

Then ask:

- When, in this story, was the Holy Spirit working in John Wesley's life? (*all of the time*)
- When, in this story, might John Wesley have been resisting or working against the Spirit? (*when he tried to reduce faith to a set of rules; when he went to Georgia even though he wasn't prepared*)
- When did John Wesley allow the Spirit to lead him? (*when he learned from the Moravians; when he went to the meeting in Aldersgate Street; as he kept wrestling with what it means to be a Christian*)
- Why, do you think, was John Wesley's experience in Aldersgate Street so powerful?

Then ask the confirmands to think of a time when they went to an event or took on an activity reluctantly or with low expectations but, to their surprise, had a positive or even life-changing experience. This might have been when they watched a movie that they found themselves thinking about for days (or that made them cry) or a church retreat where they heard God speaking to them. Allow volunteers to tell about their experiences, and be prepared to tell a story from your experience.

Say: "The meeting that John Wesley went to on Aldersgate Street was pretty ordinary. It was the sort of meeting that happened frequently. The same can be said for Pentecost. Pentecost is another name for the Jewish holiday Shavuot (shuh-VOO-oht), an annual celebration that recalls the event when God gave Moses and the Israelites the Torah on Mt. Sinai. What was different about that particular meeting on Aldersgate Street and that particular Pentecost celebration was the way that the Holy Spirit made something ordinary into something quite extraordinary."

SUPPLIES

- ❑ pens or pencils
- ❑ copies of "Spirit Moving in John Wesley" worksheets
- ❑ optional: Mentos®, 2-liter bottle of diet cola, towels for cleanup, and a basin (See the option, below.)

PREPARATION: Make copies of the worksheet for small groups of youth and a copy of the narrative for yourself.

OPTION: For a visual demonstration of turning the ordinary into the extraordinary, make a Mentos® rocket. Place a 2-liter bottle of diet cola in a basin, and remove the bottle cap. Then drop a few mint-flavored Mentos candies into soda, and watch the resulting eruption. (Other carbonated soft drinks will work, but experiments have shown that diet cola creates the most impressive eruption. In addition, since diet cola contains no sticky sugar or corn syrup, any eruption spillage is easier to clean up.) Information about this experiment and videos of impressive diet-cola-and-Mentos eruptions abound on the Internet.

SUPPLIES

- ❑ Bibles
- ❑ guest speaker
- ❑ cutouts of shapes from colored paper
- ❑ masking tape (or ropes if the activity will be done outdoors)
- ❑ blindfolds (one per pair of youth)

PREPARATION: Locate an empty room near your regular meeting space, and use masking tape to mark on the floor a line parallel to two opposite walls.

Cut out shapes from pieces of colored paper so that you have one shape for every two participants. Scatter these shapes on the floor. Be sure to use a color or shape only once so that the pairs will know which piece of paper is theirs.

NOTE: Be sure to recycle the paper later.

Balls or other items may be used instead of the paper if you choose. Just be sure that these items are all different from one another.

* To add difficulty, after the blindfolds are in place, scramble the non-blindfolded players so that they are not directly across from their partner.

LISTENING FOR THE SPIRIT

(15 minutes)

Say: "God communicates with us through the Holy Spirit. But it can be hard to hear the Spirit's voice amid all of the other voices competing for our attention."

Remind the confirmands of the earlier discussion about times when they felt pulled to do something that they didn't want to do. Ask them to talk about who or what persuaded them to attend that event or to participate in that activity.

Say: "Discernment is a way in which Christians make decisions by listening for and being faithful to the Spirit."(You might mention that you'll be talking about discernment in more detail during the "Wesleyan Quadrilateral" session, in the "Confirm Your Faith" unit.)

Move the class to the room in which you've scattered colored shapes on the floor. Divide the youth into pairs; and have the pairs split up and move to designated opposite ends of the room. Blindfold the confirmands on one end of the room. Assign to each of the non-blindfolded confirmands one of the shapes on the floor. (If you have an odd number of students, you will need to be the non-blindfolded person in one pair.)

When you say, "Go," the sighted confirmands should direct their blindfolded partners to their assigned shape. The non-blindfolded confirmands may say whatever they want, but they must stand still at their end of the room.* The purpose of this activity is for the blindfolded persons to discern their partners' voices amid other voices. If you only have one or two pairs, create other distractions by turning on a radio, inviting assorted adults to come into the room and carry on a conversation, playing music or a video, and so forth.

When the blindfolded students have found their paper, have the partners swap roles and repeat this activity. Move the shapes around after the blindfolds are in place. Then return to your regular meeting space. Ask:

- How difficult was it to discern your partner's voice?
- How did you focus on your partner's voice?
- How difficult was it to give your partner directions?

Wrap up by pointing out that, to be successful in this activity, both parties had to persevere. That is, they had to stay focused and determined even when the activity became frustrating.

Say: "We can't turn off the other voices and distractions in our lives. But we need to focus on what the Holy Spirit is saying to us, even when we have trouble hearing the Spirit at all. Fortunately, as we saw in John Wesley's story, the Spirit is persistent."

Then ask:

- In what ways does the Spirit speak to us? (*through Scripture, through worship, through other people, through our experiences,* and so forth)
- What can we do to stay focused on the Spirit? (*spend time in prayer, read and study Scripture, spend time with Christian friends, participate in worship,* and so forth)

SUPPLIES
- ❑ "Spirit Movement" cards

PREPARATION: Make a copy of the "Spirit Movement" cards, on the website; and cut the cards apart.

THE SPIRIT ON THE MOVE

(15 minutes)

Say: "As we learned in Scripture, the Spirit has been at work in the world since Creation. We've looked specifically at the Pentecost story and John Wesley's experience. Now we'll look at some other Spirit-filled moments in history."

Give each person one or more of the "Spirit Movement" cards, from the website. If you have more than four confirmands, have some of them work in pairs.

Give the youth a few minutes to read the stories on their cards. Then invite each person to report what he or she learned and how the Holy Spirit was at work in the life of the person on his or her card. After you've gone over all of the cards, invite the youth to name additional examples of persons they know personally or know of who have been touched by the Holy Spirit.

Then say: "These people we've discussed were just like John Wesley and the disciples on Pentecost: They were followers of Christ who had opened their ears, eyes, minds, and hearts to the Holy Spirit. We should follow their example by opening our ears, eyes, minds, and hearts to the Spirit."

NOTE: Before you dismiss, instruct the confirmands to read, reflect on, and journal about the material in the "Holy Spirit" section of the *Credo Confirmation Student Journal* before your next session. Also encourage them to try to do the activities related to "Holy Spirit" on the confirmand website.

NOW WHAT?

SUPPLIES
- ❑ markerboard
- ❑ marker

PREPARATION: Write the benediction, "John Wesley's Rule," on a markerboard; or print out the poster from the website.

CLOSING RITUAL

(10 minutes)

Gather the confirmands into a circle. Lead the youth in prayer, giving thanks to God for your time together and all that the group has learned and experienced. Then go around the circle, inviting each person to pray aloud one word or phrase that describes something he or she learned during the past week of confirmation.

After every person has had a chance to contribute a word or phrase, say a brief closing prayer. Then invite the confirmands to say aloud and in unison the benediction, "John Wesley's Rule."

Church

INTRODUCTION

You may be familiar with this rhyme and finger play: "Here is the church. Here is the steeple. Open the doors, and see all the people." (Go ahead and do the finger motions. We'll wait.)

The problem with this finger play is that it equates the church with a building. An alternative ending to the rhyme—"Open the doors, and where are the people?"—even implies that the church can exist without the people. In reality, the church is the people, dictionary definitions notwithstanding. The people may own a building with a steeple on top, but they are greater than the sum of their real estate.

What's more, if the people are spending all of their time inside the church building, they really aren't fulfilling their mission as church. They really aren't being church. The Great Commission doesn't tell us to go and hold Sunday school classes or potluck dinners or committee meetings or even worship services. It says, "Go and make disciples" (**Matthew 28:19,** NIV). That is our mission as church.

DEFINING CHURCH

The distinction between people and a building or institution is not as obvious as it seems—even to adult Christians. Oh sure, we honor it in principle; but we don't always agree with it in practice. We say "go to church" at First United Methodist Church just as we'd say we "go to dinner" at Bob's Steak House. Or we act as though we're members of the body of Christ when we're in the church building but not when we're at the office. Or we develop church budgets that are more inwardly focused than mission oriented.

Our first goal in this lesson is to define *church*. Here's what *The Book of Discipline of The United Methodist Church* says in the Preamble to The Constitution:

> The church is a community of all true believers under the Lordship of Christ. It is the redeemed and redeeming fellowship in which the Word of God is preached by persons divinely called, and the sacraments are duly administered according to Christ's own appointment. Under the discipline of the Holy Spirit the church seeks to provide for the maintenance of worship, the edification of believers, and the redemption of the world.

That's a dense definition, but it explains *who* the church is (the community of all believers) and *why* it exists (for worship, teaching, and service). Later sessions will explore the "why" in more detail. This session focuses on the "who."

Learning Our History

In the United Methodist tradition, persons become baptized members of the church upon baptism. Baptized members may become professing members by professing their faith and taking the vows of membership. Confirmation is, among other things, an opportunity for young people to become professing members of three bodies: Christ's universal church, The United Methodist Church, and the local church.

This session will look at the church on all three levels, starting with the symbolic birth of the church during the first Christian Pentecost (**Acts 2**). It looks at the growth of the church and some of the major divisions in the body of Christ. It looks briefly at the origins of some of the many Christian denominations that are active today. Then it looks specifically at the development of The United Methodist Church. Finally, this session challenges you to explore the story and ministries of your congregation.

The Body of Christ

Paul describes the church as the body of Christ. Each member of the church is a part of the body; and the many parts of the body have different, yet equally vital, functions. Confirmation is a great time for youth to claim their roles in the body of Christ and to reflect on ways God calls them to contribute to the body. This session emphasizes that God calls all persons in the church to be ministers—not just those who become ordained clergy. Christians serve as ministers when they sing in the children's or youth choir, when they participate in a service project, when they listen patiently to a friend who is hurting, or when they engage in a discussion in a Sunday school class. Young Christians should see themselves as ministers whom God has equipped to do the work of God's kingdom.

SUPPLIES AND PREPARATION

BASIC SUPPLIES

- ❑ Bibles of various translations
- ❑ markerboard or large sheets of paper
- ❑ markers
- ❑ pens or pencils
- ❑ clear tape and/or glue
- ❑ masking tape
- ❑ index cards or paper cut about the same size (3-by-5 or 4-by-6)
- ❑ sheets of posterboard
- ❑ paper (Use paper that has already been used on one side as much as possible, depending on the activity.)
- ❑ scissors

ACTIVITY	PREPARATION	OTHER SUPPLIES
WHAT?		
Opening Ritual	Write the opening meditation—which is adapted from 1 Chronicles 16:8, 12, 15, 23—on a markerboard; or project the meditation, using the slide on the website.	❑ vine from previous sessions ❑ vine branches (1 for each student)
Defining Church	Gather supplies.	❑ optional: *The Book of Discipline of The United Methodist Church*
SO WHAT? PART 1		
The Church in the Bible	Gather supplies.	
The Church Expands	Optional: Download the slide show "The Church Expands," on the website.	❑ optional: the slide show "The Church Expands" and equipment with which to show it
SO WHAT? PART 2		
Forefathers, Mothers, and Others	Make copies of and cut apart the "Forefathers, Mothers and Others Biographies" handout and "Forefathers, Mothers and Others Cards" on the website.	❑ "Forefathers, Mothers and Others Biographies" handout ❑ "Forefathers, Mothers and Others Cards"
Our Story	Invite someone who has been a member of your congregation for years to tell the history of your congregation.	❑ guest speaker
NOW WHAT?		
The Members and the Body	Gather supplies.	
Playing Our Part	Gather supplies.	❑ 3 rubber balls
Closing Ritual	Write the benediction, "John Wesley's Rule," on a markerboard; or print out the poster on the website.	

WHAT?

opening ritual

(10 minutes)

As confirmands arrive, point them to the confirmation vine and give each person a branch. Invite the confirmands to reflect on the previous session and to write on their branch something they learned or experienced during that session. Ask the confirmands to attach their branch to the vine. Remind the youth that this vine and its branches represent God's story, a story that they are a part of.

When all of the confirmands have arrived, invite each person to talk briefly about what he or she wrote on his or her branch. Then invite the youth to read aloud the opening meditation, which is adapted from **1 Chronicles 16:8, 12, 15, 23:**

> Give thanks to the LORD,
> and make God's deeds known among the peoples.
> Remember the wonderful works that God has done;
> remember God's covenant forever.
> Sing to the LORD, all the earth.
> Tell of God's salvation every day.

supplies
- ❑ vine from previous sessions
- ❑ vine branches (1 for each student)
- ❑ markers or pens

preparation: Have on hand supplies for the youth to add branches to the vine. Write the opening meditation—which is adapted from 1 Chronicles 16:8, 12, 15, 23—on a markerboard; or project the meditation, using the slide on the website.

note: Take time before you get started to talk with the confirmands about what they read and wrote in the "Holy Spirit" section of their *Credo Confirmation Student Journals.*

defining church

(15 minutes)

Say: "We've followed the story of God and God's people from Creation to sin and estrangement to redemption through the death and resurrection of Christ and to the coming of the Holy Spirit on the first Christian Pentecost. Along the way, we've discussed each person of the Trinity and the ways in which God connects with God's people. This week, we continue this story by talking about the church, which is an important way that we connect with God. But before we talk about church, we need to define what church is."

Point out that defining *church* is not as easy as it might seem. Read this quotation from John Wesley's sermon "Of the Church" (Sermon 74): "How much do we almost continually hear about the Church! With many it is a matter of daily conversation. And yet how few understand what they talk of! How few know what the term means! A more ambiguous word than this, the Church, is scarce to be found in the English language."

You might paraphrase Wesley's quotation as: "We hear a lot about church. But a lot of the time, we have no idea what people are saying when they talk about church. Most of us don't even know what *church* means, because *church* is one of the hardest words in the English language to define and understand."

supplies
- ❑ markerboard or paper
- ❑ marker or pen
- ❑ optional: *The Book of Discipline of The United Methodist Church*

Ask the confirmands to spend a few minutes brainstorming words and short phrases that describe or define *church,* as you list them on a markerboard or paper. Once you have a good list, have the confirmands work together, using the words and phrases they've identified, to come up with a good definition of *church.*

Possible definitions might include the following:

- *"A group of people who love God and come together to worship, learn about God, and serve God's people"*
- *"A congregation, or body of people, united together in the service of God"* (This is John Wesley's definition, from his "Of the Church" sermon.)

Write the definition across the top of the markerboard or paper so that you can refer to it throughout the session.

Then read aloud the definition of *church* that is in the Preamble to The Constitution in *The Book of Discipline*. Ask the youth to compare their definition with the definition from *The Book of Discipline*.

SO WHAT? PART 1

SUPPLIES
- ❑ Bibles

THE CHURCH IN THE BIBLE

(10 minutes)

Say: "The Bible says a lot about what it means to be the church."

If your confirmands already have a good knowledge of the Bible, ask them where in the Bible they might find information about the history of the church and about what it means to be the church.

Point out these books:

- The **Acts of the Apostles** gives the history of the early church, from its beginnings in Jerusalem to its spread throughout the Roman Empire.
- Paul's general letters (**Romans** through **2 Thessalonians**) contain advice to specific churches about theology (salvation, who Christ is, and so forth) and how to live in communion with one another.
- The "Pastoral Epistles," **1 and 2 Timothy** and **Titus,** give advice to specific church leaders about caring for their congregations.
- **Revelation 2** and 3 contain messages to seven specific churches in Asia Minor.

Say: "One of the best descriptions of what it means to be the church appears in **Acts 2:43-47,** which follows the Pentecost story."

Invite a volunteer to read aloud **Acts 2:43-47,** while the others students follow along in their Bibles.

Ask:

- How is this description of the early church similar to our definition of *church*?
- How is it different?

THE CHURCH EXPANDS

(30–40 minutes)

Say: "At the beginning of Acts, the people who made up the church could fit in a single room. But through the power of the Holy Spirit—and the hard work of early Christians—the church grew."

Make sure that each person has a Bible, and tell everyone to turn to **Acts 1.** Challenge the confirmands to be the first to find a reference to the church's size in that chapter. Tell them that, when they find it, they are to raise their hand. When the first youth raises a hand, ask him or her to name the verse and read it aloud. (***Acts 1:15*** *gives the size of the church as "about one hundred twenty persons."*)

Then challenge the confirmands to be the first to find in **Acts 2** the reference to the church's size. Again, call on the first youth to raise his or her hand to name the verse and read it aloud. (***Acts 2:41*** *says, "About three thousand persons were added* [to the church].")

Continue with **Acts 4.** (***Acts 4:4*** *says, "But many of those who heard the word believed; and they numbered about five thousand."*)

Say: "Shortly after Jesus' ascension to heaven, the church had about 120 members. At Pentecost, they added three thousand more; and a little while later, they added another five thousand. So, in a very short time, the church grew from 120 people to several thousand. Within a few decades, the good news of Christ had reached Rome, which was the center of the civilized world. In the fourth century Christianity became the official religion of the Roman Empire. Today there are more than two billion Christians in the world, and the church has a major presence on every continent."

Ask:

- Why, do you think, did the church grow and spread so rapidly?

To begin, ask the confirmands to call out the names of various Christian traditions and denominations. Write these on one side of a markerboard. Don't make any comments, except to make corrections and add clarifications.

Then say: "Let's look at where some of these denominations and traditions came from and how we, as United Methodists, fit into the Christian family tree."

SUPPLIES

- ❑ Bibles
- ❑ optional: the church history slide shows from the website and and equipment to show them

PREPARATION:

Optional: Download the church history slide shows on the website.

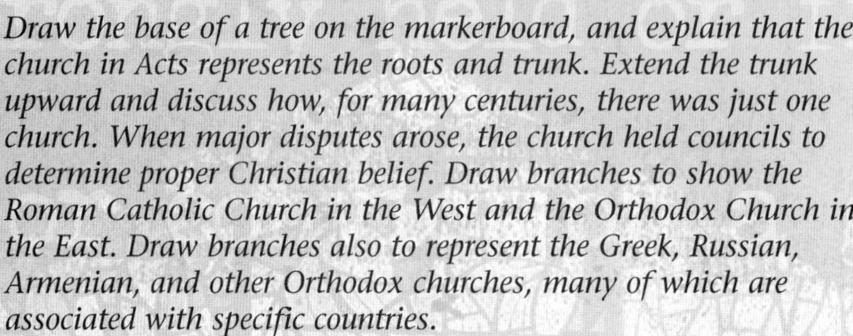

Draw the base of a tree on the markerboard, and explain that the church in Acts represents the roots and trunk. Extend the trunk upward and discuss how, for many centuries, there was just one church. When major disputes arose, the church held councils to determine proper Christian belief. Draw branches to show the Roman Catholic Church in the West and the Orthodox Church in the East. Draw branches also to represent the Greek, Russian, Armenian, and other Orthodox churches, many of which are associated with specific countries.

Then say: "Because the church was (and is) made up of imperfect people, the church in the West developed some imperfect practices. In 1517, a monk named Martin Luther posted his "95 Theses," calling for reform of the Catholic Church, on the church door in Wittenberg, Germany. Luther felt that the church had put so much emphasis on church tradition that it had distorted the truth of Scripture."

Split the Catholic branch to represent the Protestant Reformation, the split in the church that followed Luther's protest. Then split the Protestant branch into smaller branches labeled Lutheran, Calvinist *(including the Reformed and Presbyterian), and* Anabaptist *(including Mennonites and Amish).*

Say: "Again, because the church is made up of imperfect people, the church also split in England. King Henry VIII was a Roman Catholic until the pope would not allow him to divorce. In 1554, Henry left the Catholic Church and started the Church of England. The king ended up getting divorced several times and kicked the Catholic Church out of England. Despite its controversial beginnings, the Church of England became an important Christian denomination in England and elsewhere in the world. (In the United States, the Church of England is known as the Episcopal Church.)"

Split the Catholic branch again to represent the beginning of the Church of England.

Say: "Once again, because the church is made up of imperfect people, the Church of England eventually needed to be reformed. John Wesley, a minister in the Church of England in the eighteenth century, emphasized God's grace, personal holiness, and social responsibility. Those who followed Wesley's method for holy living earned the nickname 'Methodists,' and the Methodist movement began. The Church of England stopped sending clergy to the American colonies during the Revolutionary War, prompting Wesley to ordain in 1784 the first United States Methodist superintendent, Thomas Coke. Coke then ordained Francis Asbury, and Coke and Asbury became the first two bishops of the newly formed Methodist Episcopal Church."

Split the Church of England branch to represent the Methodist movement in England and the subsequent birth of the Methodist Episcopal Church in the United States.

Say: "Not long after the Methodist Episcopal Church took shape, a pair of German-speaking preachers, Philip William Otterbein and Martin Boehm (baym), started a movement of their own among German immigrants. In 1800, Otterbein, who came from the Reformed tradition, and Boehm, who was a Mennonite, formed the Church of the United Brethren in Christ." Shortly thereafter, Jacob Albright, a Methodist, began another ministry among German immigrants, which led to the formation of the Evangelical Association.

Draw branches from the Reformed and Anabaptist branches that join to form a United Brethren branch; draw an Evangelical Association branch off of the Methodist Episcopal Church branch.

Say: "The Methodist Episcopal Church took a strong stand against slavery, but didn't always live up to its welcoming message. As congregations segregated black and white worshipers and as individual Methodists bought slaves, some African American Methodists left the church to form two new denominations: The African Methodist Episcopal Church and the African Methodist Episcopal Zion Church."

Draw branches from the Methodist Episcopal Church branch representing the African Methodist Episcopal and African Methodist Episcopal Zion Churches.

Say: "The Methodist Episcopal Church, the Church of the United Brethren in Christ, and the Evangelical Association were two of many traditions that would ultimately come together to form The United Methodist Church. As recently as 2004, the Protestant Methodist Church of Côte d'Ivoire, in West Africa, officially joined our denomination."

Have theses branches join to form a new branch.

Tell the youth that this drawing is only a rough sketch of church history. Many more splits and mergers took place to get us to the religious landscape we know today. (More information on the formation of The United Methodist Church is available on the website.)

As needed, draw additional branches to the tree to represent additional Christian traditions that the confirmands named earlier. If you are unsure about where a certain branch fits, tell the youth that you don't know and challenge the youth to do some research to find out.

Then say: "The denominations and Christian traditions that we've represented on here are organized differently, worship differently, have different understandings of baptism and Holy Communion, and emphasize different spiritual practices. But all of these churches share some essential beliefs. They all believe in one God who is three persons; that Jesus Christ was fully divine and fully human; and that Jesus Christ, by his death and resurrection, defeated sin and death to reconcile the world to God."

NOTE: If you choose to divide this session into two one-hour classes, break here.

SUPPLIES

- ❑ "Forefathers, Mothers and Others Biographies" handout
- ❑ "Forefathers, Mothers and Others Cards"

PREPARATION: Make copies of the "Forefathers, Mothers and Others Biographies" handout and "Forefathers, Mothers and Others Cards," on the website. Cut apart the cards so that each box on the grid is a separate card.

SUPPLIES

- ❑ "guest speaker

PREPARATION: Invite someone who has been a member of your congregation for years to tell the history of your congregation. Give your guest the list of points from the activity so that he or she can include that information in his or her talk. Be sure to tell your guest that the students will have a chance to ask questions afterward.

SO WHAT? PART 2

Forefathers, Mothers, and Others

(20 minutes)

Say: "Countless people, some well-known and others anonymous, have made The United Methodist Church what it is today. We're going to take a quick look at four of these persons."

Hand out copies of the biographies of the following four persons, from the website.

- Francis Asbury
- Barbara Heck
- John Stewart
- William Wadé Harris

Give the confirmands a few minutes to read over the biographies. While they're doing this, spread out on the floor, face down, the 20 cards cut from the "Forefathers, Mothers, and Others" handout from the website. Have them leave the biographies handout behind as they move to the floor to work together to match the cards to the person whom they describe. Give them plenty of time to work, then check their answers against the information on the biographies handout.

Our Story

(15 minutes)

Introduce your guest, someone who has been a member of your congregation for several years (if possible, since the congregation was founded) and who will tell the group the story of your congregation. This person should talk about the following:

- When and why the congregation was founded
- How some of the church's ministries came into being
- Ways in which the church has served the community over the years
- Ways that the church has ministered to people around the world
- How the church building and property have changed over the years
- How the church's children's, youth, and confirmation ministries have changed over the years

Allow plenty of time for the confirmands to ask questions.

NOW WHAT?

THE MEMBERS AND THE BODY

(20 minutes)

SUPPLIES
- ❑ scratch paper
- ❑ pens and pencils

Tell the youth that they'll be taking a pop quiz.

Distribute scratch paper, and ask the confirmands to write down two numbers: the number of ministers in your congregation and the number of people it takes to put on a worship service in your congregation. (Do not differentiate between ministers and pastors at this time.)

Ask volunteers to give their answers to these two questions, but don't indicate whether the answers are right or wrong.

Say: "Let's work together to figure out how many people it takes to put on a worship service in our congregation."

Invite volunteers to call out a specific job (for example, "preach the sermon," "select the hymns," or "clean the sanctuary") and how many people do that job for the worship service. List these jobs and the number of people required to do them on a markerboard. Don't worry if the youth don't know precise numbers (such as how many choir members there are). Just write down a rough estimate and move on.

When the youth have run out of ideas, suggest additional jobs from the following list, modifying it to fit your church's structure:

- pastor
- liturgist
- music director
- musicians
- sound technicians
- ushers
- greeters
- custodians or others who prepare the worship space
- parking lot attendants
- whoever prepares and reproduces the worship bulletins
- nursery workers

Add the numbers to get a grand total. Regardless of your church's size, this should be a fairly large number relative to worship attendance.

Then ask:

- In addition to worship, what are some things that our congregation does? (*outreach in the community and around the world, care for members of the congregation who are ill or grieving, providing educational opportunities,* and so forth)

Ask the confirmands to name some of the persons who are involved in each of these ministries of the church. Offer help as needed.

Return to the first question and ask whether any of the confirmands would like to revise his or her answers to the first question (the number of ministers in your congregation). Chances are good that at least one student will realize that the number of ministers in your congregation is a lot larger than the number of ordained clergy.

Discuss these questions:

- How many people listed on the board are ministers? (*all of them*)
- How many people in our congregation are ministers? (*all who play a role in carrying out the work of the church—whether in worship or in their day-to-day lives*)
- How many people in our congregation are called to be ministers? (*all of them*)

Point out two or three of the ministry roles you've talked about that some people might consider "lesser" jobs. Talk about what would happen if these jobs didn't get done. (For example, without nursery workers, families with small children might not attend worship or be involved in certain ministries of the church. Without someone to print bulletins or project content on video screens, worshipers wouldn't know what to say or sing.)

Say: "Church is not like a play or concert, where you pay money to see a performance. Church is more like a team sport, where everybody has a job to do and every job is critical to the team's success."

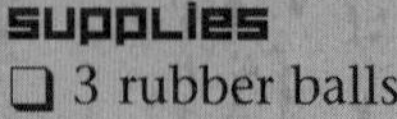

supplies
❑ 3 rubber balls

preparation: Involve as many people as possible (including adults, children, and older youth) in this activity.

Playing Our Part

(20 minutes)

Since the purpose of this activity is to illustrate that the church is a community of believers who must come together to do the work God has called them to do, involve as many participants as possible. Make sure that any adult volunteers and parents who are present participate and, if feasible, invite children and older youth to join in.

Ask all of the participants to stand in a circle, facing inward. Hand a rubber ball to one player; and have the players pass the ball, hand-to-hand, around the circle. Emphasize that accurately passing the ball is more important than speed. After a minute, add a second ball on the opposite side of the circle from the first one, then a third. Once the players have mastered the game, announce that all of the players with a birthday in July are to leave the game by dropping their hands and taking two steps backward.

Every minute or so, announce that players with another characteristic are to leave the game—persons wearing glasses, persons wearing red shirts, and so on. (You might try to limit the characteristics to items that few have in common so as to keep the game going longer.) Keep the game going until everyone is out and all of the balls are dropped.

Say: "The church is a lot like this game. If everyone does his or her part, we can do a lot of things well. If a lot of people don't participate, we aren't very effective. Paul talked about the importance of everybody participating in one of his letters to the church in Corinth."

Invite a volunteer to read aloud **1 Corinthians 12:12-27,** while the other students follow along.

Then ask:

- How does this passage relate to the game we just played?
- How does this passage relate to our discussions about the people involved in planning worship and the other ministries of the church?

Say: "As we continue this journey together, we will talk more about our gifts and how God calls us to use them in ministry. For now, know that you each have important gifts and are a critical part of our congregation, of The United Methodist Church, and of the church universal."

NOTE: Before you dismiss, instruct the confirmands to read, reflect on, and journal about the material in the "Church" section of the *Credo Confirmation Student Journal* before your next session. Also encourage them to try to do the activities related to "Church" on the confirmand website.

CLOSING RITUAL

(10 minutes)

SUPPLIES

- ❑ markerboard
- ❑ marker

PREPARATION: Write the benediction, "John Wesley's Rule," on a markerboard; or print out the poster from the website.

Gather the confirmands into a circle. Lead the youth in prayer, giving thanks to God for your time together and all that the group has learned and experienced. Then go around the circle, inviting each person to pray aloud one word or phrase that describes something he or she learned during the past week of confirmation.

After every person has had a chance to contribute a word or phrase, say a brief closing prayer. Then invite the confirmands to say aloud and in unison the benediction, "John Wesley's Rule."

New Creation

INTRODUCTION

Quick! How many Creation stories does the Bible contain? Casual observers will say one. Those who have read Genesis carefully (and Bible scholars who have practiced source criticism) will say two: the one where God creates the world in six days and rests on the seventh (**Genesis 1:1–2:3**) and the one where God forms Adam and Eve in the Garden and gives them basic instructions for how to live (**Genesis 2:4-25**). Those who know the Bible cover to cover—or who have skipped ahead—will add a third Creation story: the one where God creates a new heaven and a new earth at the end of days (**Revelation 21:1–22:5**).

Three Stories, Three Plot Lines, One Central Character

With each of these stories, it's easy to get caught up in the details. Were the days of Creation literally 24-hour days? What does the Adam and Eve story say about the relationship between man and woman? How many karats will the gold be that paves the streets of the new Jerusalem?

But the real power of the stories lies in the power source: the God who can create a universe from nothing, a man from mud, a new Creation from the mess we humans have made of the old one.

New Creations

This theme continues in the Bible's other Creation stories: the ones where God's creatures become new creations through the saving power of Jesus Christ. Consider the Samaritan woman Jesus met at Jacob's well (**John 4:1-42**): She was undoubtedly a new creation after her brief encounter with Jesus. So was the tax collector Levi (known in other sources as Matthew, in **Luke 6:27-28**), Zacchaeus (**Luke 19:1-10**), and Paul (also known as Saul, in **Acts 9:1-19**). As Paul himself wrote, "So if anyone is in Christ, there is a new creation; everything old has passed away; see, everything has become new" (**2 Corinthians 5:17**).

Christ didn't stop doing extreme personal makeovers after his death, resurrection, and ascension: Paul's encounter on the Damascus road was with the risen Christ. And Christ didn't stop transforming people when the biblical canon was closed: We know people—perhaps we *are* the people—whose lives have been radically transformed by encounters with Christ. Paul's words from **2 Corinthians** are just as true today.

The Kingdom of God

Look carefully at Paul's words in **2 Corinthians 5,** and another important truth emerges. Many translations say, "*He* is a new creation"; but the New Revised Standard Version says, "*There* is a new creation." The original Greek may be translated either way. The distinction is significant. Christ's extreme personal makeovers aren't just personal; people who are transformed inevitably transform those around them. Like candles in the darkness, their light shines beyond themselves. In ways large or small, they help usher in the kingdom of God.

To many Christians, the kingdom of God is synonymous with heaven and is entirely removed from the here and now. But God's kingdom is not so remote. God's will can be done on earth as it is in heaven, just as we pray in the Lord's Prayer.

Luke 17:20-21 describes an encounter between Jesus and a group of Pharisees. They ask him when the kingdom is coming, as though he's going to whip out his planner and point to the date when the angel armies will arrive to install him on the throne. His response? "The kingdom of God is not coming with things that can be observed; nor will they say, 'Look, here it is!' or 'There it is!' For, in fact, the kingdom of God is *among* you."

That word *among* can mean two things: 1) within a person; or 2) throughout a group of people. Typically, both are true—and in that order. As mentioned earlier, an individual is transformed and, in turn, transforms his or her surroundings. At first, bystanders might not notice a difference; but eventually, everyone will see that the kingdom is breaking through.

It's something like what can happen in a blighted neighborhood when a Habitat for Humanity house goes up. The next-door neighbor paints her house. The family across the street remodels their living room. A store goes up on a nearby vacant lot. Stable families become involved in the community. The changes mount until you can't help but notice the entire neighborhood's transformation.

Transforming in More Ways Than One

Adolescence is a time of identity formation. Even younger youth begin thinking of themselves and expressing themselves in new ways. The prospect of being made new, of claiming a new way of living and a new perspective on life, may be quite appealing to young people who are eagerly looking for ways to define themselves.

At the same time, many young people yearn to be a part of something bigger than themselves and to have an impact on the world around them. They need to see examples of people transformed by Christ who have transformed their communities and their world. They need to understand how living a life of Christian discipleship not only draws them closer to God but also gives the world a sense of the power of the Holy Spirit.

SUPPLIES AND PREPARATION

BASIC SUPPLIES

❑ Bibles of various translations ❑ markerboard or large sheets of paper ❑ markers ❑ pens or pencils	❑ clear tape and/or glue ❑ masking tape ❑ index cards or paper cut about the same size (3-by-5 or 4-by-6) ❑ sheets of posterboard	❑ paper (Use paper that has already been used on one side as much as possible, depending on the activity.) ❑ scissors

ACTIVITY	PREPARATION	OTHER SUPPLIES
WHAT?		
Opening Ritual	Write the opening meditation—which is adapted from 1 Chronicles 16:8, 12, 15, 23—on a markerboard; or project the meditation, using the slide on the website.	❑ vine from previous sessions ❑ vine branches (1 for each student)
New Creation	Gather supplies.	❑ colored pencils
SO WHAT? PART 1		
Old Creatures, New Creations	Optional: Have on hand extra adult leaders.	❑ optional: extra adult leaders
Transformed and Transforming	Gather supplies.	
SO WHAT? PART 2		
Defining the Kingdom	Gather supplies.	
Finding the Kingdom	Gather supplies.	❑ access to newspapers, news magazines, or Internet news sources
Characteristics of the Kingdom	Gather supplies.	
NOW WHAT?		
Playing Our Part	Gather supplies.	
Closing Ritual	Write the benediction, "John Wesley's Rule," on a markerboard; or print out the poster on the website.	

WHAT?

Opening Ritual

(10 minutes)

As confirmands arrive, point them to the confirmation vine and give each person a branch. Invite the confirmands to reflect on the previous session and to write on their branch something they learned or experienced during that session. Ask the confirmands to attach their branch to the vine. Remind the youth that this vine and its branches represent God's story, a story that they are a part of.

When all of the confirmands have arrived, invite each person to talk briefly about what he or she wrote on his or her branch. Then invite the youth to read aloud the opening meditation, which is adapted from **1 Chronicles 16:8, 12, 15, 23:**

> Give thanks to the LORD,
> and make God's deeds known among the peoples.
> Remember the wonderful works that God has done;
> remember God's covenant forever.
> Sing to the LORD, all the earth.
> Tell of God's salvation every day.

supplies
- ❑ vine from previous sessions
- ❑ vine branches (1 for each student)
- ❑ markers or pens

preparation: Have on hand supplies for the youth to add branches to the vine. Write the opening meditation—which is adapted from 1 Chronicles 16:8, 12, 15, 23—on a markerboard; or project the meditation, using the slide on the website.

note: Take time before you get started to talk with the confirmands about what they read and wrote in the "Church" section of their *Credo Confirmation Student Journal.*

New Creation

(15 minutes)

Before introducing the concept of new creation, review with the confirmands the Creation stories in **Genesis 1–2.** Give them time to read the passage in their Bible, looking for three things:

- Characteristics of the Creation (see the examples below)
- Ways that God's power is at work
- God's relationship with the people whom God creates

After several minutes, invite volunteers to talk about what they found. Write their responses on a markerboard. Characteristics of Creation might include *good, diverse, no sin or pain or death,* and so on. Examples of God's power at work might include *creating the universe from a "formless void," creating countless creatures, separating the land from the water,* and so on. Indications of God's relationship with humankind might include *creating a bountiful garden for them to live in, giving them a role in tending to Creation,* and *giving them rules to live by*. Feel free to offer examples of your own.

Say: "As we know, it didn't take long for people to rebel against God. Scripture is full of examples of people betraying God's trust, disobeying God's commands, and acting contrary to God's will. This rebellion has continued throughout history, but the **Book of Revelation** points to a day in which it will end. Much of **Revelation** is hard to understand; but the ending, which describes the new Creation that God will bring about, is very clear."

supplies
- ❑ Bibles
- ❑ markerboard
- ❑ markers
- ❑ colored pencils
- ❑ paper

Have a volunteer read aloud **Revelation 21:1-5** and **22:1-15,** while the other students follow along. Hand out paper and markers and/or colored pencils; and have the confirmands draw pictures of the new Creation described in Revelation. Then ask the students to name any common elements between the Creation stories in **Genesis** and the story of new Creation in **Revelation.**

Say: "The Bible begins and ends in a garden, and it begins and ends with people living in right relationship with God. In between is very different; but even then, God is able to take the messes people have made and turn them into something beautiful."

SO WHAT? PART 1

OLD CREATURES, NEW CREATIONS

(15 minutes)

SUPPLIES
- ❑ Bibles
- ❑ paper
- ❑ pens and pencils
- ❑ optional: extra adult leaders

PREPARATION:
Optional: Have on hand extra adult leaders.

Say: "The **Book of Revelation** tells the story of God making all things new. But we don't need to wait to experience God's new Creation. God is always making things new—including individuals. Let's look at some persons who became new creations when they encountered Jesus."

Assign each of the Scriptures below to a youth. If possible, assign an adult leader to each confirmand to help them better understand their assigned Scripture. Scriptures may be assigned to more than one person.

- **John 4:1-42** (the Samaritan woman at the well)
- **Luke 19:1-10** (Zacchaeus)
- **Acts 9:1-19** (Saul's conversion—Point out that Saul was also known as Paul.)

Have each person read the assigned Scripture with the following questions in mind:

- Who was changed?
- Why did he or she need to be changed?
- How did Jesus transform him or her?
- What happened next?

Give the youth a few minutes to work. Then have each person report to the group.

Point out that, while the Bible tells several stories of people transformed by an encounter with Christ, these stories are not limited to Scripture. Christians throughout history (and today) have been made new in Christ. Remind the youth of John Wesley's Aldersgate experience, which they learned about in Session 4 ("The Holy Spirit"). Also emphasize that transformation doesn't happen in a single moment. Many people are made new gradually, over the course of their lives. And even those who have a dramatic conversion experience continue to grow and change long after their initial experience with Christ.

Transformed and Transforming

(10 minutes)

Explain that Paul (called Saul in **Acts 9:1-19,** in the previous activity) helped spread Christianity throughout the Roman Empire and wrote many letters that are included in the New Testament.

Read aloud **2 Corinthians 5:17** from two translations:

—New International Version: "Therefore, if anyone is in Christ, he is a new creation; the old has gone, the new has come!"
—New Revised Standard Version: "So if anyone is in Christ, there is a new creation: everything old has passed away; see, everything has become new!"

Ask:

- What is the difference between these two versions? (*The NIV uses the word* he, *while the NRSV uses* there.)

Say: "When someone has a relationship with Christ, he or she is made new. But that new creation is not limited to an individual person. When one person is transformed by Christ, that person—through his or her attitude and behavior—transforms those whom he or she encounters. There is a new creation: It starts with the individual, but it doesn't end with the individual."

Ask:

- How does God use persons such as the woman at the well and Paul and Zacchaeus to transform others? (*The woman at the well told the people in her town about Jesus, and many believed because of her testimony. Paul became an important leader of the church, took the gospel message to many places throughout the Roman world, and wrote several letters included in the New Testament that have touched people's lives for nearly 2,000 years. Zacchaeus set an important example by repenting of his sins and promising to live differently.*)

Supplies
- ❑ NRSV Bible
- ❑ NIV Bible

SO WHAT? PART 2

NOTE: If you choose to divide this session into two one-hour classes, break here.

Defining the Kingdom

(15 minutes)

Say: "Jesus often talked about the kingdom of God when explaining how God was making all things new."

Ask the group about kingdoms they've heard about in books, movies, TV shows, and so forth. Then ask a volunteer to read aloud **Revelation 21:10-21,** while the others follow along in their Bibles.

Say: "This vision of the New Jerusalem fits pretty well with what we imagine kingdoms should look like. Some of Jesus' followers thought that he would bring about such a kingdom in their lifetime."

supplies
- ❑ access to newspapers, news magazines, or Internet news sources
- ❑ optional: posterboard, scissors, tape or glue

Finding the Kingdom

(15 minutes)

Read aloud **Luke 17:20-21.**

Ask:

- Jesus says in this Scripture that the kingdom of God is "among" us. What, do you think, does he mean by this? In what ways is God's kingdom *among* us?

Challenge the youth to look through newspapers and magazines or Internet news sources to find stories about people who are working in godly ways to transform the world around them. Provide publications or suggest websites that specialize in such inspirational stories. Give the youth several minutes to look for and read through such stories. Then invite each person to present one news story about a person doing the work of the Kingdom.

Option: Have the youth make a poster by mounting on a large posterboard all of these stories about kingdom-building. Hang the poster somewhere in your church building. Or have the confirmands come up with a plan for drawing attention to these stories on the Internet.

supplies
- ❑ Bibles
- ❑ scratch paper
- ❑ pens and pencils
- ❑ markerboard
- ❑ marker

Characteristics of the Kingdom

(15 minutes)

Assign to each youth a pair of the following Scriptures. Divide into pairs as needed:

- **Matthew 13:31-33** (parables of the mustard seed and of the yeast) and **Matthew 18:23-35** (parable of the unforgiving servant)
- **Matthew 13:44-45** (parables of the hidden treasure and of the pearl of great price) and **Matthew 20:1-16** (parable of the laborers in the vineyard)
- **Matthew 13:1-9, 18-23** (parable of the sower) and **Matthew 25:1-13** (parable of the ten bridesmaids)
- **Matthew 18:1-5** (greatest in the kingdom) and **Matthew 25:31-45** (judgment of the nations)

Have the confirmands read their assigned Scriptures and pay attention to what these passages say about the kingdom of God. Give them plenty of time to read and discuss, then ask them to name some of the characteristics of God's kingdom that they discovered in their assigned Scriptures. List their responses on a markerboard.

Then ask:

- How does the kingdom of God compare to the other kingdoms with which you're familiar?
- How do these parables show us ways in which the kingdom of God is among us?

NOW WHAT?

Playing Our Part

(25 minutes)

Say: "The Scriptures you read and studied tell us a lot about God, but they also teach us about how we should live and act in God's kingdom."

Have the confirmands work together to create a skit that puts one of the parables they read into a current-day setting and a familiar location (such as school or church).

Give the youth about 10 minutes to prepare, then invite them to perform their skit(s).

Say: "When we claim God's grace and establish a relationship with Christ, we become new creations. As new creations in Christ, we have an obligation to be kingdom people and to help bring about God's kingdom at home, at school, at church, in our community, and throughout the world."

(If the youth agree, have them perform their skit on Confirmation Sunday. Someone will have to write down their lines and a description of the skit so they remember when it's time for their Confirmation worship service.)

Supplies
- ❑ Bibles
- ❑ scratch paper
- ❑ pens and pencils

Note: Before you dismiss, instruct the confirmands to read, reflect on, and journal about the material in the "New Creation" section of the *Credo Confirmation Student Journal* before your next session. Also encourage them to try to do the activities related to "New Creation" on the confirmand website.

Closing Ritual

(10 minutes)

Gather the confirmands into a circle. Lead the youth in prayer, giving thanks to God for your time together and all that the group has learned and experienced. Then go around the circle, inviting each person to pray aloud one word or phrase that describes something he or she learned during the past week of confirmation.

After every person has had a chance to contribute a word or phrase, say a brief closing prayer. Then invite the confirmands to say aloud and in unison the benediction, "John Wesley's Rule."

Supplies
- ❑ markerboard
- ❑ marker

Preparation: Write the benediction, "John Wesley's Rule," on a markerboard; or print out the poster from the website.

Way of Discipleship

INTRODUCTION

Younger youth are in a development stage in which they try on identities to see what fits. This experimentation might involve trying on new clothing styles, new ways of speaking, new activities, and new habits that fit their trial identities.

Christians also have a way, a well-trodden path that disciples have taken generation after generation. One way to chart this path is to look at four spiritual practices: the personal practices of devotion and compassion and the corporate practices of worship and justice.

devotion

Devotion is the name for private activities that draw us in to Scripture, focus our attention on prayer, and help us be mindful of God's presence. Devotion is much more than just spending a few minutes each day reading from a daily devotional guide, although such resources certainly have merit. It also includes spending time each day in personal prayer; reading, studying, and reflecting on Scripture; and spending time in silence and solitude.

worship

Like devotion, worship is directed toward God. But unlike devotion, which is personal, worship is done as a community of faith. In worship, a faith community joins together for praise, prayer, and hearing God's Word. Although many individuals think of worship as a private act (ever heard, "I can worship at home . . . or on the golf course"?), it is not. We confess our sin in the presence of God *and* one another. We pray for one another as we hear the concerns of the people of God. We hear together the interpretation of Scripture, and we leave empowered to minister to the world.

compassion

Compassion represents practices of caring for the physical, emotional, and spiritual needs of others. Some refer to such care as "acts of mercy." Through compassion, we put our gifts, blessings, and talents to use on a personal level, caring and extending God's grace to individuals. Acts of mercy and compassion are important ways in which we follow the biblical commandment to love our neighbor as ourselves (**Leviticus 19:18; Matthew 22:34-40**).

Justice

Justice is the corporate side of compassion. It involves seeking peace and wholeness for all people and all of God's creation. When the church seeks justice, it moves beyond meeting the needs of individuals and looks at the root causes of social ills, such as poverty, hunger, slavery, sickness, and oppression. The work of justice sometimes means getting involved in politics, economics, and law; and it often involves being an advocate for those who lack the power and resources to make their voices heard. By striving for justice, we honor a God who is just and who desires the well-being of all people.

Practices for a Lifetime

These four easy-to-remember concepts—devotion, worship, compassion, and justice—give Christians of all ages a structure for Christlike living. Jesus spent much time in solitude and private prayer but also worshiped with a community of followers. Jesus met the immediate needs of the sick and hungry but also said that the Spirit of the Lord had anointed him to "bring good news to the poor," "proclaim release to the captives," and to "let the oppressed go free."

This session will give your confirmands an opportunity not only to learn about but to experience each of these four practices of faith. Challenge the youth to find new ways to incorporate devotion, worship, compassion, and justice into their daily lives.

These four pillars of Christian living are most commonly associated with Covenant Discipleship groups. A Covenant Discipleship group is a small group of Christians (usually no more than 7) who develop a covenant—focused on devotion, worship, compassion, and justice—and meet regularly to hold one another accountable to this covenant. Following this session, you might facilitate Covenant Discipleship groups for the confirmands and all youth and adult volunteers. Resources for doing this are available at *www.credoconfirmation.com.*

SUPPLIES AND PREPARATION

BASIC SUPPLIES

❑ Bibles of various translations ❑ markerboard or large sheets of paper ❑ markers ❑ pens or pencils	❑ clear tape and/or glue ❑ masking tape ❑ index cards or paper cut about the same size (3-by-5 or 4-by-6) ❑ sheets of posterboard	❑ paper (Use paper that has already been used on one side as much as possible, depending on the activity.) ❑ scissors

ACTIVITY	PREPARATION	OTHER SUPPLIES
WHAT?		
Opening Ritual	Write the opening meditation—which is adapted from Psalm 67—on a markerboard; or project the meditation, using the slide on the website.	❑ vine from previous sessions ❑ vine leaves (1 for each student)
Gathering: Tell Me the Way		
Private and Corporate	Gather supplies.	
SO WHAT? PART 1		
Devotion	Make copies of "Devotional," from the website. Optional: Buy subscriptions to a devotional resource such as *Devo'Zine,* available from Upper Room.	❑ copies of "Devotional," from the website ❑ bell or other signal of your choice ❑ optional: a devotional resource such as *Devo'Zine*
Create a Devotional Space (Optional)	Gather supplies.	❑ assorted craft supplies (See activity.)
SO WHAT? PART 2		
Worship	Gather supplies.	❑ copies of a recent church bulletin or order of worship
Compassion	Preparation depends on your choice of option.	❑ supplies for whatever option you choose
Justice	Look on the website for information about church agencies.	❑ newspapers and news magazines ❑ optional: computer with Internet access
NOW WHAT?		
Putting It All Together		❑ newspapers and news magazines ❑ optional: computer with Internet access
Closing Ritual	Write the benediction, "John Wesley's Rule," on a markerboard; or print out the poster on the website.	

WHAT?

OPENING RITUAL

(10 minutes)

During the first unit, Know Your Story, your confirmands added branches to a vine (or tree trunk) as part of a ritual inspired by **John 15:1-9.** During the second unit, Confirm Your Faith, they will add leaves to the branches.

As the confirmands arrive give each person a leaf. Invite each person to write on his or her leaf something that he or she learned, gained, or experienced during the Know Your Story unit. Instruct the confirmands to affix their leaf to a branch.

Say: "Healthy branches bear leaves, and the leaves collect the sunlight and carbon dioxide that plants need to grow. In this unit, we'll look at some of the traditions and practices that have helped Christianity and United Methodism grow and stay healthy."

Then invite the youth to read aloud this opening meditation, adapted from **Psalm 67:**

> O God, be gracious to us and bless us
> and make your face to shine upon us,
> that your way may be known upon earth,
> your saving power among all nations.
> Let the peoples praise you, O God;
> let all the peoples praise you!
> Let the nations be glad and sing for joy,
> for you judge the people with equity
> and guide the nations upon earth.

SUPPLIES
- ❑ vine from previous sessions
- ❑ vine leaves (1 for each student)
- ❑ markers or pens

PREPARATION: Have on hand supplies for the youth to add leaves to the vine. Write the opening meditation—which is adapted from Psalm 67—on a markerboard; or project the meditation, using the slide on the website.

NOTE: Take time before you get started to talk with the confirmands about what they read and wrote in the "New Creation" section of their *Credo Confirmation Student Journal*.

GATHERING: TELL ME THE WAY

(10–15 minutes)

Engage the youth in conversation about interesting things that they know how to do and could clearly describe to others. Be sure to use in your conversation the phrase *the way*. For example, youth might describe *the way* to be a good babysitter, *the way* to add music to a portable music player, *the way* to throw a football in a spiral, or *the way* to make the best chocolate chip cookies ever.

Give the confirmands a few minutes to prepare a presentation that teaches others *the way* to do something.

After everyone has had a chance to make a presentation, ask:

- What are some of the ways that people learn how to do something? (*trial and error, read books, have a parent show you, find instructions online,* and so forth)
- Which style works best for you? Why?

- Suppose I wanted to know the way to (*insert the name of a large town a hundred miles or so from you*). How could I go about learning the way? Would there be just one way to get there? What would be most helpful or least helpful in giving instructions to someone who wanted directions?
- In **John 14:6,** Jesus says that he is "the way" to God. What are some possible ways to understand that statement? (*He himself provides a way to God; his way of life is the way that we should follow; if we want to grow closer to God, Jesus' way is the way to do that;* and so forth.)

Say: "The earliest people who abided by Jesus' teaching were called 'followers of the way.' Today we're going to take a closer look at the way of discipleship, the way a disciple today can follow Jesus. We're going to look especially at four parts of being a Christian disciple: devotion, worship, compassion, and justice."

supplies
- ❑ markerboard or paper
- ❑ marker

private and corporate

(10 minutes)

Say: "There are some activities that we do privately, either alone or with a small number of people." Ask:

- What are some things that people usually do alone?
- What are some things that people usually do with only a few other people?

Then say: "There are also activities that we do corporately, or as part of a large group." Ask:

- What are some things that people usually do as part of a large group?

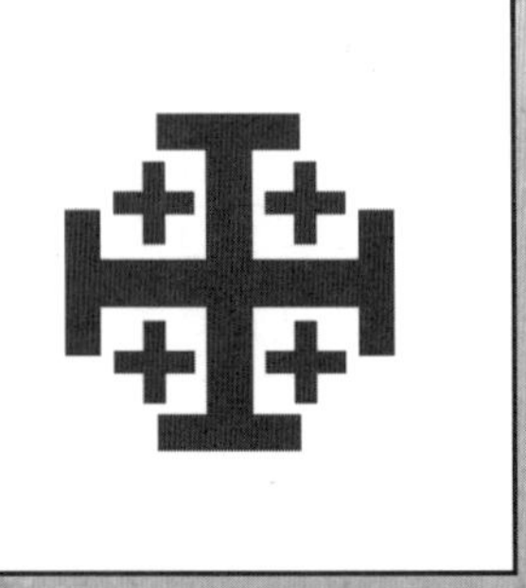

Then challenge the confirmands to think about activities that could be done privately or corporately. For example, one could watch football alone at home on television (private) or one could watch football with thousands of other people in a stadium (corporate). Discuss some of the differences between doing these things privately and corporately.

Before moving on, draw on a markerboard or paper a Jerusalem cross, pictured in the margin.

SO WHAT? PART 1

devotion

(10–15 minutes)

Write the word *devotion* in the center of a markerboard or paper. Set out markers, and ask the confirmands to write any words or phrases that come to mind when they see that word.

Read aloud the words and phrases the youth wrote. Ask the youth for clarifications, as needed. The confirmands might describe personal prayer or daily spiritual reading, being devoted to an art or a sport, persons they feel are devoted to a cause, and so forth. If the range of answers is fairly limited, draw out other possibilities by asking questions such as "Whom do you know who is very devoted to something or someone?"

Then ask:

- For a Christian, what, do you think, does the word *devotion* mean? (If the youth are unsure about how to answer the question, help them make connections to the words and phrases they wrote earlier.)

Say: "Devotion is spending time alone with God. Often this involves prayer, meditation, and reading and reflecting on Scripture and inspirational writings. Jesus often made time for devotion."

Ask volunteers to read aloud **Mark 1:35; 6:45-46;** and **14:32-39.**

Then hand out Bibles, pens or pencils; paper; and a copy of the "Devotional" handout, from the website, or copies of a devotional resource such as *Devo'Zine* (a monthly devotional magazine for young people published by The Upper Room).

Invite the confirmands to find a quiet place in the room or elsewhere in the church building or on the grounds where they can silently read and reflect on Scripture and devotional material and spend time in prayer. Tell them that you would like them to spend 12 minutes in silence, reading and reflecting on the devotional material, and writing down their reflections on the paper. Tell them that you'll ring a bell (or give another signal) to let them know when the time is up. Assure them that they will not have to talk about what they write.

After 12 minutes, gather everyone back together. Ask:

- What was that experience like for you? Was it easy or hard? What made it easy or difficult for you?
- Do you think that you could set aside 12 minutes or more of devotional time each day? What would you need to change to set aside this time each day? What barriers would you have to overcome?

Label one of the small crosses on the Jerusalem cross you drew earlier "Devotion." (See the example in the margin.)

create a devotional space (optional)

(15–20 minutes)

Have the class sit in a circle at a table. Have the members of each group talk together about their bedrooms or other parts of their homes that they've had a chance to personalize. Invite them to discuss how these spaces reflect their personalities and interests.

supplies

- ❑ Bibles
- ❑ markerboard or paper
- ❑ markers
- ❑ pens and pencils
- ❑ paper
- ❑ copies of "Devotional," from the website
- ❑ bell or other signal of your choice
- ❑ optional: a devotional resource such as *Devo'Zine*

preparation: Make copies of "Devotional," from the website.

optional: Buy subscriptions to a devotional resource such as *Devo'Zine,* available from Upper Room.

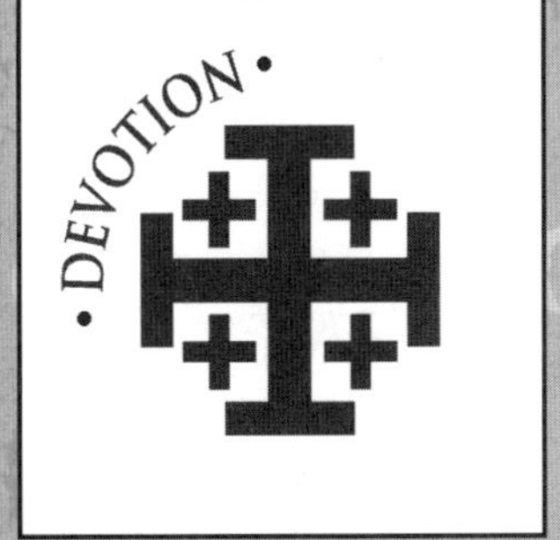

supplies
- ❑ assorted craft supplies (See "Preparation," below.)

preparation: Gather assorted art and craft supplies such as color paper, scissors, markers, craft clay, polished or smooth rocks, driftwood or small branches, glue, journals, fabric swatches, votive candle holders.

Then say: "Just as we take time to create a space in our homes that speaks to our personality and interests, many people find it meaningful to have a special place set aside for their devotional life. It could be a desk, a corner of a room, or a shelf on a bookcase. This space would include items that would help one connect with God, such as a Bible, a cross, a photo, a candle, a rock from a special place, a journal. In the coming week, work on setting up such a space in your house. To get you started, each of you is going to create an item for *someone else* to use in his or her devotional space."

Instruct each confirmand to use the art and craft supplies to create something for the person on his or her right. This might be a cross, a candle holder, a sign with a favorite Bible verse. Urge them to use their creativity to make their unique item.

Give the confirmands 10–15 minutes to work. Then have each person present the item he or she created to the person on his or her right.

note: If you choose to divide this session into two one-hour classes, break here.

SO WHAT? PART 2

supplies
- ❑ Bibles
- ❑ copies of a recent church bulletin or order of worship
- ❑ paper
- ❑ markers or colored pencils

worship

(10 minutes)

Note: Because worship is covered much more extensively in another lesson in this unit, please feel free to keep this part of the lesson briefer than the other three sections.

Ask:

- Devotion is spending private time with God. What activity involves spending time with God as part of a group of people? (*worship*)

Label another one of the small crosses on your Jerusalem cross—one that is adjacent to the "Devotion" cross—"Worship."

Ask a volunteer to read aloud **Acts 2:37-47.**

Say: "This Scripture comes right after the story of the birth of the church on Pentecost." (As needed, review the Pentecost story, using the information from the "Holy Spirit" session in the "Know Your Story" unit.)

Then say: "Right after the first Christian community came together, the people joined one another in worship."

Ask:

- Why, do you think, is it important for Christians to worship together on a regular basis?

Hand out copies of a recent church bulletin or order of worship.

Ask:

- What parts of our worship service are corporate (done as a group)? Which are private?

As a group, go to your congregation's sanctuary or worship space. Ask the youth to walk around, looking at each part of the worship space. Tell them to pay attention to ways that the worship space enhances the feeling of being together in community (such as how pews or chairs are arranged and hymnals or monitors that allow everyone to read the same songs and prayers).

Then ask:

- If you were going to design a worship space, what would you do to bring people together as a community and get everyone involved in worship?

Hand out paper and markers or colored pencils, and ask the youth to draw (or write about) the worship space they would design. Give them about 5 minutes to work, then invite each person to present his or her planned worship space.

Compassion

(Time will vary, depending on the project you choose.)

Determine a service project that the youth can do together. Ideally, try to find something that directly affects a particular individual or identifiable group of people (as opposed to a church-maintenance project).

Option 1: In-Class Project
Examples of possible projects include:

- Assemble mission kits to areas recovering from a disaster.
- Write "thinking of you" notes to persons in the congregation who are ill.
- Create teacher-appreciation gifts (for school teachers or Sunday school teachers).
- Sort donated canned gifts for a food pantry.

Option 2: Project During Non-Class Time
Send details to youth and parents at least a week in advance of your project. Be sure to indicate the start and end times of your project, any special instructions (such as what to wear or bring), and details about what the youth are doing and how the project relates to this particular session.

Examples of possible projects include:

- Visit members of the congregation who are at home or residents of a retirement center. Take everything necessary for Holy Communion (get the help of an ordained elder, who will consecrate the Communion elements) and spend some time just talking with them.

Supplies

- ❑ supplies for whatever option you choose
- ❑ large sheet of paper
- ❑ markers

Preparation: This activity involves having the confirmands do a short service project. You may choose to do this during the regular class session or at another time.

If using Option 2, send details to youth and parents at least a week in advance.

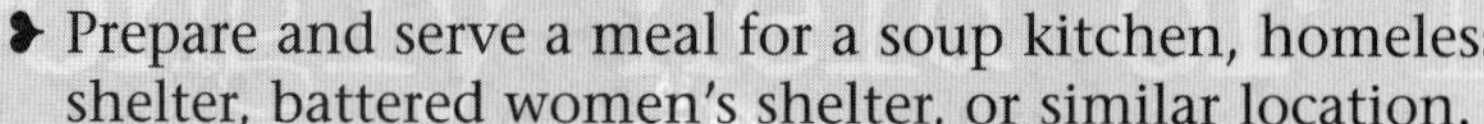

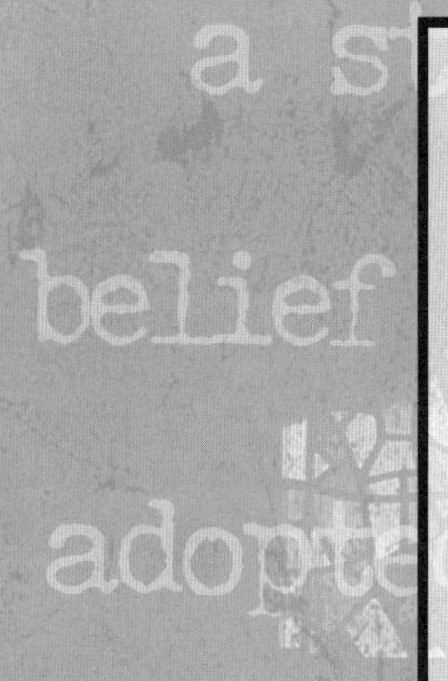

- Prepare and serve a meal for a soup kitchen, homeless shelter, battered women's shelter, or similar location.
- Walk around town, with the help of parents and adult volunteers, to get donations of non-perishable goods for a food pantry.
- Pull weeds or do other needed work at a community garden.

Class Time
During or following your project, ask the confirmands to talk about times when they have done something helpful for someone or when someone did something helpful for them. Talk about why people serve one another, how helping one another makes a difference, and how we experience God's love through acts of service.

Label a third small cross on your Jerusalem cross—the cross that is next to the "Devotion" cross and opposite the "Worship" cross—"Compassion." Explain that compassion, like devotion, is a private spiritual practice. But unlike devotion, which is directed toward God, compassion is directed toward others.

Say: "The word *compassion* came from two words that would literally be translated as 'to feel with.' When we have compassion for someone, we try to feel what they are feeling and to meet their needs and heal their pain. Sometimes we show compassion through service projects, such as the one we worked on today. But each day, we have countless opportunities to show compassion to others."

Read aloud **Philippians 2:1-5.**

Then ask the youth to brainstorm ways that they can show compassion for others in the coming week. List these items on a large sheet of paper.

Once you have a good list, ask the confirmands to look through the list and select at least one thing that they don't normally do that they will commit to doing in the coming week. Tell everyone to put his or her initials next to the action(s) he or she is committing to. Keep the sheet of paper, and check up on their commitments during the following session.

JUSTICE

(15–20 minutes)

Say: "The last part of the way of discipleship is justice. *Justice* is one of those words that is used in many different ways."

Label the fourth cross on your Jerusalem cross "Justice." Then ask:

- What comes to mind when you hear the word *justice*?

Say: "Scripture has quite a bit to say about justice."

Ask volunteers to look up and read aloud the following Scriptures:

- **Deuteronomy 16:19-20**
- **Isaiah 42:1-4**
- **Amos 5:15**
- **Micah 6:8**

Say: "These Scriptures tell us that God cares about justice and that we should care about justice; but they don't really tell us what justice is."

Suggest this simple definition of *justice*: *Justice* is God, all people, and all of creation living in right relationship with one another.

Ask:

- How, do you think, can we tell whether we're in right relationship with God, others, and all of creation?

Say: "Mary, Jesus' mother, gives us a good description of God's justice in the song she sings after learning that she will give birth to the Messiah."

Ask a volunteer to read aloud **Luke 1:46-55.** Then ask:

- What does Mary's song tell us about justice?

Say: "Like compassion, justice involves loving others. And like worship, justice is corporate. We work with other people to bring about justice for all people."

Another way to understand justice is to understand injustice. If justice refers to making things right, then injustice refers to what is wrong.

Have the confirmands search newspapers and news magazines for examples of injustice. (If Internet access is available, have the youth search Internet news sites.) Have each person select one story of injustice. After everyone has had time to find a story, have each person present his or her example of injustice. Challenge the confirmands to think of ways that each injustice could be eliminated and justice could prevail.

Then say: "Compassion and justice are closely related. Sometimes it's hard to tell where one stops and the other begins. Here's one way to explain the difference between the two: Compassion is about meeting people's needs by feeding the hungry, caring for the sick, providing shelter for the homeless, and so on. Justice deals with the causes of hunger, sickness, poverty, and homelessness and tries to eliminate these problems altogether. Both are equally important. For example, we need to feed people *and* work to end hunger."

Explain to the confirmands that The United Methodist Church is devoted to both compassion and justice. Our

supplies
- ❑ Bible
- ❑ newspapers and news magazines
- ❑ optional: computer with Internet access

preparation: Look on the website for information about church agencies.

General Board of Global Ministries operates Volunteers in Mission, which gives people opportunities to serve persons in need throughout the country and around the world. Our General Board of Church and Society works for justice by educating United Methodists and the general public about injustices in the world and why Christians have a responsibility to respond to these injustices, working with elected officials and international organizations to address injustices, and helping congregations respond to injustices in their communities and elsewhere in the world.

NOW WHAT?

Putting It All Together

(10–15 minutes)

Point to your picture of the Jerusalem cross, and say: "Devotion, worship, compassion, and justice give us a structure for being faithful disciples of Jesus Christ."

Ask the confirmands to spend a minute in silence reflecting on what they have learned about these 4 aspects of discipleship.

Then have the confirmands pair off to discuss the following questions.

- In what ways are you already practicing devotion, worship, compassion, and justice?
- What are some things that you will start doing because of what you've learned today?
- What are some things that you will stop doing because of what you've learned today?

Encourage partners to hold each other accountable to the commitments they've made.

Note: Before you dismiss, instruct the confirmands to read, reflect on, and journal about the material in the "Way of Discipleship" section of the *Credo Confirmation Student Journal* before your next session. Also encourage them to try to do the activities related to "Way of Discipleship" on the confirmand website.

Closing Ritual

(10 minutes)

Supplies
- ❑ markerboard
- ❑ marker

Preparation: Write the benediction, "John Wesley's Rule," on a markerboard; or print it out from the website.

Gather the confirmands into a circle. Lead the youth in prayer, giving thanks to God for your time together and for all that the group has learned and experienced. Then go around the circle, inviting each person to pray aloud one word or phrase that describes something he or she learned during the past week of confirmation. After every person has had a chance to contribute a word or phrase, say a brief closing prayer. Then invite the confirmands to say aloud and in unison the benediction, "John Wesley's Rule."

Way of Salvation

INTRODUCTION

A center point of United Methodist theology is our Wesleyan understanding of grace. We affirm that salvation comes entirely through God's grace and that God's grace is with us throughout our lives and at every stage of our faith journey.

Grace can be defined as God's favor or as a gift from God that we have done nothing to earn. But a more complete definition of *grace* would be the way in which we experience God's extraordinary love and forgiveness.

Prevenient Grace

John Wesley identified three movements of grace, each of which has significant implications for ministry. The first movement is prevenient grace. This is the grace of God that is present in all of our lives, even before we are aware of it. God constantly seeks each of us, through other people, through our experiences, and through our consciences. Those of us who are in ministry with young people must always remember that God's grace is present in and with children and youth, even those who are not active in church. Parents, teachers, congregation members, coaches—and you!—are agents of God's grace for youth. For young people, many of whom yearn for meaningful relationships, the knowledge that God is seeking them out is good news!

Justifying Grace

Justifying grace is the second movement of grace. For many Christians, this is the most familiar form of grace. Justifying grace is the grace that brings us into right relationship with God. This, too, is a gift of God, who has acted in and through the life of Jesus. Our responsibility is to respond to God's grace in faith, to make a decision for Christ. Our ministries with youth should include events that offer youth opportunities to make significant faith decisions. But we can't stop there.

Sanctifying Grace

The final movement of God's grace is sanctifying grace. United Methodists understand salvation to be a process, not

just a one-time event. Gradually, God transforms us into the persons whom God intends for us to be. This gradual transformation is called sanctification. Prayer, service to others, study and reflection, fellowship with the family of faith, worship, and many other spiritual practices empower us to grow and mature in our faith, so that we may be more like Jesus. Actions such as these are also evidence that we are aware of our union with God and our need to grow. Our programs and ministries for youth should help youth mature in perfect love, and they should vary in spiritual depth because youth are at different stages in their spiritual development.

Tackling the Tough Questions

This complex topic is difficult to cover in a single confirmation lesson or two. And frankly, it's not a subject that is likely to enthrall most youth. Yet youth often have questions related to this topic. For example, a youth may want to know why your church does not do an altar call every week, when, at her friend's church or youth group, such events happen frequently. Another youth may have heard that he will go to hell if he doesn't "pray the sinner's prayer." Questions may arise about whether persons of other faiths are saved or loved by God. To questions like these, Wesley's theology of grace provides a significant way of approaching the character and activity of God in the world.

As you explore this topic with youth, please remember the following:

- First, it is not your job to "convert" youth. Remember that grace is a gift from God.
- Second, youth should never be made to feel guilty if they have not accepted Christ's love for themselves or if they are unsure whether they want to. The process of spiritual development is on the Holy Spirit's timetable, not yours.
- Finally, it is not the names of the three movements of grace that are critical for youth to know (although it's great when they do memorize them). Rather, youth need to hear that God is truly at work in them—and in their friends and family members—and will continue to be so throughout their lives.

SUPPLIES AND PREPARATION

BASIC SUPPLIES

❑ Bibles of various translations ❑ markerboard or large sheets of paper ❑ markers ❑ pens or pencils	❑ clear tape and/or glue ❑ masking tape ❑ index cards or paper cut about the same size (3-by-5 or 4-by-6) ❑ sheets of posterboard	❑ paper (Use paper that has already been used on one side as much as possible, depending on the activity.) ❑ scissors

ACTIVITY	PREPARATION	OTHER SUPPLIES
WHAT?		
Opening Ritual	Write the meditation—adapted from Psalm 67—on a markerboard; or project the meditation, using the slide on the website.	❑ vine from previous sessions ❑ vine leaves (1 for each student)
Opener: Faith Walk	Plan the route for the walk. Have on hand extra adults.	❑ blindfolds, 1 for every 2 youth ❑ extra adult helpers
SO WHAT? PART 1		
My Faith Timeline	Make your own timeline to use as an example.	❑ hard surface for the youth to write on
House of Salvation	Make copies of "House of Salvation" handout, from the website.	❑ copies of the "House of Salvation" handout
Prevenient Clays	Optional: Create your own sculpture as an example.	❑ copies of "House of Salvation" from the previous activity ❑ modeling clay ❑ tools for modeling the clay
I Just Want to Say Thanks	Wrap a small box in gift wrap that isn't for birthday, Christmas, or some other specific event.	❑ gift-wrapped box ❑ optional: thank-you cards ❑ optional: postage stamps
SO WHAT? PART 2		
Amazing, Justifying Grace	Gather supplies.	❑ hymnals or copies of the song "Amazing Grace"
Sanctifying Grace: An Object Lesson	Gather supplies.	❑ plastic bag full of water ❑ needle
Growing Toward Perfection	Draw or create with paper a bare tree (with branches but no leaves) that is at least three feet tall. Make copies of the "Growth in Grace" handout from the website.	❑ drawn or created tree ❑ green paper ❑ leaf template or real leaves ❑ optional: note card ❑ copies of the "Growth in Grace"
Bible Study: What Kind of Grace?	Make copies of the "What Kind of Grace?" handout from the website.	❑ copies of the "What Kind of Grace?" handout
NOW WHAT?		
Thorny Issues	Copy "Thorny Issues" from the website, and cut it apart. Write on nametags: "Hello, I'm a Wesleyan Theologian."	❑ copies of "Thorny Issues" ❑ hat or bowl ❑ nametag labels ❑ pair of dice
Closing Ritual	Write the benediction, "John Wesley's Rule," on a markerboard; or print out the poster on the website.	

WHAT?

Opening Ritual

(10 minutes)

As confirmands arrive, point them to your confirmation vine; and give each person a leaf. Invite the confirmands to reflect on the previous session and to write on their leaf something they learned or experienced during that session. Ask the confirmands to affix their leaf to the vine. Remind them that these leaves represent ways that we, as Christians and United Methodists, grow in our faith and more fully experience God's grace.

Then invite the youth to read aloud this opening meditation, adapted from **Psalm 67:**

> O God, be gracious to us and bless us
> and make your face to shine upon us,
> that your way may be known upon earth,
> your saving power among all nations.
> Let the peoples praise you, O God;
> let all the peoples praise you!
> Let the nations be glad and sing for joy,
> for you judge the people with equity
> and guide the nations upon earth.

Supplies
- ❑ vine from previous sessions
- ❑ vine leaves (1 for each student)
- ❑ markers or pens

Preparation: Write the opening meditation—which is adapted from Psalm 67—on a markerboard; or project the meditation, using the slide on the website.

Note: Take time before you get started to talk with the confirmands about what they read and wrote in the "Way of Discipleship" section of their *Credo Confirmation Student Journal.*

Opener: Faith Walk

(10–15 minutes)

Have the confirmands pair up and decide which person in the pair will be a tour guide and which will be a tourist in this activity. Adult volunteers should participate to ensure that every student has a partner. (Don't tell them what you are planning to do.) Hand out blindfolds to the tourists, and have them sit down.

Say: "We are going to go for a walk together. Those of you who are tourists will be blindfolded, so you obviously won't know where you are going. But you will be gently guided. Those of you who are tour guides, come with me."

Take the tour guides to a place out of earshot of the tourists, and explain the activity. Tell them that they are to guide the tourists as gently, as softly, and with as little direct (hands-on) interference as possible. They also should be very encouraging and uncritical of the tourists. The tour guides may whisper or speak quietly to their tourist; and they may, when necessary, very gently guide with a touch of the hand. But they should not constantly talk to or touch their tourist. They should watch out for obstacles, and slow down or stop as necessary so that everyone has plenty of room.

Explain that everyone must follow you on the journey.

Supplies
- ❑ blindfolds, enough for half of your group
- ❑ extra adult helpers

Preparation: Think about the route that you will lead the youth through. (See the note in the margin on page 139.) Other adults should act as spotters, as necessary.

Answer any questions the tour guides may have. Then allow the guides to go back to get their partners and follow you.

Guide the whole group. When everyone has reached the destination, ask the tourists to leave their blindfolds on. Ask the tourists:

- Tourists, where do you think you are? (Let them make a few guesses.)

Have the tourists take their blindfolds off. Then ask them questions such as the following that will help them describe their experience:

- What did your tour guide do that helped you get to this place safely?
- What was unusual or surprising about how you were guided?
- Did you need more guidance, or did you get the right amount?

Ask the tour guides questions such as the following to describe their experience:

- What was it like trying to be quiet, gentle, and as hands-off as possible during this activity?
- If I hadn't given you instructions but had just told you to lead your partner however you wanted to, what, do you think, might you have done instead?

Say: "Today we're going to talk about the life of faith and how God's grace guides us every step of the way."

Then ask the whole group:

- How, do you think, is this activity like or unlike the way that God guides people?

NOTE: If you meet during a time when other classes or events are taking place at your church, you may choose to map out a route for the youth to take. Choose or create a route that has some challenges (obstacles, a few stairs) but that will not put the youth in harm's way. The route should take about 10 minutes to complete at a slow pace. When planning this, be sensitive to and respectful of any physical limitations of members of your group. Plan ahead for the rest of your class session: Will you circle the group back during this activity, walk back after you're done, or hold the rest of the session at your destination?

SO WHAT? PART 1

MY FAITH TIMELINE

(15–20 minutes)

Give each person a sheet of paper and a pen or pencil. If necessary, also provide a hard surface for them to write on.

Say: "Today we will talk about God's grace, presence, and work in our lives. Some of you might feel as though you have been growing in your relationship with God for your whole life, while others of you may feel as though you are just starting to form a relationship with God. As we'll discover later, God has been present and active in your whole life, even if you weren't always aware of it."

Continue: "To get us thinking about the high and low points in our faith, we're going to create timelines that illustrate

supplies

- ❑ paper
- ❑ pens and pencils
- ❑ optional: hard surface for the youth to write on

preparation: Do the activity so that you can show an example of a timeline. Be prepared to give a quick summary of your own faith story, using your timeline.

some of the key moments of our lives."

Give the youth the following instructions:

> Imagine that the left side of the page is your birth and that the right side of the page is the present. You'll draw a line to represent the ups and downs of your life, especially as it relates to your walk with God. During times that you felt especially close to God or you had a significant faith experience, your line will probably go up. In times when you felt distant from God or had negative faith experiences, your line might go down. There's no right or wrong way to do your line, so draw it the way you think it should be done. Also, mark some of the points on your line with words that will help you remember what your various points stand for.

Show your own timeline as an example, and give the youth a few highlights, especially from your younger years. Then give the youth several minutes to quietly complete their own timeline. Some youth might finish very quickly, while others may need significantly longer. So keep an eye on their progress and, if necessary, let the youth know that they may finish their timelines later.

Invite those who feel comfortable to tell about their timelines. Then ask:

- What did you notice about the timelines?
- Were there are lot of similarities between your timelines? Why, or why not?
- Use your imagination for a moment and think about what these timelines would be like in ten years. Would they be likely to become more similar or more different from one another? Why? What does that suggest to you about how God works in our lives?

supplies

- ❑ markerboard
- ❑ marker
- ❑ copies of "House of Salvation" handout

preparation: Make copies of the "House of Salvation" handout from the website.

HOUSE OF SALVATION

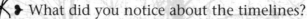

(10 minutes)

Ask:

- What comes to mind when you hear the word *grace*?
- How would you define the word *grace*? (Possible definitions might include *"an undeserved gift," "a prayer given before a meal,"* or *"patience and forgiveness."*)

Then say: "For Christians, grace is the way we experience God's extraordinary love and forgiveness. God's grace allows us to feel God's presence and to understand what God is calling us to do. In the United Methodist tradition, we recognize three types, or movements, of grace: prevenient grace, justifying grace, and sanctifying grace."

Write each of these types of grace on a markerboard.

Hand each youth a copy of the "House of Salvation" handout from the website. Explain that John Wesley used the metaphor of a house to illustrate God's grace and salvation. Throughout this session, you'll refer to the house illustration.

Prevenient Clays

(10–15 minutes)

Say: "United Methodists believe that we experience God's grace throughout our lives, even before we are aware of God or have any idea what grace is. The grace that we experience before we are aware of it is called prevenient grace. *Prevenient* means 'going before.' Through prevenient grace, God seeks us out and invites us into a relationship. God's prevenient grace also helps us to make wise choices and discern the difference between good and evil."

Point to the "House of Salvation" handout.

Say: "John Wesley compared prevenient grace to the porch in front of the house. When we experience prevenient grace, God has invited us into the house; but we haven't yet accepted the invitation."

To further illustrate prevenient grace, hand out the clay and instruments for shaping it. Then read aloud **Isaiah 64:8.**

Give these instructions:

> Imagine that this clay is you and that God is the potter who shapes the clay. Think of a simple object that represents who you are. Use the tools to carve and/or mold the object from the clay, but carve or mold only on the left half. (It's OK for them to mold the right side, instead of the left, if they'd rather.) Without splitting the lump of clay in half, leave the other side alone so that it remains an unshaped block.
>
> The half you carve represents the ways that God's grace has already been active in your life, so if you wish the object you sculpt can relate to your faith in some way. The other half represents the fact that God's grace will continue to work in your life in the future, in ways you can't now imagine."

Give the youth several minutes to work on their sculptures. Then regroup and allow volunteers to describe their sculptures to the rest of the group. Be particularly sensitive to the discussions, for youth might tell very personal stories.

Supplies

- ❑ Bible
- ❑ copies of "House of Salvation" handout from the previous activity
- ❑ modeling clay (at least a 1- by 2-inch chunk)
- ❑ tools for modeling with clay, such as craft sticks, butter knives, spoons

Preparation:

Optional: Create your own sculpture as an example.

SUPPLIES
- ❑ gift-wrapped box
- ❑ optional: thank-you cards
- ❑ optional: postage stamps

PREPARATION: Wrap a small box in gift wrap that isn't for birthday, Christmas, or some other specific event.

NOTE: If you have more than 10 people in your group, you may choose to divide into two or more groups to save time. But if possible, stay together so that the youth can hear a wide number of stories.

I JUST WANT TO SAY THANKS

(10 minutes)

Hold the gift-wrapped box, and say: "Many of us have had people in our lives who have been agents of God's prevenient grace. For example, they may have taught us about God's love, helped us in unexpected ways because of their faith, or helped us to know what to do when we were facing an important decision. I'd like for you to take a moment now to think of a story of grace from your life."

After a few moments, say: "I'm going to toss this gift box to one of you. When you catch it, I hope that you will tell us your story of grace. It doesn't have to be a long story or a super-detailed one. Just speak from your heart about what you experienced. Then toss the box to someone else in the room to hear his or her story. We'll continue until everyone has had a chance to speak."

Ask for a volunteer to start, or just choose an individual to begin the storytelling process. Continue until everyone has had a chance to share.

Optional: After everyone has finished, or as an alternative to sharing aloud, hand out thank-you cards. Ask the youth to write either a thank-you card to a person who was an agent of God's grace for them, or to write a thank-you note to God for the grace they have experienced from God. Encourage the youth to mail the notes if they wrote to a specific person, or to keep the note in their Bible if they wrote it to God.

NOTE: If you choose to divide this session into two one-hour classes, break here.

SO WHAT? PART 2

SUPPLIES
- ❑ hymnals or copies of the song "Amazing Grace"
- ❑ markerboard or paper
- ❑ marker
- ❑ copies of the "House of Salvation" handout

AMAZING, JUSTIFYING GRACE

(15 minutes)

Hand out hymnals or copies of the song "Amazing Grace." Sing the song together or listen to a recording of the song.

Ask:

- What does the author of the song understand to be true about God's grace?

Make a list of the students' responses on a markerboard or paper. Then ask:

- Have you ever heard your friends or some people of faith talk about being saved? What, do you think, did they mean by that phrase?

Return to the "House of Salvation" handout.

Say: "When we respond to God's invitation and open the door into God's house, we experience the second movement of God's grace: *justifying grace*. Justifying grace pardons our sins and makes us right with God. This is God's gift to us. God has acted in and through Jesus Christ, who made atonement for our sins, and that's the amazing grace we sang about earlier. We do not earn God's justifying grace. The choice we have is whether we will or will not respond to God's grace in faith and whether we will confess Jesus Christ as our Lord and Savior."

To help the confirmands remember the meaning of justifying grace, write the following on a markerboard:

> Justified
> Just-if-ied
> Just-if-I'd (as in "just [as] if I'd never sinned")

Ask:

- How can we respond to God's grace and accept God's invitation to live a new life? (Possible answers: *by repenting of our sins, by committing to spend time each day alone with God, by trying to do God's will in all situations, by leaving behind habits that have a negative effect on our relationship with God and others.*)
- How do our lives change when we experience God's justifying grace and know that God forgives all of our sins?

Sanctifying Grace: An Object Lesson

(10 minutes)

Supplies

- ❑ plastic bag full of water
- ❑ needle
- ❑ copies of the "House of Salvation" handout
- ❑ tape

Refer again to the "House of Salvation" handout.

Say: "When we experience justifying grace, we enter the house. And once we're in the house, we find a lot of rooms for us to explore. The type of grace we experience after we have responded to God's invitation and been assured that our sins are forgiven is called *sanctifying grace*. To help you understand sanctifying grace, we're going to step away from the house metaphor and do a little demonstration."

Ask for two volunteers. Give the first volunteer a plastic bag full of water and the second volunteer a needle.

Say: "This bag of water represents you, filled with all of the talents and goodness and gifts that God has given you. This needle represents sin, those actions we do that interfere with our relationship with God and others."

Ask the volunteer with the needle to poke the bag of water, then ask the confirmand with the bag, "What has happened to you?"

Say: "Sin causes us to deflate a bit, and it prevents us from living the whole, full life that God intends for us. The good news is that God forgives us of our sin."

Use tape to cover the hole so that the bag doesn't leak. Then ask the person with the bag: "This tape represents God's forgiveness. Now, are you back to where you started?" (*No, you are still deflated.*)

Say: "The thing is, we need a way for our lives to be refilled and for grace to grow in our lives. That's what Wesley called sanctifying grace—God's grace that helps us grow throughout our entire life to be more like God."

Growing Toward Perfection

(10 minutes)

Supplies

- ❑ drawn or created tree (See "preparation, below.)
- ❑ green paper
- ❑ leaf template to make leaves of the appropriate size for the tree (Or have the youth use real leaves as templates.)
- ❑ optional: note card
- ❑ pens or pencils
- ❑ scissors
- ❑ glue or tape
- ❑ copies of the "Growth in Grace" handout

Preparation: Draw or create with paper a bare tree (with branches but no leaves) that is at least three feet tall. Make copies of the "Growth in Grace" handout from the website.

Say: "We've been creating a (vine/tree) as part of our Confirmation experience. Today, we're going to add another tree that will illustrate to the congregation the idea of sanctifying grace. We'll work together to draw icons on tree leaves for various ways that people can continue to grow in grace throughout their lives."

Set out green paper and (if you have them) leaf templates and ask the confirmands to trace and cut out leaves. While the youth are working, hand out copies of the "Growth in Grace" handout from the website.

Tell the confirmands to select an item from the "Growth in Grace" list, write it on a leaf, and draw a small picture on the leaf to represent that item. For example, a leaf that said, "Worship each Sunday," might include a picture of a candle or an altar or the outside of a church sanctuary.

As the confirmands finish the leaves, have the youth use glue or tape to add the leaves to the tree. Allow confirmands to work on multiple leaves, and encourage the youth to work together to make sure that each of the items on the list is included on at least one leaf.

Then ask:

- Which of these practices of faith are you most familiar with? least familiar with?
- How do these practices help us grow closer to God and better do God's will?
- How, do you think, can we as a class help teach the rest of the congregation about sanctifying grace and these practices of faith?

For the last question, in particular, take some time to talk about their answers and to begin making some initial plans, as appropriate.

Optional: Place your tree where the entire congregation can see it. Ask a volunteer to write on a note card an explanation of the tree and what it represents.

Ask:

- Are any of you perfect?
- Is it possible for a human to be perfect? Explain.

Say: "John Wesley believed that Christians could reach perfection, or entire sanctification. Reaching Christian perfection does not mean that a person no longer sins, but it does mean that one is completely in tune with God's will and has complete faith that God can deliver him or her from sin."

Bible Study: What Kind of Grace?

(15 minutes)

Hand out copies of the handout "What Kind of Grace?" to each youth, and divide the group into pairs.

Say: "Now that you're getting to be experts on grace, let's see whether you can identify the kind of grace mentioned in some passages from the Bible. With your partner, look up the passages and write either *prevenient, justifying,* or *sanctifying* grace next to each verse."

Give the youth several minutes to work, and then go through their answers together. If there is disagreement on some of the Scriptures, ask the confirmands to talk about why they chose to call the item a certain type of grace. As needed, clarify the differences between prevenient, justifying, and sanctifying grace.

Supplies
- ❑ Bibles
- ❑ copies of the "What Kind of Grace?" handout
- ❑ pens or pencils
- ❑ scissors
- ❑ glue or tape

Preparation: Make copies of the "What Kind of Grace?" handout from the website.

Now What?

Thorny Issues

(10–15 minutes)

Say: "A theologian is someone who thinks deeply about God and God's actions in the world. A person doesn't have to be a pastor or college professor to be a theologian. You can be a theologian too. And now that you know about prevenient, justifying, and sanctifying grace, you're especially well equipped to think theologically from a Wesleyan point of view."

Give each person a nametag label that says, "Hello, I'm a Wesleyan Theologian"; and have the class sit in a circle.

Say: "In this hat [or bowl] are some really difficult questions. Using what you've learned about God and God's grace in this session and in previous sessions, you're going to do some theological reflection. I'm going to pass around a pair of dice and the hat [or bowl] with questions in it. Draw a strip, read the question aloud, then roll the dice. If you roll a 6 or lower, you must do your best to answer the question. If you roll a 7 or higher, you may answer the question or put the question back in the hat."

SUPPLIES
- ❑ copy of "Thorny Issues"
- ❑ hat or bowl
- ❑ nametag labels
- ❑ pair of dice

PREPARATION: Make a copy of "Thorny Issues," from the website. Cut apart the slips, and place them in a hat or bowl. One slip is blank so that you can write a question of your own. Write on the nametags: "Hello, I'm a Wesleyan Theologian."

Start play with the student who has the most family members (including pets). Play will proceed to his or her right. Encourage each youth as he or she answers. These are tough questions, and it's OK if the youth don't have profound answers.

After a youth has given his or her best answer, open up the question to further conversation by asking each of the other participants, "What do the rest of you think?" You also may choose to add commentary of your own, based on the introductory material from this session and your understanding of Wesley's theology of grace.

CLOSING RITUAL

(10 minutes)

NOTE: Before you dismiss, instruct the confirmands to read, reflect on, and journal about the material in the "Way of Salvation" section of the *Credo Confirmation Student Journal* before your next session. Also encourage them to try to do the activities related to "Way of Salvation" on the confirmand website.

SUPPLIES
- ❑ markerboard
- ❑ marker

PREPARATION: Write the benediction, "John Wesley's Rule," on a markerboard; or print it out from the website.

Gather the confirmands into a circle. Lead the youth in prayer, giving thanks to God for your time together and for all that the group has learned and experienced. Then go around the circle, inviting each person to pray aloud one word or phrase that describes something he or she learned during the past week of confirmation. After every person has had a chance to contribute a word or phrase, say a brief closing prayer, such as this one:

> God who goes before us, we're grateful to you for your action in our lives. God who moves us to moments of decision, we invite you to act anew in us today. God who will guide us throughout all of our lives, we promise to do our part to grow in faith. We're grateful for the fact that our salvation is a process, and that your grace will never leave us. Amen.

Then invite the confirmands to say aloud and in unison the benediction, "John Wesley's Rule."

Wesleyan Quadrilateral

INTRODUCTION

Let's face it: Youth are frequently not the best decision-makers. Lots of factors come into play here, factors such as hormones, social identity, inexperience, and the process of individuation (separating oneself from one's parents and taking on an individual identity). Additionally, brain research has shown that the frontal cortex of the brain—the logic center—essentially shuts down during much of the teenage years. So if a teenager has ever exasperated you by the choices he or she made, take heart; it will get better.

Youth can certainly learn ways to become better decision-makers, and one way to explore this with youth is to introduce (or re-introduce) them to a process called "discernment." Discernment is a process of prayer, study, and reflection for the purpose of clarifying one's path in life, making decisions, and knowing God's will. Through discernment, we begin to sort out those impulses and inclinations that simply arise from our own ego or other influences from the ones that have their origination in God. Discernment is also a process that is useful for a community of people as they seek together a way forward that is faithful to God and is wholly loving.

In this session, the youth will use a Wesleyan tool for discernment, the Quadrilateral. Although the term *quadrilateral* was not one used by John Wesley (the concept of the Wesleyan Quadrilateral was introduced by twentieth-century Methodist scholar Albert Outler), the elements of the Quadrilateral were certainly common in his writing. Wesley encouraged us to use Scripture, tradition, reason, and experience when making decisions and determining God's will for us today.

Scripture

By the time the youth reach their middle school years, many of them have figured out that Christians have a lot of differences of opinion, especially when it comes to the Bible. This session gives you a chance to talk briefly with the youth about what Scripture is and how we should read it.

Try to resist the temptation to spend a great deal of time on the topic of the Bible. Keep in mind that the youth will learn about the Bible in other sessions; in other education and formation settings, such as Sunday school and youth group;

at home; in worship. Special focus should be on how Scripture is foundational for discernment and decision-making, not for turning youth into Bible scholars. However, that doesn't mean that you should squelch dialogue when it comes up.

For United Methodists, Scripture—as represented in the Old and New Testaments—is foundational to our process of discernment. Christians disagree tremendously at times on what Scripture is and how it should be read, understood, and applied. But Christians are universally in agreement that the Bible is our foundational document, is important for our lives today, and (as stated in The Articles of Religion of The Methodist Church) contains "all things necessary to salvation."

Tradition

For Wesley, tradition primarily had to do with the traditions of both the early church and the Church of England. Early Christian writings and the authority of the Church of England had a profound influence on him and on his writing, as he was an Anglican minister his entire life. When we use tradition as a tool for discernment, we must look at all of Christian history, including more than two hundred years of United Methodist history, and consider how others have approached the issues we face today. While Scripture is our foundation, we cannot discount the witness of faithful Christians who have answered God's call in the centuries since the Old and New Testaments were written and compiled. God continues to work though individual Christians and through the church, teaching us how to respond faithfully to new issues and realities.

Experience

Wesley understood that our ideas are based on our experiences, but he had a particular interest in our religious experience. He believed that we could objectively evaluate those experiences of God, and thus they are an authoritative source for one's faith and life.

Unless we make note of the "God moments" in our lives, we're likely to forget them or to downplay their significance. Many youth have had significant moments of spiritual insight or occasions when they have felt God's presence in their lives. Other youth might not recall such experiences, but that doesn't mean that God was not present throughout the events of their life. In the "Experience" section of the session, the youth will make an "Experience Journal," a tool to mark the significant moments of their lives when they had an encounter with God, came to a new understanding, or lived through an important event.

Discernment from experience should not be limited to only our own experience. Young people need to understand that their individual experience is valuable, but they also must be aware of what they haven't experienced and how much they have to learn. One way to gain perspective is to hear the stories of others so that they will also have a chance to hear from those who have a long experience with the life of faith and with the church.

reason

Wesley felt that we are called by God to use our God-given rational abilities, but he also warned us against thinking that we can rely on reason alone. Our tradition is one in which we are allowed and encouraged to ask, "Does that make sense?" We may determine, for example, whether a particular position on a social issue is reasonable, that is, consistent with our understanding of the Bible, the teaching of the Christian church, and the best information we have from contemporary humanities and sciences.

The Work of Discernment

Discernment often requires careful listening to others, as well as a willingness to be moved toward a way of thinking and acting that is best for others and not just best for oneself. Individual congregations and entire denominations wrestle with many controversial topics. But even in the midst of our differences, we still can learn to value the other person, to respect the integrity of different points of view, and to move toward those positions that unite rather than divide us. During this session, the youth will have an opportunity to reason things out within the context of community.

SUPPLIES AND PREPARATION

BASIC SUPPLIES		
❑ Bibles of various translations ❑ markerboard or large sheets of paper ❑ markers ❑ pens or pencils	❑ clear tape and/or glue ❑ masking tape ❑ index cards or paper cut about the same size (3-by-5 or 4-by-6) ❑ sheets of posterboard	❑ paper (Use paper that has already been used on one side as much as possible, depending on the activity.) ❑ scissors

ACTIVITY	PREPARATION	OTHER SUPPLIES
WHAT?		
Opening Ritual	Write the meditation—adapted from Psalm 67—on a markerboard; or project the meditation, using the slide on the website.	❑ vine from previous sessions ❑ vine leaves (1 for each student)
Moving Beyond the Magic 8 Ball	If you don't have a Magic 8 Ball, look online for a website that has a Magic 8 Ball that answers questions.	❑ Magic 8 Ball or Internet access
Introducing the Quadrilateral	Optional: Hang the wind chimes in the meeting space.	❑ wind chime with 3 chimes or a photo of one ❑ optional: a way to hang the wind chimes
Lectio Divina		
SO WHAT? PART 1		
Scripture as I See It	Make copies of the "Bible Statements" handout, from the website.	❑ copies of the "Bible Statements" handout
Scripture on Scripture	Make copies of the "Scripture on Scripture" handout, from the website.	❑ copies of the "Scripture on Scripture" handout
Tradition: Lingo	Make copies of the "UMC From *A* to *Z*" handout, from the website only.	❑ copies of the "UMC From *A* to *Z*" handout
Our Church Is Changing		
SO WHAT? PART 2		
Experience Journals	Work with the church office and parents to gather significant dates for the youth. (See the activity.)	❑ *Credo Confirmation Student Journals* ❑ optional: blank journals
Wisdom From the Elders	Invite long-time church members. (See the activity.)	❑ guests ❑ extra chairs, as needed
Reason: We're in Agreement That . . .		
NOW WHAT?		
Putting It All Together	Make copies of the "Scenarios for Putting It All Together" handouts, from the website, making 1 copy of each handout for every 2 youth.	❑ copies of the "Scenarios for Putting It All Together" handouts
Closing Ritual	Write the benediction, "John Wesley's Rule," on a markerboard; or print out the poster on the website.	

WHAT?

Opening Ritual

(10 minutes)

As confirmands arrive, point them to your confirmation vine; and give each person a leaf. Invite the confirmands to reflect on the previous session and to write on their leaf something they learned or experienced during that session. Ask the confirmands to affix their leaf to the vine. Remind them that these leaves represent ways that we, as Christians and United Methodists, grow in our faith and more fully experience God's grace.

Then invite the youth to read aloud this opening meditation, adapted from **Psalm 67:**

> O God, be gracious to us and bless us
> and make your face to shine upon us,
> that your way may be known upon earth,
> your saving power among all nations.
> Let the peoples praise you, O God;
> let all the peoples praise you!
> Let the nations be glad and sing for joy,
> for you judge the people with equity
> and guide the nations upon earth.

Supplies
- ❑ vine from previous sessions
- ❑ vine leaves (1 for each student)
- ❑ markers or pens

Preparation: Write the opening meditation—which is adapted from Psalm 67—on a markerboard; or project the meditation, using the slide on the website.

Note: Take time before you get started to talk with the confirmands about what they read and wrote in the "Way of Salvation" section of their *Credo Confirmation Student Journal*.

Moving Beyond the Magic 8 Ball

(10 minutes)

In this activity, the youth will have an opportunity to laugh at some of the bad advice and decision-making processes that they and others have heard and perhaps even used.

Ask:

- How many of you have or have had a Magic 8 Ball?
- What are your memories of using one?
- What about a Magic 8 Ball would a child find funny?"

If you have a Magic 8 Ball or can use one online, have some youth toss out a few yes-or-no questions for it to "answer."

Say: "A Magic 8 Ball might not be the best way to make decisions or to figure out what God's will is for our lives, but it's also not the only poor way to go about it. We're going to have a little fun thinking about some of the bad advice we've received and some poor ways to make decisions. To do this, we're going to come up with some questions and create our own Magic 8 Ball-type responses to them. For example, to the question, 'Should I go to college?' our Magic 8 Ball might answer, 'Pluck the petals of a daisy to decide.' "

Divide the class into 2 groups. (It is OK if a "group" includes only one person.) Give each group a couple of markers and two large sheets of paper, one labeled "Questions" and the

Supplies
- ❑ Magic 8 Ball or Internet access
- ❑ large sheets of paper
- ❑ markers

Optional Preparation: If you don't have access to a Magic 8 Ball, look online for a website that has a Magic 8 Ball that answers questions so that you can show the class.

other labeled "Answers." Ask the groups to think up 7 questions one might ask a Magic 8 Ball about decision-making, God's will for our lives, or what we should believe about certain issues.

Have the groups write these questions on the "Questions" page. Then, have them create a list of "Answers" that are based on bad advice they have heard, methods of decision-making that are silly, and answers that are really non-answers.

After a few minutes, take turns having one group ask a question and the other group responding with one of its answers. Enjoy the laughter.

Say: "We have named a few ways of making decisions that are pretty silly, so let's shift gears and think about some decision-making tools that are more useful."

Ask:

- What are some examples of how a person can make better decisions?

Introducing the Quadrilateral

(5–10 minutes)

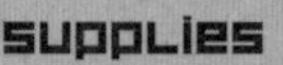

Supplies
- ❑ wind chime with 3 chimes or a photo of one
- ❑ optional: a way to hang the wind chimes

Optional preparation: Hang the wind chimes in the meeting space.

Say: "We will now think about the word *discernment* and a distinctly United Methodist way of making decisions. Discernment is a process of prayer, study, and reflection that helps us clarify our path in life, make decisions, and know God's will. It helps us know the difference between what *we* want and what *God* wants. And while discernment is important for personal decisions, it also is useful for a community of people as they seek together a way to live that is faithful to God."

Then say: "As United Methodists, we have a unique approach to making better decisions that is sometimes referred to as the *Quadrilateral,* which is a fancy word for saying something that has four parts. We follow the advice of John Wesley to consider Scripture, tradition, experience, and reason when making decisions and trying to discern God's will for our lives. Today, we'll look at each of those four elements of decision-making."

Show the youth a wind chime—an actual one or a photo or drawing of one. Be sure to show a wind chime that has three chimes. (If you can bring in a wind chime, hang it from a doorway or window in the room before class.)

Ask:

- Suppose that the four parts of the Quadrilateral—Scripture, tradition, experience, and reason—are the parts of this wind chime. Which part of the Quadrilateral, do you think, would Wesley say is this part, the part that holds the chimes? Why?

After a short time for discussion, let the youth know that Wesley considered Scripture to be foundational and the "primary source and criterion for Christian doctrine and life."

Ask:

- What else, do you think, is important about wind chimes that might help us understand how this is a good metaphor for the Quadrilateral? (*There may be many answers; but be sure to point out, if no one else does, that wind is an essential part. The wind, which in this metaphor represents the movement of the Holy Spirit within the community of faith, helps the wind chime ultimately fulfill its purpose: making music or, in our case, the "music" of theological reflection.*)

If you have a photo or drawing of wind chimes, label each of the parts according to the Quadrilateral.

Say, "Scripture, the Old and New Testaments, is where we as Christians look first when trying to discern what to do or think. Our tradition is our faith heritage, the history of God's continuing presence with followers of Christ. It includes the things the church has believed or done or said in the past. Experience refers to what we know to be true about God and the world from our own experience.

"We use our reasoning, or thinking, abilities to ask questions of faith, evaluate what we read in Scripture and what we learn from our tradition, and compare all of that with our experience. Remember, too, that all of these work together as you work to grow in your understanding of them. Being raised in or out of the church doesn't change the gifts tradition gives us—just your awareness of them. Time in the church and in relationship with other responsible people of faith will improve your use of all the pieces of the Quadrilateral."

Lectio Divina

(10 minutes)

Supplies

- ❑ Bibles

Tell the youth that you're going to lead them in a Scripture-reading exercise called *Lectio Divina* (LEK-tee-oh dih-VEE-nah). Ask them to turn to **Luke 24:13-35,** or have them close their eyes and sit comfortably.

Explain that *Lectio Divina* is a meditative way of reading Scripture. You'll read the Scripture three times, with different instructions each time.

The first time, ask the confirmands to listen to the story and to pay special attention to any word or phrase that catches their interest. Read the passage slowly and with feeling.

Then ask the youth to call out the word or phrase that stood out for them. It is not critical that everyone respond.

Pause a short time; then tell the youth to listen to the story again and consider the question, "How does this Scripture touch my life?" Have one of the youth read the Scripture aloud. Then pause for a moment of silence while the class reflects.

Ask the youth to tell something about how the Scripture touched their life or how they heard God's voice in the passage. Again, it's not critical that every youth participate; but be sure to allow them the space and time to do so.

Have someone read the Scripture aloud the third time. This time the youth should listen while keeping in mind the question, "What in this Scripture do I hear God inviting me to do or to change?"

Ask the youth to reflect on the question in silence for a minute. Then ask them to tell what invitation they heard in the Scripture.

Close with a simple prayer.

SO WHAT? PART 1

SUPPLIES

- ❑ copies of the "Bible Statements" handout

PREPARATION: Make copies of the "Bible Statements" handout, from the website.

SCRIPTURE: AS I SEE IT

(10–15 minutes)

The purpose of this activity is to help you gauge the youth's knowledge and opinions with regard to Scripture. In addition, it will allow youth to begin to see how their views are similar to or different from their classmates.

Say, "When it comes to the Bible, people have lots of different opinions about what it is, what is says, and what we're supposed to do with it. To help us explore the Bible as a starting point for our discernment and decision-making, let's think about where we stand right now on various questions about the Bible."

Point to 2 walls or chairs on opposite ends of the room, and explain that one side (*point to it*) represents "true," and the other side (*point to it*) represents "false." The youth should decide where along the spectrum they are—on one side or the other or somewhere in between.

Read the statements, one at a time, from the "Bible Statements" handout. After each statement, allow time for the youth to choose where they will stand. (Adult leaders—except the leader of this activity—may also participate.) Do not read the answers or the explanations at this point in the exercise.

Before reading the next statement, have a brief conversation with the youth about why they chose to stand where they did. Youth may, at any point, change their position and move to another point on the spectrum if they choose to do so.

After you have read each of the statements, have the youth take a seat. Give the youth a copy of the "Bible Statements" handout.

Have youth volunteers read aloud the statements and explanations. Notice that some of the items are definitively true or false, while others are more subjective. Allow the youth to debate with one another a bit if there are diverse opinions on some statements.

Scripture on Scripture

(10 minutes)

In this activity, we'll look at a few of the passages in the Bible that describe what Scripture is and that relate to the theme of discernment.

Distribute Bibles and copies of the "Scripture on Scripture" handout.

Ask the youth to read and talk briefly about all four of the passages, answering the questions on the handout. Give the them about 6–7 minutes to work.

supplies
- ❑ Bibles
- ❑ copies of the "Bible Statements" handout
- ❑ optional: large sheets of paper and art supplies

preparation: Make copies of the "Bible Statements" handout, from the website.

Tradition: Lingo

(10 minutes)

Help confirmands think about some words and phrases associated with The United Methodist Church even if they do not understand their meanings.

Write the letters *A* thru *Z* from top to bottom on a large sheet of paper.

Say: "The United Methodist Church, like any denomination, has its own lingo that can sometimes seem strange to those who are not 'in the know.' I'm guessing that you might have added a few of these terms, names, acronyms, and so forth to your vocabulary. So work together to try to come up with at least one answer for each letter. When possible try to think of things that relate specifically to The United Methodist Church and not all churches." Pause for a moment to answer any questions.

Give the group about 5 minutes to come up with ideas. Answers such as "God," "salvation," and "church" are good; but answers such as "General Conference," "sanctifying grace," and "cross and flame" are better examples of the lingo associated with United Methodism. Some letters will be difficult. (You might suggest "quadrennium" for Q.) Be willing to accept names of persons from church history for especially tough letters. (You might suggest Andrew Zeller, an important early United Brethren bishop for *Z*.) For *X*, tell the confirmands that *X* resembles the Greek letter *chi*, which is the first letter in the Greek words for "Christ" and "Christian."

It is OK if you don't come up with something for every letter. The point of the activity is that every religious tradition has its own language and uses this language to describe its beliefs.

supplies
- ❑ a markerboard or large sheet of paper
- ❑ marker

Our Church Is Changing

(10–15 minutes)

In this activity, you can do a little (non-statistical) sampling of your group to see what trends are emerging in your community.

Explain that you'd like to take a poll that will help to uncover possible ways that your church and other churches in your town are changing. Ask the youth to stand for any statement that is true for them and to remain standing for a moment. Then everyone may sit down together.

Read the following statements, pausing after each one for youth to stand and sit. "Stand if you. . . ."

. . . have been a part of this church for 5 years or more
. . . have been a part of The United Methodist Church for 5 years or more
. . . have spent your entire life going to only a United Methodist church
. . . and your family have ever done some "church shopping" in your lifetime
. . . think that you have a pretty good idea of what makes The United Methodist Church different from other churches
. . . have friends who are part of other Christian churches
. . . have friends that rarely or never go to church
. . . have never invited a friend to come with you to worship or to another church activity
. . . regularly go to more than one church
. . . are excited about joining The United Methodist Church as a professing member when you are confirmed

Next, talk with the youth about their reactions to the poll. Ask:

- What did you notice in our responses? Were there very many statements for which our responses were similar? Why, do you think, is that?
- If the way we answered the questions is typical for United Methodists, what conclusions, if any, can be drawn about what might be changing in our denomination?
- The United Methodist Church has changed a lot over the years. What, do you think, is valuable about being familiar with and knowing our tradition? What can we learn from our past that is useful in the present?"

Note: If you choose to divide this session into two one-hour classes, break here.

SO WHAT? PART 2

Experience Journals

(10–15 minutes)

If the confirmands are not regularly bringing their *Credo Confirmation Student Journals* with them, instruct them beforehand to bring their journals for this session.

Invite the youth to thumb through their student journals, paying attention to what they have written in them so far.

Ask:

- Have you gotten into the habit of writing in your confirmation student journal? What has this experience been like?
- How can journaling help us connect to God and grow in faith?

Invite volunteers to read aloud some of the things they have written in their journals.

Hand out the page of dates that you had put together for each youth. Explain that these are some dates that the church and their parents had thought were significant dates to include in these journals. Give the youth time to record these events in their journals.

Encourage the youth to keep these journals in a place where they can regularly see and add to them. Ideally, they should turn the pages daily and write down with regularity where they have seen or experienced God in their lives.

Option: Give each confirmand a blank journal that has one page for every day of the year (if the pages are small) or one page for every two days of the year (if the pages are large). Challenge them to keep a "perpetual journal" in which they record significant experiences in their lives and times when they feel God's presence. Each date should get its own page or half-page in the journal, and they should write on a date's page or half-page whenever that date comes around. (For example, the March 29 page would make note of things that happened in different years but that all happened on March 29.)

SUPPLIES
- ❑ *Credo Confirmation Student Journals*
- ❑ pens or pencils
- ❑ optional: blank journals

PREPARATION: Work with the church office and parents to put together a list of significant events in the life of each youth: birth date, baptism date, date of first attendance in this congregation, and any other dates that seem to parents to be especially significant in the faith lives of the youth. Type these dates and details for each student so that you can hand them out.

Wisdom From the Elders

(15–20 minutes)

Invite the guests into the classroom, and rearrange the chairs as necessary so that the guests and the students can easily see one another.

Tell the youth that the special guests in your class are going to tell a story about their own discernment. Let the confirmands know that they may ask of the guests any questions they have.

Have the guests tell their stories. After each guest, allow a time for the confirmands' questions.

Then surprise the confirmands by telling them that the guests have questions for them as well. Then allow the guests to ask their questions and any follow-up questions related to what they want to know about the youth.

When everyone has finished, thank the guests for their participation, and allow them to leave.

SUPPLIES
- ❑ guests
- ❑ extra chairs, as needed

PREPARATION: Invite some long-time, active members of the congregation to join your class for a short while. Choose to invite individuals who articulate their faith well, who have been leaders in the congregation, or who simply have a quiet wisdom in the way they live. Ask these guests to be prepared to tell a story or two about discernment in their life or in the life of the congregation. In addition, invite them to ask the youth a question or two related to discernment, decision-making, or experiences of faith.

SUPPLIES
- ❑ markerboard
- ❑ marker
- ❑ large sheets of paper

REASON: WE'RE IN AGREEMENT THAT . . .

(10–15 minutes)

Ask the youth to suggest topics that are highly controversial for young people, topics about which their friends often take opposite sides and have strong opinions. The topics may be serious, such as whether towns should have curfews for teens, or they may be silly, such as whether fish or gerbils make the best pets.

Write their suggestions—at least 6 of them—on a markerboard. Then ask the youth to narrow the list to one topic for every confirmand. Take a final vote on which topics the group will debate. Have the confirmands break into two groups including adult leaders. (A group here could consist of a single youth working with an adult leader.)

The two groups should have opposite opinions and prepare an argument supporting their positions. Give the teams about 2 minutes to prepare their arguments. Then call the start of the debate.

After about 3 minutes of debate, stop the conversations (or arguments) and tell the groups that they need to switch gears. They now should determine what they can both agree on, using their reasoning skills to create a unified "position statement" on the issue being discussed. Have the unified groups write their statement of agreement on their large sheet of paper.

Discuss with the confirmands about the process they used and how this is good process that a group of church members or Christian groups could use when they have disagreements.

Ask:

- What role does our faith play when it comes to controversial topics?
- How does focusing on what we agree on move us forward?

NOW WHAT?

PUTTING IT ALL TOGETHER

(10 minutes)

Say: "Now that we've had a chance to explore all four parts of the Quadrilateral, we're going to try applying them to a real-life scenario. Before we do that, let's review just a bit." Ask:

- What are the four parts of the Quadrilateral? (*Scripture, tradition, experience, reason*)
- To what does each part refer? (***Scripture** refers to the fact that our first, foundational resource in discernment is the Bible. Our **tradition** is the historic church and what Christians have done and believed throughout the ages. Our*

experience *refers to our own experiences of faith and the depth of experience we've had in our own life.* **Reason** *is our ability to think through rationally all of these and to come to a decision that is reasonable.*)

Select one of the "Scenarios for Putting It All Together" from the handout on the website. Ask the youth to read the scenario and then, as a group, use Scripture, tradition, experience, and reason to discern a good course of action. Provide concordances, Bible dictionaries, or access to online Bibles and copies of *The Book of Discipline* or *The Social Principles* as available.

Allow the youth several minutes to work together then talk to them about what they concluded to be a good course of action.

SUPPLIES
- ❏ copies of the "Scenarios for Putting It All Together" handouts

PREPARATION: Make copies of the "Scenarios for Putting It All Together" handouts, from the website, making 1 copy of each handout for every 2 youth.

CLOSING RITUAL
(10 minutes)

Gather the confirmands into a circle. Lead the youth in prayer, giving thanks to God for your time together and for all that the group has learned and experienced. Then go around the circle, inviting each person to pray aloud one word or phrase that describes something he or she learned during the past week of confirmation. After every person has had a chance to contribute a word or phrase, say a brief closing prayer, such as this one:

> God who goes before us, we're grateful to you for your action in our lives. God who moves us to moments of decision, we invite you to act anew in us today. God who will guide us throughout all of our lives, we promise to do our part to grow in faith. We're grateful for the fact that our salvation is a process, and that your grace will never leave us. Amen.

Then invite the confirmands to say aloud and in unison the benediction, "John Wesley's Rule."

NOTE: Before you dismiss, instruct the confirmands to read, reflect on, and journal about the material in the "Wesleyan Quadrilateral" section of the *Credo Confirmation Student Journal* before your next session. Also encourage them to try to do the activities related to "Wesleyan Quadrilateral" on the confirmand website.

SUPPLIES
- ❏ markerboard
- ❏ marker

PREPARATION: Write the benediction, "John Wesley's Rule," on a markerboard; or print it out from the website.

Worship

INTRODUCTION

Regular worship with a community of faith is essential to being a follower of Christ and living a holy life. Worship is the most comprehensive way in which a congregation rehearses its faith and is recharged by God. In his three General Rules, John Wesley named worship as an "ordinance of God" that faithful Christians should attend to.

"Above All Sing Spiritually"

Music is an important element in many worship services. St. Augustine, in his commentary on **Psalm 73,** explained that, when you sing to God, not only does it praise God, but it also changes your heart.

Singing is not just something that we do to fill time during a worship service. The songs we sing, particularly hymns, are rich in Scripture and theology. Hymns and songs of praise can convey and interpret biblical passages, lift up common beliefs and practices, and be a conversation with God.

For John and Charles Wesley, music was a means of knowing, understanding, and communicating their faith. Within each of Charles Wesley's hymns are layers of scriptural references and theological concepts such as grace, the Trinity, salvation.

John Wesley wrote in his "Directions for Singing," which is still included in *The United Methodist Hymnal* (page vii), "Above all sing spiritually. Have an eye to God in every word you sing. Aim at pleasing him more than yourself." These words apply not only to the hymns and other songs we sing but also to every other aspect of our worship. Worship is not about performance or entertainment, but about having an eye to God.

Worshiping as the Body of Christ

Worship also is about what God is doing through and among the community of faith. While we all should strive to make worship a part of our daily lives—through daily prayer, Scripture reading, and spending time alone with God—worshiping as part of the body of Christ is an essential part of Christian discipleship. (The importance of worship in a faith community also is discussed in the "Way of Discipleship" session.)

Worshiping as a community makes us accountable to one another, supporting one another and growing together as we strive for personal holiness. Christian disciples are stronger together.

Young Christians who are considering confirming their faith and making a commitment to a life of discipleship need to get into the habit of worshiping each week with their congregation. John Wesley named many aspects of community worship—participating in sacraments, praying with the congregation, listening to sermons, and the reading of Scripture—as means of grace, ordinary ways in which God conveys grace to humankind. Participating in weekly worship opens young Christians to God's grace, allowing them to mature in faith.

Different Style, Same Purpose

Congregations vary in their style of worship. Some worship in large, ornate sanctuaries with wooden pews and stained-glass windows; others worship in spaces rented from schools or community centers. Some sing classic hymns from a printed hymnal; others sing contemporary praise songs projected on a screen. Some celebrate Holy Communion each week; others celebrate the sacrament once a month. Despite these stylistic differences, certain patterns and elements are common across most United Methodist congregations. You can read a detailed description of the United Methodist pattern of worship in the "Worship" section of this resource.

Young Christians will have different tastes when it comes to music and worship space. This is OK, and we should celebrate such diversity of aesthetic preferences. But youth need to understand that, regardless of the songs we sing or the architecture of the buildings where we gather, our worship should involve gathering, praise, the reading and proclaiming of Scripture, the affirmation of faith, prayers for the congregation and the world, thanksgiving, and a sending forth into the world to live as faithful disciples of Christ.

This session is an opportunity to teach youth about why we worship, about why worshiping with a community of faith is essential to Christian discipleship, and about the common patterns and elements of Christian worship.

SUPPLIES AND PREPARATION

BASIC SUPPLIES

❑ Bibles of various translations ❑ markerboard or large sheets of paper ❑ markers ❑ pens or pencils	❑ clear tape and/or glue ❑ masking tape ❑ index cards or paper cut about the same size (3-by-5 or 4-by-6) ❑ sheets of posterboard	❑ paper (Use paper that has already been used on one side as much as possible, depending on the activity.) ❑ scissors

ACTIVITY	PREPARATION	OTHER SUPPLIES
WHAT?		
Opening Ritual	Write the meditation—adapted from Psalm 67—on a markerboard; or project the meditation, using the slide on the website.	❑ vine from previous sessions ❑ vine leaves (1 for each student)
Listen to Me		
SO WHAT? PART 1		
Rules Rule	Copy John Wesley's "Directions for Singing" from page *vii* of *The United Methodist Hymnal* or print it from the website. Cut apart the 7 directions and attach them to index cards.	❑ 7 index cards (4-by-6) or card stock cut to at least 2-by-6 ❑ *The United Methodist Hymnal*
Do You Know Hymn?	Make copies of the "Do You Know Hymn?" quiz, from the website.	❑ copies of the "Do You Know Hymn?" quiz ❑ *The United Methodist Hymnal*
Noteworthy Composers	Gather supplies.	❑ *The United Methodist Hymnal*
SO WHAT? PART 2		
Solo and Community		
Worship Scavenger Hunt	Choose an option. If you choose Option B, gather appropriate supplies.	❑ optional: supplies for Option B only
A Color for Every Season		❑ optional: church paraments
Liturgical Doughnuts (Optional)	Gather supplies. Prepare an area where as many students as possible can decorate the doughnuts or cake.	❑ unfrosted doughnuts or a ring-shaped cake ❑ tubes of various colors of frosting (blue, green, purple, red, and white or gold); or the same colors of frosting, butter knives, and/or pastry bags with piping tips ❑ copies of the "Liturgical Doughnuts" handout
Person, Place, or Thing	Copy the 5 questions at the top of page 170 onto a sheet of paper. Cut the questions apart into strips, fold them, and put them into a hat or basket.	❑ 5 strips of paper with questions from page 170 ❑ hat or basket
You're in Charge	Choose an option. If you choose Option B, gather appropriate supplies.	❑ variety of worship bulletins ❑ *The United Methodist Hymnal*
NOW WHAT?		
Journalist to the Aliens	Gather supplies.	
Closing Ritual	Write the benediction, "John Wesley's Rule," on a markerboard; or print out the poster on the website.	

WHAT?

OPENING RITUAL

(10 minutes)

As confirmands arrive, point them to your confirmation vine; and give each person a leaf. Invite the confirmands to reflect on the previous session and to write on their leaf something they learned or experienced during that session. Ask the confirmands to affix their leaf to the vine. Remind them that these leaves represent ways that we, as Christians and United Methodists, grow in our faith and more fully experience God's grace.

Then invite the youth to read aloud this opening meditation, adapted from **Psalm 67:**

> O God, be gracious to us and bless us
> and make your face to shine upon us,
> that your way may be known upon earth,
> your saving power among all nations.
> Let the peoples praise you, O God;
> let all the peoples praise you!
> Let the nations be glad and sing for joy,
> for you judge the people with equity
> and guide the nations upon earth.

SUPPLIES

- ❑ vine from previous sessions
- ❑ vine leaves (1 for each student)
- ❑ markers or pens

PREPARATION: Write the opening meditation—which is adapted from Psalm 67—on a markerboard; or project the meditation, using the slide on the website.

NOTE: Take time before you get started to talk with the confirmands about what they read and wrote in the "Wesleyan Quadrilateral" section of their *Credo Confirmation Student Journals.*

LISTEN TO ME

(10 minutes)

SUPPLIES

- ❑ Bibles

Discuss with the confirmands songs and singing, asking some or all of the questions below.

- What is your favorite song? Why do you like it?
- When your favorite song is playing, what do you do?
- What songs do you sing, even if you are not a singer? (Examples might include *"Take Me Out to the Ball Game," "Happy Birthday," "The Star-Spangled Banner"*)
- How is the experience of singing with a group different from singing alone? (Have the group take into consideration singing to honor someone at his or her birthday, singing at a sporting event because it is part of a tradition.)

Then read aloud **Psalm 100** in unison as a group, or ask for a volunteer to read it aloud to the group. Then ask:

- What does this Scripture say about the importance of songs as worship?

SO WHAT? PART 1

supplies
- ❑ 7 index cards (4-by-6) or card stock cut into pieces that are at least 2-by-6 (See "Preparation," below.)
- ❑ copies of *The United Methodist Hymnal*

preparation: Copy John Wesley's "Directions for Singing" from page *vii* of *The United Methodist Hymnal.* Cut apart the 7 directions and attach them to index cards.

rules rule!

(20 minutes)

Say: "For people who sing a lot, there are rules: no yelling or you'll damage your voice; sit up straight; breathe deeply; and so on. But did you know that John Wesley even had rules for singing hymns?"

Ask volunteers to read aloud John Wesley's "Directions for Singing" from page *vii* of *The United Methodist Hymnal.* Choosing a youth with an ability to read them dramatically can make the activity more entertaining. As an alternative, you may invite someone from your congregation to recite the rules dressed up in full eighteenth-century English garb.

Give each student a hymnal. Place the cards or slips on which Wesley's rules are written in a hat or jar. Have one person draw a rule from the container. That person should select a hymn from the hymnal for the class sing in a manner that blatantly disobeys their rule. (For example, they might violate the second rule by altering lyrics or melodies of their hymn; they might break the fifth rule by singing to "be heard above the congregation" and destroying the harmony.)

Ask each person to select another rule to break and another hymn to sing improperly. Repeat this process until each rule has been broken.

Then ask:

- Why, do you think, did Wesley write these rules?
- Which of these rules, do you think, are relevant and need to be followed? Which, if any, seem over the top or outdated?
- Why does the way in which we sing a song matter?

supplies
- ❑ copies of the "Do You Know Hymn?" quiz
- ❑ copies of *The United Methodist Hymnal*

preparation: Make copies of the "Do You Know Hymn?" quiz, from the website.

do you know hymn?

(10 minutes):

Say: "You might or might not pay close attention to the hymns and songs used in church, but they are usually chosen to correspond to a particular Scripture or season of the Christian year. Today, you'll have a chance to look up some hymns and see what part of Christian life they talk about."

Give each youth a copy of the "Do You Know Hymn?" quiz and a *United Methodist Hymnal*. Have each youth match the hymn in the hymnal with its corresponding theme.

The answers are as follows (numbers refer to the hymns' location in *The United Methodist Hymnal*):

- **Trinity:** "Maker, in Whom We Live" (88)
- **Repentance:** "Pass Me Not, O Gentle Savior" (351)
- **Creation:** "All Things Bright and Beautiful" (147)
- **Church:** "The Church's One Foundation" (545)
- **Salvation:** "All Hail the Power of Jesus' Name" (155)
- **Justice:** "Lift Every Voice and Sing" (519)
- **God's Call:** "Lord, You Have Come to the Lakeshore" (344)
- **Holiness:** "Jesu, Jesu" (432)

Noteworthy Composers

(10 minutes)

Supplies

- ❑ copies of *The United Methodist Hymnal*

Read aloud the indented paragraph, below, about Charles Wesley; then ask the corresponding questions. Have the youth race to see which of them is able to answer first. Build excitement by saying, "On your mark, get set, go!" before allowing the students to open their hymnals.

If students have trouble locating the answers, show them the index on page 914, which lists hymns by the name of the composer, arranger, author, translator, and source. Then repeat the activity with the paragraph about Fanny Crosby.

> **Charles Wesley** was born December 18, 1707, and died March 29, 1788. He was the eighteenth child of his parents, Samuel and Susanna Wesley, and was John Wesley's younger brother. Charles was instrumental in the Methodist movement as a fellow member of the Oxford "Methodist group." He accompanied John in his ministry and went all over the country with him and even on John's first trip to the colony of Georgia. Devoted to bringing the message of Jesus Christ to the poor, Charles continued to work with John for the next 50 years in ministry. While John preached theology, Charles put theology to music. He wrote more than 7,000 hymns and poems in his lifetime.

Ask the following questions:

- What Charles Wesley hymn would you sing at Christmas? (*"Hark! The Herald Angles Sing," 240*)
- Which Charles Wesley hymn would you sing at Easter? (*"Christ the Lord Is Risen Today," 302*)

> Lifelong Methodist **Fanny Crosby** was born March 24, 1820, and died February 12, 1915. Despite being blinded at only 6 weeks old, she went on to write 8,000 hymns. Fanny wrote under almost 100 different pseudonyms because she was worried that music publishers might not want to select too many hymns from one composer.

Ask the following question:

- Which one of Fanny Crosby's hymns would you sing to celebrate a baptism? (*"Blessed Assurance," 369*).

NOTE: If you choose to divide this session into two one-hour classes, break here.

SO WHAT? PART 2

SOLO AND COMMUNITY

(10 minutes)

SUPPLIES
- ❑ Bible

Read aloud **1 Corinthians 1:2-3.** Ask each student to take three minutes in silence to think about the Scripture and pray. It will feel like a long time. You can read aloud the Scripture a second time if necessary to refocus the group.

Ask the following questions to the class, pausing for discussion after each question:

- How was your 3-minute devotion time similar to and different from the rituals that we do at the beginning and end of each session?
- What is "worship"?
- Why, do you think, does God call us to be in a group when we worship?

Say: "Worship is the way that Christians come together as a community of faith to tell our story, offer praise and thanks to God, and support one another as we grow in faith."

WORSHIP SCAVENGER HUNT

(20 minutes)

SUPPLIES FOR OPTION B
- ❑ paper
- ❑ pens or pencils
- ❑ copies of your choice of sanctuary layout, from the website

PREPARATION: Option A requires no supplies, just access to the sanctuary. Option B requires copies of a download from the website of a sanctuary layout or paper and pens and pencils for students to draw a sanctuary.

If your sanctuary or main worship space is available during class time, proceed to Option A and ignore Option B. If it is not available, skip Option A and continue with Option B. You may need to make some adjustments to this activity to reflect the layout of your worship space.

Option A
Take your class to the sanctuary, and gather in the center. Call out a word from the list on page 167 and have the confirmands identify the item by going to it and placing a hand on it.

Once the confirmands have correctly identified the item, ask them to define its purpose in worship. Read the item's corresponding paragraph.

Option B
1. Download from the website the sanctuary layout that best resembles your church. Or give the students a sheet of paper, and have them design a sanctuary inspired from a current or past church.
2. If the students design a sanctuary, be sure that each student includes the following items in his or her drawing: altar,

cross, pulpit, baptismal font, Communion rail. Have them add paraments later, after you discuss what paraments are.

3. Go over each item with the students and make that sure it is correctly labeled in the sanctuary. Ask the confirmands whether they know the purpose of each item. Before moving on to the next word, give the youth the information associated with each item, below.

For Both Options

- **Altar:** The Israelites used the altar as a place to give offerings to God. This included the best items someone might possess, such as crops from the harvest, precious metals, and even livestock. As Christians, we recognize that Christ has made the ultimate sacrifice and that God no longer desires these items as a sacrifice. Instead, we offer the one thing to God that is desired most, our heart. Today, the altar continues to represent the grace Christ offers through the sacrament of Holy Communion.

- **Cross** (or other symbols)**:** The cross is one of many symbols in the Christian church. The empty cross is a reminder of Christ's resurrection and victory over sin and death. Many church sanctuaries also use fire to symbolize another person of the Trinity, the Holy Spirit. In many congregations, acolytes bring in the light at the beginning of a worship service to light candles that burn throughout the service. Some churches have a perpetual light, a light that hangs in the corner of the sanctuary and is continually lit. It also reminds us that the Holy Spirit is constantly with us.

- **Pulpit:** The pulpit is where the pastor addresses the congregation and (in many churches) delivers the sermon. In many sanctuaries, a similar structure, called a lectern, stands on the opposite side of the chancel (front of the sanctuary). Lay persons stand at the lectern when they read Scripture or lead responsive readings.

- **Baptismal Font:** This is the basin of water used in baptism. United Methodists affirm baptism by affusion (pouring) and immersion. However, most United Methodist baptisms are done by aspersion (sprinkling), because of its gentleness to infants and its simplicity in worship. Churches that baptize by immersion, such as Baptist churches, often have a baptismal pool in the sanctuary.

- **Communion Rail:** Kneeling before the Lord as we celebrate the sacrament of Holy Communion shows humility and honors God.

- **Paraments:** The seasons of the Christian calendar year, or liturgical year, each have a corresponding color, or colors. The colors in the sanctuary remind us of what we are celebrating and observing in worship.

supplies
- ❑ optional: church paraments

preparation:
Optional: If you can, gather examples of church paraments in the various colors of the seasons of the church.

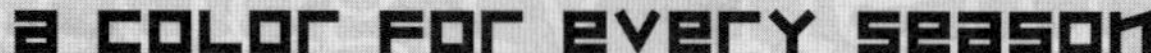

a color for every season

Building on your discussion of paraments from the previous activity, say: "The colors of paraments and other sanctuary decorations correspond to the different seasons of the Christian calendar, or liturgical year. These seasons tell the story of our faith year after year and help us structure our worship services."

Ask the youth to name some seasons of the Christian year. Offer help as needed and work together until you've talked about each of the following seasons and the meaning behind each of these seasons. Show the paraments for each season as you discuss them if you have brought in paraments.

- **Advent:** a season of preparation for Christ's promised coming. Advent begins on the fourth Sunday before Christmas.
- **Christmas:** celebrates Jesus' birth. This season lasts from Christmas Eve until January 5, the day before Epiphany.
- **The Season After Epiphany:** celebrates Christ's divinity (frankincense), royalty (gold), and sacrifice (myrrh—used for anointing and embalming). This season begins on Epiphany, January 6, and continues until the Tuesday before Ash Wednesday.
- **Lent:** recalls Jesus' 40-day temptation in the wilderness and journey toward Jerusalem and the cross. The 40 days (not including Sundays) of Lent begin with Ash Wednesday and continue through Holy Week.
- **Easter:** celebrates Christ's resurrection. The Easter season goes from Easter Sunday until Pentecost.
- **Pentecost:** commemorates the outpouring of the Holy Spirit and the establishment of the church. Pentecost is the fiftieth day after Easter.
- **Ordinary Time:** a time to reflect on doing the work of God's kingdom and growing spiritually.

Name each of these seasons, and ask the confirmands to guess which color (or colors) the church associates with them. Answers and descriptions are below.

- **Advent:** Purple or blue (*Purple is the color of royalty, as we prepare for the coming of Jesus the King. Some churches today use blue to separate Advent from another liturgical season. Blue is the color of pre-dawn light.*)
- **Christmas:** White or gold (*These colors together signify a celebration, reserved for only the most important Christian holidays. These colors are also used on Epiphany, the day marking the arrival of the three wise men, typically celebrated on the first Sunday of January but, technically, January 6 each year.*)

- **Season After Epiphany:** Green (*Green is the color of growth, as we study the life of Jesus from child to man.*)
- **Lent:** Purple (*Purple is also the color of penitence.*)
- **Easter:** White or gold (*Like Christmas, this is one of the holiest and most celebrated days of the Christian year, Christ's resurrection.*)
- **Pentecost:** Red (*Red is the color of fire, which represents the Holy Spirit. Red may also be used in evangelistic or other services special to Christ's church, such as ordination.*)
- **Ordinary Time** (the time between Pentecost and Advent)**:** Green (*Green is the color of growth and symbolizes our growth in faith and understanding in the general teachings of Christ.*)
- **Communion** and **baptism** are not seasons, but they are represented by what color? White (*These sacraments signify the cleansing of the soul, through the grace of Jesus Christ.*)

Liturgical Doughnuts (Optional)*

Provide doughnuts and various colors of frosting—blue, green, purple, red, white, and possibly gold—and implements to apply the frosting. Invite the confirmands to make "liturgical doughnuts" by piping or spreading icing on the doughnuts to represent the seasons of the liturgical year.

Distribute copies of the "Liturgical Doughnuts" handout, and instruct the confirmands to frost their doughnuts so that the pastries match the liturgical calendar diagram. Tell them to focus on making sure that all of the seasons are represented by the proper colors and not to worry whether they have the precise ratio of green icing to purple icing and so forth. The colors and seasons, in order, are:

- **Purple or Blue (Advent)**
- **White or Gold (Christmas)**
- **Green (Season After Epiphany)**
- **Purple (Lent)**
- **White or Gold (Easter)**
- **Red (Pentecost)**
- **Green (Ordinary Time)**

Give the confirmands plenty of time to work, then invite them to eat their freshly frosted Christian calendars.

Person, Place, or Thing?

(10 minutes)

Discuss each of the following questions:

Supplies

- ❑ unfrosted doughnuts or a ring-shaped cake, such as angel food or a bundt cake
- ❑ tubes of various colors of frosting (blue, green, purple, red, and white or gold); or the same colors of frosting, butter knives, and/or pastry bags with piping tips
- ❑ copies of the "Liturgical Doughnuts" handout

Preparation: Prepare an area where as many students as possible can decorate the doughnuts or help decorate the cake. Make as many copies as you think that you'll need of the "Liturgical Doughnuts" handout.

* "Liturgical Doughnuts" activity was created by Sarah Herron.

SUPPLIES
- ❑ 5 strips of paper prepared as described below
- ❑ hat or basket

PREPARATION: Copy the 5 questions at right onto a sheet of paper. Cut the questions apart in strips, fold them, and put them into a hat or basket.

1. What are we doing during worship?
2. How is what we do during worship different from what we do while watching a football game or other sporting event?
3. How is a sermon different from a lecture in a classroom?
4. How is a sanctuary or other worship space different from a movie theater?
5. Where can you hold a worship service?

SUPPLIES
- ❑ Bibles
- ❑ various copies of your church's worship bulletin and from other churches, if possible
- ❑ pens or pencils
- ❑ paper
- ❑ markerboard or paper
- ❑ marker
- ❑ copies of *The United Methodist Hymnal*

PREPARATION: Collect worship bulletins from your local church and other congregations. As much as possible, have a wide variety available. It is important to offer several examples of services.

YOU'RE IN CHARGE

(15 minutes)

Say, "Now that we've learned about the different parts of worship, the setting, and the reasons we worship, we're going to plan our own worship service."

Parts planned may be used in their confirmation worship service or used at some other appropriate time.

1. Give each student a worship bulletin as an example.
2. Write on a markerboard or paper the four movements of a worship service: 1) Entrance or Gathering, 2) Proclamation & Response, 3) Thanksgiving and Communion, 4) Sending Forth.
3. Have students share as a group where they see all four movements in the worship services on their bulletins. There may be multiple answers to each movement.
4. Divide into two groups and have each group work on 2 aspects of the service. Suggested tasks are: write a call to worship, write an offertory prayer, pick hymns for the service, design a bulletin cover, write additional confirmation vows, and design worship paraments or other visuals for the altar.

NOW WHAT?

SUPPLIES
- ❑ paper
- ❑ pens or pencils

JOURNALIST TO THE ALIENS

(10 minutes)

Say: "Knowing about our own ways of worship is one thing; but teaching someone else about worship, how and why we do it, is much harder."

Give each student a pen or pencil and a piece of paper. Then say: "Aliens have landed in our church parking lot, and the greeters have invited them to our congregation's worship service. The only problem is that the aliens do not want to go, unless they understand what a worship service is about and what to expect. What would you say to them? How would you describe a worship service and all that it entails? Be sure to answer the important questions of why, what, where, and with whom?" (Assume that the aliens can understand English.)

Give the confirmands about 5 minutes to come up with their description and how they will present it to the space aliens. Then invite volunteers to try to explain worship to your extra-terrestrial visitors.

Closing Ritual

(10 minutes)

Gather the confirmands into a circle. Lead the youth in prayer, giving thanks to God for your time together and for all that the group has learned and experienced. Then go around the circle, inviting each person to pray aloud one word or phrase that describes something he or she learned during the past week of confirmation. After every person has had a chance to contribute a word or phrase, say a brief closing prayer, such as this one:

> God who goes before us, we're grateful to you for your action in our lives. God who moves us to moments of decision, we invite you to act anew in us today. God who will guide us throughout all of our lives, we promise to do our part to grow in faith. We're grateful for the fact that our salvation is a process, and that your grace will never leave us. Amen.

Then invite the confirmands to say aloud and in unison the benediction, "John Wesley's Rule."

Note: Before you dismiss, instruct the confirmands to read, reflect on, and journal about the material in the "Worship" section of the *Credo Confirmation Student Journal* before your next session. Also encourage them to try to do the activities related to "Worship" on the confirmand website.

Supplies

- ❑ markerboard
- ❑ marker

Preparation: Write the benediction, "John Wesley's Rule," on a markerboard; or print out the poster from the website.

Sacraments

INTRODUCTION

In the United Methodist tradition, confirmation cannot be separated from baptism. Through the rite of confirmation, Christians confirm their baptism and renew their baptismal vows. This connection to baptism is essential because baptism is one of the two sacraments.

Sacraments are rites ordained by Jesus Christ, through which we experience God's grace. The Confession of Faith of the Evangelical United Brethren Church (one of the two denominations that merged to form The United Methodist Church), in our *Book of Discipline* says:

> We believe the Sacraments, ordained by Christ, are symbols and pledges of the Christian's profession and of God's love toward us. They are means of grace by which God works invisibly in us, quickening, strengthening and confirming our faith in him. Two Sacraments are ordained by Christ our Lord, namely Baptism and the Lord's Supper.

a HOLY MYSTERY

Sacraments are not the only ways in which we receive God's grace, but they are unique in that they were ordained by Jesus himself. Jesus was baptized by John (**Mark 1:9**) and told his followers to go and baptize people "in the name of the Father and of the Son and of the Holy Spirit" (**Matthew 28:19**). And during his final meal with his disciples before his crucifixion, Jesus instituted the sacrament of Holy Communion, instructing his disciples to partake of his body and blood—the bread and cup—"in remembrance" of him (**1 Corinthians 11:23-26**).

Following the celebration of Holy Communion in The United Methodist Church, we pray, "Eternal God, we give you thanks for this holy mystery in which you have given yourself to us." For many young people, "mystery" is an apt description of baptism and Holy Communion. What exactly happens when the pastor applies the waters of baptism to an infant or to an adult who is new to the faith? What is going on during the consecration of the Communion elements? Why do we approach these rites with such reverence?

To answer these questions, confirmands need to understand that we revere baptism and Communion—not because of what we do or what the pastor does but because of what God is

doing. The breaking of the bread, the pouring of the water, the laying on of hands, and the drinking from the cup are all outward, visible signs of the unseen work of God. When Christians are baptized or celebrate Communion, the Holy Spirit works within us, drawing us closer to God, strengthening our faith, and reminding us of God's promises.

Cleansed by the Waters of Baptism

Baptism is an initiation. It is the sacrament that draws us into the body of Christ as a member of the universal church, The United Methodist Church, and the local congregation. Baptism is an act of the Holy Spirit, and persons of any age may be baptized. Because we affirm God's prevenient grace—the grace by which God seeks us out and prepares us for faith—we often baptize infants and small children who are too young to take the baptismal vows for themselves. Their parents take the vows on their behalf. "By Water and the Spirit: A United Methodist Understanding of Baptism," a document that the church adopted in 1996 and has since been reaffirmed, says, "The church affirms that children being born into the brokenness of the world should receive the cleansing and renewing forgiveness of God no less than adults."

Since baptism is an initiation into the church, the entire worshiping congregation participates in the sacrament. Members of the congregation reaffirm their faith and promise to support and nurture the person being baptized.

If they choose to be confirmed, some of your confirmands may be affirming the baptismal vows taken on their behalf when they were babies. Others may be receiving the sacrament of baptism during the confirmation service. In either case, they need to understand that baptism is a means of grace, and act of the Spirit, and an initiation into Christ's body, the church.

Nourished by the Lord's Supper

While a person may be baptized only once, Christians may and should partake frequently in the sacrament of Holy Communion. Through Communion, we are nourished by God's saving grace and reminded of the sacrifice Jesus made for our redemption.

As with baptism, the Holy Spirit is at work in Holy Communion. And, as with baptism, Holy Communion requires the participation of a community of faith. (Notice that *Communion* and *community* share a root word.) Celebrating Communion not only draws us closer to God, but also draws us closer to one another.

The United Methodist Church upholds an open table. *The United Methodist Book of Worship* explains: "All who intend to lead a Christian life, together with their children, are invited to receive the bread and cup." Confirmands may be nourished by Holy Communion even before they take their confirmation vows and should understand that this sacrament is an important part of the life of all Christian disciples.

SUPPLIES AND PREPARATION

BASIC SUPPLIES		
❑ Bibles of various translations ❑ markerboard or large sheets of paper ❑ markers ❑ pens or pencils	❑ clear tape and/or glue ❑ masking tape ❑ index cards or paper cut about the same size (3-by-5 or 4-by-6) ❑ sheets of posterboard	❑ paper (Use paper that has already been used on one side as much as possible, depending on the activity.) ❑ scissors

ACTIVITY	PREPARATION	OTHER SUPPLIES
WHAT?		
Opening Ritual	Write the opening meditation—which is adapted from Psalm 67—on a markerboard; or project the meditation, using the slide on the website.	❑ vine from previous sessions ❑ vine leaves (1 for each student)
Question Ball	Inflate the ball or balloon, and write on it questions related to baptism and Holy Communion.	❑ beach ball or balloon ❑ permanent marker
SO WHAT? PART 1		
What Is Baptism?	Gather supplies.	❑ *The United Methodist Hymnal*
Babies and Believers		
¡Agua Va!	Gather supplies.	❑ small cup ❑ containers of water
Remember Your Baptism	Prepare an altar setting.	❑ *The United Methodist Hymnal* ❑ pitcher filled with water ❑ basin ❑ small, smooth stones
SO WHAT? PART 2		
What Is Holy Communion?	Gather supplies.	❑ *The United Methodist Hymnal*
How It All Started	Gather supplies.	
Sacramental Vocabulary	Gather supplies.	
The Table Is Open	Gather supplies.	
But Why?	Invite an ordained elder to answer questions.	❑ several pads of sticky notes ❑ ordained elder
NOW WHAT?		
Celebration of Holy Communion	Gather supplies. Invite an ordained elder to administer Communion.	❑ Communion elements ❑ ordained elder ❑ *The United Methodist Hymnal*
Closing Ritual	Write the benediction, "John Wesley's Rule," on a markerboard; or print out the poster on the website.	

WHAT?

Opening Ritual

(10 minutes)

As confirmands arrive, point them to your confirmation vine; and give each person a leaf. Invite the confirmands to reflect on the previous session and to write on their leaf something they learned or experienced during that session. Ask the confirmands to affix their leaf to the vine. Remind them that these leaves represent ways that we, as Christians and United Methodists, grow in our faith and more fully experience God's grace.

Then invite the youth to read aloud this opening meditation, adapted from **Psalm 67:**

> O God, be gracious to us and bless us
> and make your face to shine upon us,
> that your way may be known upon earth,
> your saving power among all nations.
> Let the peoples praise you, O God;
> let all the peoples praise you!
> Let the nations be glad and sing for joy,
> for you judge the people with equity
> and guide the nations upon earth.

Supplies

- ❑ vine from previous sessions
- ❑ vine leaves (1 for each student)
- ❑ markers or pens

Preparation: Write the opening meditation—which is adapted from Psalm 67—on a markerboard; or project the meditation, using the slide on the website.

Note: Take time before you get started to talk with the confirmands about what they read and wrote in the "Worship" section of their *Credo Confirmation Student Journals*.

Question Ball

(5 minutes)

Inflate a beach ball or balloon. Then use a permanent marker to write on the beach ball or balloon these questions (or others related to baptism and Holy Communion):

- How would you describe baptism to a friend who has never heard of baptism?
- How would you describe Communion to a friend who has never heard of it?
- How is baptism in our church different from baptism in some of the churches your friends attend?
- How is Communion in our church different from Communion in some of the churches your friends attend?
- Who may be baptized in our church?
- Who may take Holy Communion in our church?
- What is one question that you have about baptism?
- What is one question that you have about Holy Communion?

Throw the ball to a confirmand. Ask him or her to read aloud the question under his or her left thumb and to answer it or open the question to the others. As needed, add information about the sacraments (such as the information on pages 172–173). Then have the confirmand with the ball pass the ball to another person, and ask this person to read aloud the

Supplies

- ❑ beach ball or balloon
- ❑ permanent marker

Preparation: Inflate the ball or balloon, and write on it questions related to baptism and Holy Communion.

question under his or her thumb. Continue until you've had a chance to discuss most of the questions. It is OK if some questions are repeated.

Then say: "Baptism and Holy Communion are the two sacraments, or ways that Jesus has given us to more fully experience God's grace."

SO WHAT? PART 1

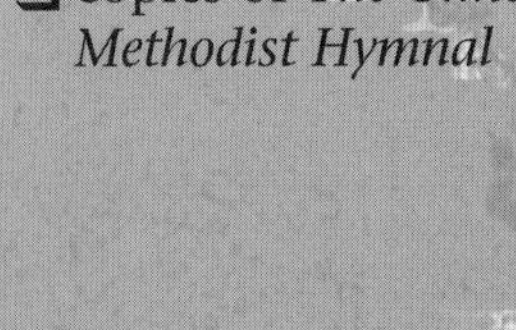

supplies
- ❑ copies of *The United Methodist Hymnal*

what is baptism?

(15 minutes)

Hand out copies of *The United Methodist Hymnal* and ask the confirmands to turn to page 33, "The Baptismal Covenant I." Read through the baptismal service together, making note of the instructions for the pastor, which are in red. After you've read through the service, ask:

- What vows are being taken (or what promises are being made) in this baptismal service?
- Who is taking these vows? (*the person being baptized or those taking the vows on his or her behalf; the congregation*)

Point out that the vows of baptism are identical to the vows of confirmation (which the confirmands will learn about in detail in the next unit, "Live Your Commitment"). Also talk about the role of the congregation in baptism, and how the congregation vows to nurture one another and the person being baptized.

babies and believers

(10 minutes)

Say: "In The United Methodist Church, we baptize people of all ages. For infants and small children, who are unable to answer for themselves, parents or sponsors take the baptismal vows on their behalf."

Invite the confirmands to talk about whether they were baptized as infants or small children (even if they were baptized in another congregation or denomination) or have not been baptized and are considering being baptized during the confirmation service. Also invite them to talk about how they were baptized. (Was water gently applied to their head? Were they fully immersed?) Assure them that all of these expressions of baptism are equally valid.

Ask:

- Why, do you think, do we baptize infants and small children in The United Methodist Church?

Use the information on page 173 to explain why our church baptizes people of all ages. Remind the confirmands of what

they learned about prevenient grace in the "Way of Salvation" session. Explain that baptism is a sign of God's grace and that God's grace is at work in a person's life even before that person responds to God's grace by professing his or her faith. Also point out that infants and children in the church experience God's prevenient grace through the members of the congregation who have vowed to support, nurture, and teach them. Thus infant baptism involves the entire congregation.

Then say: "Not all Christian traditions baptize infants. Some practice what is called 'believer's baptism,' meaning that a person can be baptized only when he or she is old enough to make a person faith commitment. They believe that baptism before a person comes to faith is invalid."

Note that, along with The United Methodist Church, the Roman Catholic, Eastern Orthodox, Anglican (Episcopal in the U.S.), Lutheran, and Presbyterian churches and the United Church of Christ baptize infants. Baptists, Anabaptists (including Mennonites and the Amish), and Churches of Christ practice believer's baptism.

Phil and Martin (Optional)

(10 minutes)

Note: This activity is most appropriate for older (eighth and ninth grade) confirmation groups.

Say: "The debate between infant baptism and believer's baptism was a matter of controversy among the founders of the Church of the United Brethren in Christ, one of the denominations that would eventually join with others to form The United Methodist Church. Philip William Otterbein, one of the founders, was a Reformed German pastor who came to America in 1752 and worked closely with Methodist preachers. Otterbein believed in infant baptism. The other founder, Martin Boehm (pronounced "baym"), was a Mennonite preacher. Mennonites practice believer's baptism. Although they had very different views on baptism, the two preachers put their differences aside to form the Church of the United Brethren in Christ. The church got its name because Otterbein was so moved by one of Boehm's sermons that he approached him after the service and said, 'Wir sind bruder,' which means, 'We are brethren.' "

Assign one person the role of Philip William Otterbein and another Martin Boehm. Have remaining confirmands act as moderators, asking Philip and Martin questions about baptism and who can be baptized. If there are no remaining confirmands, an adult leader can act as moderator. Possible questions include:

- Philip, why do you believe in baptizing infants, who aren't old enough to know what they believe?
- Martin, why do you think that people have to profess their faith before they can be baptized?
- How can two people with such different views of baptism come together in one church?

Following the panel discussion, say: "While the United Brethren felt that baptism was important, the new church did not originally take sides in the infant baptism-versus-believer's baptism debate. But over time, The United Brethren came to affirm the baptism of infants and small children."

supplies
- ❑ Bibles
- ❑ small cup
- ❑ containers of water

¡agua va!

(15–20 minutes)

The title of this activity is Spanish and literally means "water goes." Begin by having volunteers read aloud **Mark 1:1-11; Acts 8:14-24;** and **Romans 6:1-14.** Encourage the confirmands to pay close attention, because there will be a quiz.

Pour a *small amount* of water into a small cup and place the cup on a table. Have an additional container of water ready so that you can refill the cup, as needed.

Ask one of the questions below. If one of the confirmands thinks that he or she knows the answer, he or she should slap the table. Allow the first person to slap the table to answer the question.

If the answer is correct, hand the player the cup and allow him or her to splash the opposing players with the water in the cup. If the answer is incorrect, hand the cup to the person on the player's right and allow that person to splash the player who answered incorrectly. If no one answers the question correctly, reveal the answer. (No one gets wet.)

These questions come from the Scriptures above and from "Baptismal Covenant I," which you read earlier in this session.

- Complete the sentence the pastor says during a baptism: "I baptize you in the name of the Father, and of the Son, and __________________." (*of the Holy Spirit*)
- True or false—John the Baptist appeared in a city, proclaiming a baptism of mercy and justice. (*False. He appeared in the wilderness, proclaiming a baptism of repentance for the forgiveness of sins.*)
- Through the sacrament of baptism, we are initiated into ________________. (*Christ's holy church*)
- In what river did John baptize Jesus? (*The River Jordan*)
- Simon the magician tried to give the apostles ___________ so that he could receive the power of the Holy Spirit and ability to baptize. (*money* or *silver*)
- What tore apart as Jesus came up out of the water? (*the heavens*)
- John the Baptist proclaimed that he baptized with ________, but that Jesus would baptize you with the Holy Spirit. (*water*)
- According to **Romans,** if you are alive to God in Christ, you must consider yourself dead to what? (*sin*)

- True or false: When a small child is baptized, his or her parents are the only ones who take vows. (*False. The congregation also takes vows to help raise the child in the Christian faith.*)
- At Jesus' baptism, the Spirit descended on Jesus like a _______. (*dove*)

remember your baptism

(15 minutes)

Say a prayer of blessing over the water. For guidance, refer to "The Baptismal Covenant IV: Congregational Reaffirmation of the Baptismal Covenant" (pages 50–53, *The United Methodist Hymnal*).

Then remind those in the group who were baptized that, upon baptism, they received a new name—the name of Christ. Baptism is the formal entry into the body of Christ, the church. Then pour the water into the basin.

Invite participants who have been baptized to come to the water basin and touch the water. As each person touches the water, make the sign of the cross in water on his or her forehead (much like you would make the sign of the cross in ashes on Ash Wednesday); and say to him or her, "Remember your baptism and be thankful."

Invite each person to take a small stone, marble, or bead from the basin as a reminder of their reaffirmation and remembrance of baptism.

Invite participants who have not yet been baptized to also come forward to receive a blessing in anticipation of their baptism. Say to these persons, "Anticipate your baptism and be thankful."

Note: Be clear that this is not a service of baptism. It is a ritual and a blessing, but it is not a sacrament.

Option: If all of the participants have been baptized, and if they feel comfortable doing so, have them pair off and invite partners to make the sign of the cross on each other's foreheads, saying, "Remember your baptism and be thankful."

supplies

- ❑ copy of *The United Methodist Hymnal*
- ❑ pitcher filled with water
- ❑ basin
- ❑ small, smooth stones or large glass beads, marbles, or Lucite drops (available in arts and crafts stores, on the Internet, and in the craft or candle section of most large discount stores)

preparation: Prepare an altar setting that includes a pitcher with water and a basin containing the stones.

note: If you choose to divide this session into two one-hour classes, break here.

SO WHAT? PART 2

Supplies
- ❑ copies of *The United Methodist Hymnal*
- ❑ Bibles

What Is Holy Communion?

(10–15 minutes)

Hand out copies of *The United Methodist Hymnal* and ask the confirmands to turn to page 6, "A Service of Word and Table I." Read through the service of Holy Communion together, making note of the instructions for the pastor, which are in red. After you've read through the service, ask:

- What does this service tell us about Holy Communion and why we take it?
- In this service, what sorts of things do we do to prepare for Holy Communion? (*confess our sins, offer one another signs of peace and love, give thanks to God, and so on*)

Ask a volunteer to read aloud **1 Corinthians 11:23-26.** Then say: "Like baptism, Holy Communion is a sacrament that Jesus ordained as a way for us to experience God's grace."

Supplies
- ❑ Bibles

How It All Started

(20 minutes)

Say: "The sacraments are more than just rituals. They are practices given to us by Jesus himself as ways for us to more fully experience God's forgiving love and grace."

To tell the story of Jesus instituting the sacrament of Holy Communion, have the confirmands read aloud **Matthew 26:17-30,** each person reading a verse at a time.

Afterward, ask:

- What celebration brought Jesus' disciples together?
- What, do you think, does Jesus want us to remember when we take Holy Communion? (*the sacrifice he made on our behalf, the forgiveness God gives us through Christ, the covenant that God has made with us through Christ*)

Sacramental Vocabulary

(20 minutes)

Have the students—and any adults who are present—play a word-defining, guessing game that is similar to the board game Balderdash®.) Give each student small pieces of scrap paper and a pen or pencil. Write a word on a markerboard, and have each person attempt to define it. Have participants write their definition and their name on the scrap paper. Encourage creativity. The expectation is that the participants will not know the word. (Adults may need to pretend not to know the definitions and come up with an intentionally false definition for each word.)

While they are working, write on a scrap of paper the correct definition of the word, as written below. Have everyone hand in their definitions. Read aloud all of the definitions. Then as you read the definitions a second time, have the confirmands raise their hand to vote for the definition they think is correct.

Award a point to each student who guessed the correct definition. Award a point to any student for each vote he or she received for his or her definition. (You can decide whether or not to also keep points for adult players.)

SUPPLIES
- ❑ markerboard
- ❑ marker
- ❑ small pieces of scrap paper
- ❑ pens or pencils

Word	**Definition**
Eucharist	The sacrament of Holy Communion
Immanent	Existing with, close to
Omnipresent	God is everywhere.
Intinction	The act of dipping Communion bread into the cup

Following the game, say: "In The United Methodist Church, we believe that Christ is *immanent*—truly present with us—when we celebrate Holy Communion. During this celebration, also called *Eucharist,* the Holy Spirit is at work in our hearts, reminding us of the redemption we have in Christ and drawing us closer to God."

THE TABLE IS OPEN

(10 minutes)

SUPPLIES
- ❑ Bibles

Ask:

- Who is allowed to take Holy Communion in The United Methodist Church?

Allow a minute or two for answers and discussion, then read aloud this statement from *The United Methodist Book of Worship*:

> All who intend to lead a Christian life, together with their children, are invited to receive the bread and cup. We have no tradition of refusing any who present themselves desiring to receive.

Say: "United Methodists have an open table, meaning that 'All who intend to lead a Christian life' are welcome to participate in the sacrament. Not all Christian churches have an open table. Some, such as Roman Catholic, Eastern Orthodox, and certain Lutheran churches, have a closed table. These denominations serve Communion to only those persons who share their understanding of Holy Communion or who have been confirmed in their denomination."

Ask the confirmands whether they have had experiences of attending church with a friend and not being allowed to take Communion.

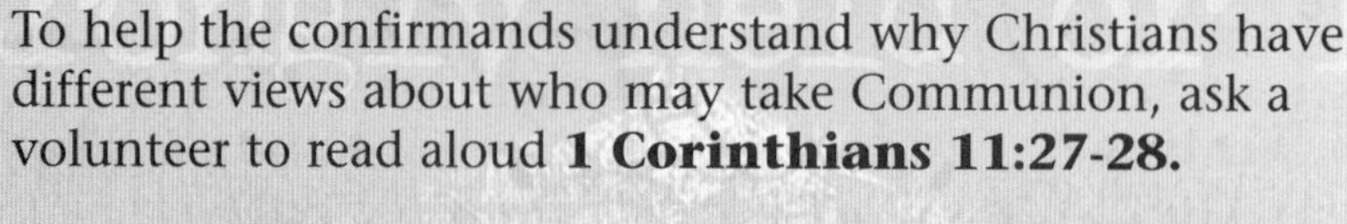

To help the confirmands understand why Christians have different views about who may take Communion, ask a volunteer to read aloud **1 Corinthians 11:27-28.**

Then explain that many churches that practice closed Communion believe that being worthy to take Holy Communion means being in a right relationship with the church and/or sharing the church's understanding of Holy Communion. United Methodists invite "all who love [God], who earnestly repent of their sin, and seek to live in peace with one another" to take Communion. It is up to the individual to determine whether he or she is worthy.

But Why?

(15 minutes)

Supplies

- ❑ several pads of sticky notes
- ❑ pens or pencils
- ❑ ordained elder (preferred but not required)

Preparation: Ask an ordained elder to attend so that he or she can answer the students' questions. If he or she cannot attend, ask him or her to answer the "common questions," listed in the activity.

Allow the youth to brainstorm "why" questions, such as "Why do stores that are open 24 hours a day every day have locks on the door?" or "Why do we drive on the right side of the road?" You may choose to try to answer some of these questions, or just allow the youth to ask.

Invite an ordained clergyperson—if you are not ordained clergy yourself—to help with the remainder of the class. Hand out sticky notes, at least 5 to each youth. Allow the youth to write down any question they would like to ask the pastor, especially about Communion and baptism. Give them 90 seconds to write and post questions. Each question should be on a separate sticky note. Each sticky note needs to be placed on a surrounding wall so that the room is decorated in questions.

Have the clergyperson answer the questions. If an ordained clergyperson is unavailable, ask the students to send in questions during the week that you can forward to him or her in advance. Or have the pastor answer the "common questions" below. Record the pastor answering the questions, and play a video of the pastor during class.

The following are common questions the youth might ask:

- What are the ways you can take Communion? (*intinction, drink, disposable cups*)
- What do you do with the leftover elements?
- Why do we use grape juice, instead of wine?
- Why do some churches use wafers and some use bread?
- Who may take Communion?
- Why do we have Communion only once a month (or however frequently your congregation does it)?

As time permits, tell the youth this anecdote related to the question of why we use grape juice: "During the nineteenth century, Methodists became very concerned about the dangers of alcohol. (The United Methodist Church today continues to take a strong stand against alcohol abuse.) Some

asked whether the church was contributing to the problem of alcohol addiction by serving fermented Communion wine. In response, Thomas Welch, a Methodist in New York, developed a method of pasteurization that would keep grapes from fermenting and that allowed him to make non-alcoholic wine. Welch called the drink, 'Methodist Unfermented Communion Wine.' It later would be known as Welch's Grape Juice."

NOW WHAT?

Celebration of Holy Communion

(5 minutes)

Have an ordained elder celebrate Holy Communion with the class. Use "A Service of Word and Table I" from page 13 of *The United Methodist Hymnal*.

supplies
- ❑ Communion elements
- ❑ ordained elder
- ❑ copies of *The United Methodist Hymnal*

preparation: Invite an ordained elder to administer Communion.

Closing Ritual

(10 minutes)

Gather the confirmands into a circle. Lead the youth in prayer, giving thanks to God for your time together and for all that the group has learned and experienced. Then go around the circle, inviting each person to pray aloud one word or phrase that describes something he or she learned during the past week of confirmation. After every person has had a chance to contribute a word or phrase, say a brief closing prayer, such as this one:

> God who goes before us, we're grateful to you for your action in our lives. God who moves us to moments of decision, we invite you to act anew in us today. God who will guide us throughout all of our lives, we promise to do our part to grow in faith. We're grateful for the fact that our salvation is a process, and that your grace will never leave us. Amen.

Then invite the confirmands to say aloud and in unison the benediction, "John Wesley's Rule."

note: Before you dismiss, instruct the confirmands to read, reflect on, and journal about the material in the "Sacraments" section of the *Credo Confirmation Student Journal* before your next session. Also encourage them to try to do the activities related to "Sacraments" on the confirmand website.

supplies
- ❑ markerboard
- ❑ marker

preparation: Write the benediction, "John Wesley's Rule," on a markerboard; or print out the poster from the website.

Living a Holy Life

INTRODUCTION

Following Christ requires more than one hour on Sundays; it is a way of life. It means living a holy life, full of faith and good works made possible through God's sanctifying grace.

Going on Toward Perfection

Through prevenient grace, God leads us to faith; through justifying grace, God assures us that we are forgiven and restored to God's favor; through sanctifying grace, God draws us toward Christian perfection.

Jesus said, in his sermon on the mount, "Be perfect, therefore, as your heavenly Father is perfect" (**Matthew 5:48**). The **Book of Hebrews** tells Christians, "Therefore let us go on toward perfection," going beyond the assurance of justification and living a holy life in obedience to God.

Perfection is an intimidating word. Some of the best pitchers in baseball history have never thrown a perfect game, and very few high school students manage to get a perfect score on the SAT. Even those people who are the very best at what they do occasionally make mistakes.

Fortunately, Christian perfection is not about being flawless. It is about being completely in tune with God's will. John Wesley described *perfection* as being "habitually filled with the love of God and neighbor." Through sanctifying grace, God changes our heart so that we desire to be like God. As a result, that change motivates us to "go on toward perfection."

Wesley believed both that Christian perfection is obtainable in our lives and that every person has the ability to obtain it. This belief boldly went against theologians such as John Calvin (the father of current-day Presbyterian and Reformed churches), who believed that God selects certain people to be saved. Wesley understood free will as a gift from God in which all may choose to grow further in grace and become perfect in love.

Be Holy, Go to Class

God's sanctifying grace draws us toward perfection through the gift of holiness. Holiness involves conforming ourselves to the example set by Christ and manifests itself in how we live and what we do.

The first Methodists were members of the Anglican Church who met in small-group class meetings that were focused on holiness. The Methodists would gather in class meetings to pray, read Scripture, and hold one another accountable. Class members would make a covenant with one another to avoid sinful behavior, to perform acts of charity, to participate in worship, and to grow in God's grace. Those who failed to live up to the covenant were expected to repent and, with the help of their fellow class members, continue striving for perfection.

Wesley had three General Rules for those in the Methodist classes: Do no harm, do good, and attend upon all the ordinances of God. By obeying these simple rules, we grow in love of God and neighbor and become holy.

"No Holiness but Social Holiness"

Holiness involves our personal relationship with God and personal habits such as prayer and devotional reading. But holiness also has a social component. "Our Doctrinal Heritage," in *The Book of Discipline,* says, "For Wesley, there is no religion but social religion, no holiness but social holiness." Our personal practices of prayer and devotion should point us to acts of mercy and justice. And these acts that we do out of our love of neighbor help us grow in our relationship with God.

Confirmands need to understand that holiness is an important part of Christian discipleship and that the church provides opportunities for them to grow in personal and social holiness. All Christians should strive for holiness—to become more like Christ and to "go on toward perfection."

SUPPLIES AND PREPARATION

BASIC SUPPLIES		
❑ Bibles of various translations ❑ markerboard or large sheets of paper ❑ markers ❑ pens or pencils	❑ clear tape and/or glue ❑ masking tape ❑ index cards or paper cut about the same size (3-by-5 or 4-by-6) ❑ sheets of posterboard	❑ paper (Use paper that has already been used on one side as much as possible, depending on the activity.) ❑ scissors

ACTIVITY	PREPARATION	OTHER SUPPLIES
WHAT?		
Opening Ritual	Write the opening meditation—which is adapted from Psalm 67—on a markerboard; or project the meditation, using the slide on the website.	❑ vine from previous sessions ❑ vine leaves (1 for each student)
Opening: Chicken or Egg?	Gather supplies.	❑ optional: toy egg, such as a plastic Easter egg ❑ optional: toy chicken
SO WHAT? PART 1		
To Know Is to Love	Cut strips from 2 colors of paper. Write love on 1 strip.	❑ 2 sets of strips of color paper
Puzzled by Holiness	Print out and cut apart copies of the "Puzzled by Holiness" sheet, from the website.	❑ copies of the "Puzzled by Holiness" sheet
It's Perfect!	Gather supplies.	
SO WHAT? PART 2		
A Wholly Holy Life	Print out copies of "A Wholly Holy Life" handout, from the website.	❑ copies of "A Wholly Holy Life" handout
Ingredients for a Holy Life	Make enough copies of "Ingredients for a Holy Life" recipe handout for each student to have one. Gather ingredients for whatever recipe(s) you choose to have the youth make.	❑ copies of the "Ingredients for a Holy Life" recipe handout ❑ ingredients and supplies for whatever recipe you choose ❑ access to a kitchen
Making Holy Choices	Gather supplies.	❑ hat or bowl
NOW WHAT?		
A Holy Reminder	Gather supplies.	❑ note cards or index cards
Closing Ritual	Write the benediction, "John Wesley's Rule," on a markerboard; or print out the poster on the website.	

WHAT?

OPENING RITUAL

(10 minutes)

As confirmands arrive, point them to your confirmation vine; and give each person a leaf. Invite the confirmands to reflect on the previous session and to write on their leaf something they learned or experienced during that session. Ask the confirmands to affix their leaf to the vine. Remind them that these leaves represent ways that we, as Christians and United Methodists, grow in our faith and more fully experience God's grace.

Then invite the youth to read aloud this opening meditation, adapted from **Psalm 67:**

> O God, be gracious to us and bless us
> and make your face to shine upon us,
> that your way may be known upon earth,
> your saving power among all nations.
> Let the peoples praise you, O God;
> let all the peoples praise you!
> Let the nations be glad and sing for joy,
> for you judge the people with equity
> and guide the nations upon earth.

SUPPLIES
- ❑ vine from previous sessions
- ❑ vine leaves (1 for each student)
- ❑ markers or pens

PREPARATION: Have on hand supplies for the youth to add leaves to the vine. Write the opening meditation—which is adapted from Psalm 67—on a markerboard; or project the meditation, using the slide on the website.

NOTE: Take time before you get started to talk with the confirmands about what they read and wrote in the "Sacraments" section of their *Credo Confirmation Student Journals*.

OPENING: CHICKEN OR EGG?

(5 minutes)

If possible, bring with you a toy egg (such as an Easter egg) and a toy chicken.

Hold up the chicken and ask: "Where do chickens come from?" (While "from farms" is technically correct, the preferred answer is "from eggs.")

Then hold up the egg and ask: "Where do eggs come from?" (The preferred answer here is "from chickens.")

Say: "The question, 'Which came first, the chicken or the egg?' is a common way to describe two things or events that completely rely on each other. In the church, the chicken-and-egg question applies to faith and works. You can't have one without the other."

Ask volunteers to read aloud **James 2:14-26.** If you need to, review the stories of Abraham offering Isaac (**Genesis 22:1-19**) and of Rahab (**Joshua 2**). Then ask:

- What does James say about faith and works?
- How does having faith in God through Christ affect the way we act and live our lives?
- How does doing good works bring us closer to God and help us grow in faith?

SUPPLIES
- ❑ optional: toy egg, such as a plastic Easter egg
- ❑ optional: toy chicken

PREPARATION: Write on a large sheet of paper, "Faith causes you to do good works." Then hang the paper on one wall in the room. On a second large sheet of paper write, "Works make you have stronger faith." And hang that paper on the wall opposite the other one.

Say: "John Wesley met Peter Bohler, a Moravian, after his return to England from Georgia, where Wesley had struggled as a missionary to Native Americans. At the time, Wesley was feeling like a failure and questioning his faith. It is at this time that Bohler gave Wesley the now famous advice: 'Preach faith till you have it, and then because you have it you will preach faith.' "

Ask:

- What, do you think, did Peter Bohler mean by "Preach faith till you have it"? (Possible answer: *If we act on our faith, even when our faith feels weak or we have doubts, our faith will grow stronger.*)

SO WHAT? PART 1

supplies
- ❑ Bible
- ❑ 2 sets of paper strips (1 set all one color, and a second set all another color)
- ❑ tape or stapler with staples
- ❑ markers

preparation: Cut 2 sets of strips from color paper, one set from one color and another set of a second color. Write the word *love* on 1 strip of paper.

TO KNOW IS TO LOVE

(10–15 minutes)

Have volunteers read aloud the following Scriptures: **John 3:16; 13:15; 1 John 4:7-8.**

Show the youth the strip of paper on which you have written the word *love*. Then form the strip into a loop, and attach the ends together with staples or tape.

Hand out markers and strips of paper. All of the strips should be the same color. Ask the students to write on their slip one thing that they love. Allow the confirmands to write on additional strips some other things they love. Have the students attach their loops together to create a paper chain.

Then hand out strips of paper of a second color. Ask the confirmands to write on these strips one way in which they show love. Again, have them attach these strips to the paper chain. Allow the confirmands to write on additional strips other ways in which they show love and to attach them to the chain.

While they work, ask:

- What do you love?
- How do you know that you love it?
- How do you show your love for the people and things you love?
- How does it feel to be loved by God?
- How do you show your love to God?

Say: "Love is a gift from God. God loves us and God gives us the ability to love. But God's love for us goes far beyond our earthly love of an activity or favorite food. God loves us unconditionally. The Greek word that the Bible uses to describe this kind of love is *agape* (uh-GAH-pay).

"We respond to God's unconditional love by loving God and loving others. And our love for God and others shows in our actions and in the way we live."

Puzzled by Holiness

(10 minutes)

Give each person a puzzle and a few minutes for assembly.

After they've had a chance to put together the puzzles, ask:

- What do all of the things named on these puzzle pieces have in common? (*They are activities we do regularly—daily or weekly—to help us long term.*)
- What is the point in doing these activities? (*They help us improve ourselves or our skills.*)
- When do these activities seem tedious or unimportant?
- How or why do people continue doing these activities even when they seem boring or difficult?
- Why, do you think, is "living a holy life" written on one of the pieces?
- How do we live a holy life on a daily basis, even while we're busy doing all of these other things?

Say: "Many daily habits involve practicing to get better at something. Living a holy life also is a matter of practice. We practice our faith so that we will mature in faith and grow in our love of God and neighbor."

Ask:

- How can we practice our faith? (Answers include: *worship; celebrate Holy Communion; pray daily; read daily devotions; read and study Scriptures; do acts of mercy and service; meet with other Christians in small groups.*)

supplies
- ❑ copies of the "Puzzled by Holiness" sheet
- ❑ optional: envelopes

preparation: Print out and cut apart copies of the "Puzzled by Holiness" sheet so that you have one puzzle for each confirmand. Optional: To keep the pieces for each puzzle together, put each set into a separate envelope.

It's Perfect!

(10 minutes)

Hand out sheets of paper and assorted markers or colored pencils. Ask the youth to draw or describe their idea of a perfect day. Give them about 5 minutes to work, then have each youth show his or her drawing to the class and explain what about it depicts a perfect day.

Ask volunteers to read aloud **Matthew 5:48** and **Hebrews 6:1-2.** Explain that **Hebrews 6:1-2** is not saying that we should disregard the "basic teaching about Christ." It is saying that this teaching is not enough. We must learn from this teaching and grow in our faith so that we can get beyond the basic and "go on toward perfection."

Ask:

- What does it mean to be perfect?
- What sorts of things do people often describe as "perfect"? (*a perfect day, a perfect game in baseball, a perfect fifth in music, and so on*)
- What, do you think, do Jesus and the author of Hebrews expect by telling us to be perfect?

supplies
- ❑ paper
- ❑ markers or colored pencils

Say: "The idea of going on to Christian perfection is important to United Methodists. This doesn't mean that we all need to become flawless, never sinning or making a mistake. Instead, it means that our hearts are completely in tune with God's will and constantly filled with love of God and neighbor. God's sanctifying grace gives us strength to go on toward perfection through the gift of holiness."

Ask:

- What comes to mind when you hear the word *holy*?
- What does it mean for a person to be holy?

NOTE: If you choose to divide this session into two one-hour classes, break here.

SO WHAT? PART 2

A WHOLLY HOLY LIFE

(10 minutes)

SUPPLIES

- ❑ copies of "A Wholly Holy Life" handout

PREPARATION: Print out copies of "A Wholly Holy Life" handout, from the website.

Say: "Holiness involves becoming more like Christ in the way we live and in all that we do. It involves practicing our faith and making faithful choices in our daily lives. Holiness is only possible with God's help; and one way that God offers help is through the support and witness of other Christians."

Explain that the first Methodists in England met in small groups, called classes, which were focused on holiness. The Methodists would gather in class meetings to pray and to read and study Scripture. Class members made a covenant with one another to avoid sinful behavior, to perform acts of charity, to participate in worship, and to grow in God's grace; and they held one another accountable to this covenant. Those who failed to live up to the covenant were expected to repent and, with the help of their fellow class members, continue striving for perfection.

While holiness was the focal point of those early Methodist class meetings, many other people have influenced The United Methodist Church by advocating holiness.

Introduce the youth to some of these people by handing out the "A Wholly Holy Life" handout. Ask volunteers to read aloud each of the stories. After each one ask:

- What can we learn from this person's example?

INGREDIENTS FOR A HOLY LIFE

(20 minutes)

Have the youth use one of the recipes on the handout to make a meal for someone who is ill at home or a family in need. As a group, deliver the dinner to the specified person(s) after the lesson. You may also choose to cook two entrées, one for the group to eat and the other to give away.

As you add each ingredient of the recipe, read aloud the ingredient for a holy life listed below whose number corresponds to the number of the food ingredient.

After you have finished the recipe, say: "Just as we followed a recipe to create an entrée, if we add the spiritual ingredients to our lives, we can create a holy life. Through the Holy Spirit, we will be molded, shaped, and created to holy perfection. The recipe for personal holiness is not immediate but takes dedication and methodical skill. With every day, however, you will see your heart grow closer to being made complete in God's love."

1. **Grace:** Grace is an essential ingredient to living a holy life. Grace allows us to have a relationship with God and to become more like Christ. Grace assures us that, because of Christ's death and resurrection, our sins are forgiven and we can leave them behind and go on toward perfection.

2. **Faith:** God's grace helps us to have faith in God's promises. As Christians we have faith that God is always with us, that the Holy Spirit guides us and strengthens us, and that we can look forward to eternal life with Christ.

3. **Works:** When we have faith, it will show in our actions and our way of life. Good works are an expression of our faith and give others an example of what it means to be a disciple of Christ.

4. **Prayer:** Through prayer we communicate with God. Communication is essential to every relationship. So living a holy life requires us to pray frequently.

5. **Sacraments:** Jesus gave us the sacraments of baptism and Holy Communion as ways in which we more fully experience God's grace. Baptism is our initiation into the body of Christ. Holy Communion provides nourishment for the Christian journey.

6. **Worship:** In worship Christians gather to remember our story, to give praise and thanks to God, to confess and repent of our sins, to hear God's message, and to prepare ourselves to go out into the world.

7. **Community:** Holiness is not something we do alone. It requires the support of a faith community, and it requires us to go out into the world and to do acts of mercy and justice.

Making Holy Choices

(10–15 minutes)

Say: "John Wesley had three General Rules for the early Methodists who met in class meetings: Do no harm; do good; and attend to the ordinances of God. The 'ordinances of God' are practices of faith through worship, prayer, reading the Bible, and celebrating Holy Communion. Still today, these rules give us guidance for living a holy life."

supplies

- ❑ copies of the "Ingredients for a Holy Life" recipe handout
- ❑ ingredients and supplies for whatever recipe you choose
- ❑ access to a kitchen
- ❑ optional: envelopes

preparation: Make enough copies of "Ingredients for a Holy Life" recipe handout for each student to have one. Gather ingredients for whatever recipe(s) you choose to have the youth make.

supplies
- ❑ markerboard or paper
- ❑ marker
- ❑ scrap paper
- ❑ pens or pencils

Write these three rules on a markerboard or paper.

Hand out scrap paper and pens or pencils. Have each person think of a difficult choice a teenager might have to make. (Examples might include: *choosing between going to church on Sunday or playing in a softball tournament or choosing whether or not to go to a party where there will be alcohol.*) Give the youth a few minutes to come up with their situations and write them on the paper.

Then ask each confirmand to read aloud his or her situation. Have the class discuss the most holy response to each situation. Encourage the youth to consider Wesley's General Rules and what they have learned in previous sessions about the way of discipleship and the Wesleyan quadrilateral.

NOW WHAT?

a holy reminder

(10 minutes)

supplies
- ❑ markerboard
- ❑ marker
- ❑ note cards or index cards
- ❑ pens or pencils

Hand out note cards or index cards and pens or pencils, and remind the confirmands of John Wesley's three General Rules (which still should be on the markerboard from the previous activity).

Instruct the confirmands to write across the top of their note card, "This week I will go on toward perfection by. . . ." Then tell them to number from *1* to *3* below that statement.

Next to the number *1,* have them complete the sentence with one way in which they will commit to doing no harm. (For example, "This week I will go on toward perfection by not hurting my younger brother.")

Next to the number *2,* have them complete the sentence with one way in which they will commit to doing good ("spending time with a friend who recently lost her grandfather").

And next to the number *3,* have them complete the sentence with one way in which they will attend to the ordinances of God ("waking up 20 minutes early to say morning prayers"). Encourage the confirmands to write goals that are achievable within the coming week.

Invite the students to tell about their commitments. Encourage your class to check up with one another during the week and to offer one another encouragement.

Tell the confirmands to keep these cards in a place where they will see them often, such as in their wallets or purses, in their Bibles, or on a desk or dresser in their rooms. Encourage them to talk with their mentors about their commitments.

Closing Ritual

(10 minutes)

Gather the confirmands into a circle. Lead the youth in prayer, giving thanks to God for your time together and for all that the group has learned and experienced. Then go around the circle, inviting each person to pray aloud one word or phrase that describes something he or she learned during the past week of confirmation.

After every person has had a chance to contribute a word or phrase, say a brief closing prayer. Then invite the confirmands to say aloud and in unison the benediction, "John Wesley's Rule."

Note: Before you dismiss, instruct the confirmands to read, reflect on, and journal about the material in the "Living a Holy Life" section of the *Credo Confirmation Student Journal* before your next session. Also encourage them to try to do the activities related to "Living a Holy Life" on the confirmand website.

Supplies

- ❑ markerboard
- ❑ marker

Preparation: Write the benediction, "John Wesley's Rule," on a markerboard; or print out the poster from the website.

Renounce, Reject, Repent

INTRODUCTION

"Do you renounce the spiritual forces of wickedness, reject the evil powers of this world, and repent of your sin?"

This statement, from "Baptismal Covenant I" in *The United Methodist Hymnal* (page 34), is the first vow your confirmands will make if they choose to be confirmed. Before they accept God's freedom and power and confess Jesus Christ as their Savior, they must reject those things that disrupt their relationships with God, with the community of faith, and with all of God's children.

While words such as *evil* and *wickedness* certainly aren't new to confirmands, some younger adolescents might not recognize how these forces are at work in the world around them. It is easy to see evil in a heartless villain in a book or movie; but how is evil at work in our world, our communities, and our hearts? Once we identify these evil and wicked forces, how do we reject and renounce them? And what does it mean to repent of our sin?

A Tradition of Rejecting Evil

United Methodists, and our spiritual forebears, traditionally have understood evil on both a personal and social level. (You covered this in the "Sin" session, in the "Know Your Story" unit.) Our Articles of Religion in *The Book of Discipline of The United Methodist Church* says that humans are "inclined to evil." Humans and the societies, systems, and institutions we create can serve as and be influenced by agents of evil. On an individual level, wickedness and evil are expressed in the mistreatment of others, materialism, and dishonesty. Because all human institutions are made up of imperfect and sinful people, we also see sin at work through structures and groups, such as those that exploit individuals and groups, create and sustain poverty, and destroy God's creation.

Our United Methodist tradition emphasizes personal piety and holiness as a means of rejecting individual wickedness. (You covered holiness and piety in the "Living a Holy Life" session, in the "Confirm Your Faith" unit.) We affirm John Wesley's General Rules for Methodist societies: Do no harm ("avoiding evil of every kind"), do good ("doing good of every possible sort . . . to all [people]"), and attend to the

ordinances of God (such as worship, Holy Communion, prayer, and reading and studying Scripture). In our tradition, rejecting evil isn't just about eliminating negative behaviors; it also involves taking on new behaviors that bring us closer to God and that demonstrate our love of others.

Eliminating social and institutional wickedness also is an important part of our United Methodist tradition. "Our Doctrinal Heritage," included in *The Book of Discipline*, says, "It is our conviction that the good news of the Kingdom must judge, redeem, and reform the sinful social structures of our time." The denominations that would come together to form The United Methodist Church have, for more than two centuries, expressed a concern for the well-being of individuals, families, communities, nations, the global community, and the natural world. In 1908, The Methodist Episcopal Church adopted a social creed affirming its faith in God, confessing its failure to use God's gifts wisely, and committing itself to justice and righteousness. Other Methodist denominations and The Evangelical United Brethren Church issued similar creeds in subsequent decades. The United Methodist Church has since established Social Principles: "a prayerful and thoughtful effort . . . to speak to the human issues in the contemporary world from a sound biblical and theological foundation as historically demonstrated in United Methodist traditions."

A Habit of Renouncing Wickedness

By vowing to "renounce the spiritual forces of wickedness," confirmands are not vowing to memorize the General Rules or Social Principles. Rejecting evil requires that they have an awareness of the ways in which sin and wickedness are at work in their lives and in the world around them. Confirmands must move beyond an understanding of evil as it is expressed in videogames and scary movies to the very real ways in which evil is at work in our world today. Rejecting evil also involves developing habits that bring them closer to God, God's will, and God's priorities.

This session identifies sources of evil and looks at ways in which confirmands can honor their vow to renounce, reject, and repent of evil—both personal and social. To honor this vow, confirmands must commit to honest and holy living and make intentional choices to steer clear of evil influences.

SUPPLIES AND PREPARATION

BASIC SUPPLIES

❑ Bibles of various translations ❑ markerboard or large sheets of paper ❑ markers ❑ pens or pencils	❑ clear tape and/or glue ❑ masking tape ❑ index cards or paper cut about the same size (3-by-5 or 4-by-6) ❑ sheets of posterboard	❑ paper (Use paper that has already been used on one side as much as possible, depending on the activity.) ❑ scissors

ACTIVITY	PREPARATION	OTHER SUPPLIES
WHAT?		
Opening Ritual	Write the responsive reading, which is adapted from Psalm 101:1-4.	❑ vine from previous sessions ❑ vine fruit (1 for each student)
SO WHAT? PART 1		
Promises, Promises	Gather supplies.	❑ wedding photo
Evil Designs	If you choose not to use the hymnal, make copies of the "Confirmation Vows" handout, from the website.	❑ copies of *The United Methodist Hymnal* or copies of the "Confirmation Vows" handout (used in 2 activities)
Wicked Words	Gather supplies.	
Hear Evil, See Evil, Do Evil?	If you choose to use printouts of the home page of various Internet news sites, print them and make copies if you choose to.	❑ newspapers, news magazines, and/or printouts from various Internet news sites ❑ optional: Internet access and a way to project the screen
SO WHAT? PART 2		
Totally Rejected	Make copies of the "D-Fining Words" and "General Rules" handouts.	❑ copies of the "D-Fining Words" and "General Rules" handouts
Rejection Letters	Make copies of the "Rejection Letters" handout.	❑ copies of the "Rejection Letters" handout ❑ copies of *The United Methodist Hymnal* or "Confirmation Vows"
Turn Your Life Around	Gather supplies.	❑ copies of *The United Methodist Hymnal*
Slavery: A Case Study		
NOW WHAT?		
Closing Ritual	Write the benediction, "John Wesley's Rule," on a markerboard; or print out the poster from the website.	

WHAT?

Opening Ritual

(10 minutes)

During the first unit, "Know Your Story," your confirmands added branches to a vine (or tree trunk) as part of a ritual inspired by **John 15:1-9.** During the second unit, "Confirm Your Faith," they added leaves to the branches. During this unit, "Live Your Commitment," the confirmands will be adding fruit. More information is available on the website.

As the confirmands arrive, give each person a cutout of a piece of fruit. Invite each person to write on his or her fruit cutout something that he or she learned, gained, or experienced during the "Confirm Your Faith" unit. Instruct the confirmands to attach their fruit to the branches.

Say: "Jesus says that, if we abide in him, we will 'bear much fruit' (**John 15:5**). For Christians, bearing fruit means living our lives according to God's will and doing God's work in the world. In this unit, we'll get a taste of some of these fruits, as we take a close look at our confirmation vows."

When all of the confirmands have arrived, invite each person to talk briefly about what he or she wrote on his or her piece of fruit. (You might also ask why he or she attached the fruit to a particular branch or near a particular leaf.) Then invite the youth to participate in the following responsive reading, adapted from **Psalm 101:1-4,** that you wrote on a markerboard beforehand:

Leader: We light this candle, remembering that Jesus is the light of the world.

We will sing to you, Lord! We will celebrate your kindness and your justice.

People: We will have nothing to do with evil.

Leader: Please help us learn to do the right thing, and we will be honest and fair in all we do.

People: We will have nothing to do with evil.

Leader: We refuse to be corrupt or to take part in anything crooked; we won't be dishonest or deceitful.

People: We will have nothing to do with evil.

Supplies

- ❑ vine from previous sessions
- ❑ vine fruit (1 for each student)
- ❑ markerboard
- ❑ markers and pens

Preparation: Have on hand supplies for the youth to add fruit to the vine. Write on a markerboard the responsive reading, adapted from Psalm 101:1-4.

Note: Take time before you get started to talk with the confirmands about what they read and wrote in the "Living a Holy Life" section of their *Credo Confirmation Student Journal*.

SO WHAT? PART 1

Supplies
- ❑ wedding photo of a couple (from your wedding album, from your friends or family, from a newspaper or an online wedding announcement)

promises, promises

(10 minutes)

Hold up the wedding picture for the students to see, then pass it around.

Ask:

- Why, do you think, am I showing you a wedding picture during a confirmation lesson?
- What do a wedding and a confirmation service (that is, a worship service in which people are confirmed) have in common? (*Both are religious services; both often take place in a church; a pastor usually presides over both; participants of both often dress up; family and friends are present at both; both have been prepared for and rehearsed; often both are followed by a reception; both involve taking vows.*)
- What vows, or promises, do couples make when they get married?
- Why are vows an important part of a wedding ceremony?

Following your discussion of vows and of the similarities between weddings and confirmation services, tell the confirmands that this unit will focus on the vows that they will have an opportunity to take during the confirmation worship service at the conclusion of your confirmation program. Make the following points:

- Just like a wedding, a service of confirmation involves vows. And, as with wedding vows, these vows must not be taken lightly. Confirmation vows are very special promises that those being confirmed make to God and to God's people, particularly those people who make up our particular faith community or local church.
- The sessions in this final unit of the CREDO CONFIRMATION program will prepare your confirmands to make these vows. It will be each student's choice whether or not to be confirmed. The purpose of the sessions in this unit is to help the confirmands make an informed decision by teaching them what these vows mean and how they will be expected to fulfill these vows.
- When a couple exchanges wedding vows (again hold up the wedding picture), the two persons are making promises to each other as they begin life together in a new relationship. If two people were to get married then say, "See ya," and went their separate ways, they obviously would not be keeping their vows. Similarly, when one is confirmed, that person enters into a new relationship with the church, a relationship marked by the vows that person makes in the presence of God and the church family.

Evil Designs

(10 minutes)

Turn to the confirmation vows on page 34 of *The United Methodist Hymnal* or hand out the "Confirmation Vows" handout from the website. Ask a volunteer to read aloud the first vow:

> On behalf of the whole church, I ask you:
>
> Do you reject the spiritual forces of wickedness,
> reject the evil powers of this world,
> and repent of your sin?

Hand out paper and markers or colored pencils.

Say: "A new band called Evil is producing a new album called *The Spiritual Forces of Wickedness,* and they've asked you to design the album cover." (For youth who have never listened to a CD, much less an actual album, explain that the album cover is the little picture that pops up when they listen to a song on their handheld digital music player.)

Continue: "The band needs a cover that does justice to the band name and album title."

Tell them to focus on the front cover; but if they have time, they might choose to create a track listing of songs that might appear on an album by a band called Evil. The song titles may be existing titles or made-up ones.

Give the students about 5 minutes to work, then invite each youth to present his or her cover ideas to the others, explaining the significance of some of the things he or she has drawn and/or the song titles included.

Supplies

- ❑ paper
- ❑ markers and/or colored pencils
- ❑ copies of *The United Methodist Hymnal* or the "Confirmation Vows" handout

Preparation: If you choose not to use the hymnal, make copies of the "Confirmation Vows" handout, from the website.

Wicked Words

(10 minutes)

Write on a markerboard or paper the words *evil* and *wickedness*. As the confirmands respond to the following questions, add their answers to the board or paper:

- What words, phrases, or images come to mind when you hear the words *wickedness* and *evil*?
- What feelings do you connect with these words?
- What actions and events come to mind when you hear the words *evil* and *wickedness*? (You might choose to add examples such as *terrorism, slavery, genocide,* and *pollution* if the confirmands do not name them.)

Invite the youth to look over what you have written then ask:

- What makes something wicked or evil?

Supplies

- ❑ markerboard or paper
- ❑ markers or pens

SUPPLIES

- ❑ newspapers, news magazines, and/or printouts of the home page of various Internet news sites
- ❑ optional: Internet access (If possible project the computer screen.)

PREPARATION: If you choose to use printouts of the home page of various Internet news sites, print them and make copies if you choose to.

HEAR EVIL, SEE EVIL, DO EVIL?

(10–15 minutes)

Say: "Sometimes when we hear words like *evil* or *wicked,* we think of villains and situations from movies, books, or videogames."

Ask:

- What are some fictional persons or situations that you would describe as evil or wicked?

Then say: "Sadly, evil and wickedness aren't confined to imaginary worlds but are a very real part of our world."

If you have Internet access in your meeting space, go to a news website. (If possible, project the computer screen so that everyone can see it well.) Scroll through the headlines and ask the youth to point out news stories where they see examples of wickedness and evil. If you do not have Internet access, bring in copies of newspapers and news magazines or print outs of the home pages of assorted news websites.

After the confirmands have selected several examples, ask:

- What makes the events and/or people in these stories wicked or evil?

Then say: "Unfortunately, some of us—or our friends and family—have experienced evil in very up-close-and-personal ways, through forces such as violence, abuse, and addiction. Wickedness and evil don't just happen in faraway places. They touch people's lives and become very real to us and to people we care about."

Ask:

- Where do you see wickedness and evil in our community? in your school?
- How can wickedness and evil affect families and/or churches?

SO WHAT? PART 2

TOTALLY REJECTED

(10 minutes)

To help the confirmands better understand evil and wickedness, raise the following points:

- **Christians affirm that evil and wickedness are present in the world.** (You've named several examples already in this session.) But Christians also believe that God is always present and active and is more powerful than evil.
- **Evil is the result of sin.** Because all people are sinful, we create structures and institutions that exploit individuals and groups, create and sustain poverty, and destroy God's creation. Rejecting evil involves both resisting the temptation to do evil and resisting the temptation to encourage or participate in evil. That is, we should strive to eliminate sin in our lives and we should also be careful not to support groups and institutions that are responsible for evil on a larger scale.
- **Obviously, we are not God, and we have trouble seeing the big picture.** We see poverty, starvation, terrorism, abuse, and murder; and we become overwhelmed. It's tempting to say, "I'm too young to do anything about all this stuff." Sometimes, we even feel powerless to address evil in our homes and schools.
- **Our United Methodist tradition, and specifically our confirmation vows, give us some help in responding to the forces of evil and wickedness.**

Hand out the "D-Fining Words" worksheet from the website.

Ask volunteers to look up in a dictionary and read aloud the definitions of *renounce, reject,* and *repent*. Have the confirmands write the definitions for each word in the "D-Fining Words" boxes on the activity sheet.

Ask:

- Think back to the news stories involving evil and wickedness that we identified earlier. How were the people you read about in these stories rejecting evil?
- Whom have you known, or known of, who has taken a stand against evil? Who were they, and what did they do?

Then distribute copies of the "General Rules" handouts from the website.

Say: "When John Wesley was organizing Methodist groups in England in the eighteenth century, one of his rules for the early Methodists was to avoid 'evil of every kind.' He gave specific examples of the evil that we should avoid."

NOTE: If you choose to divide this session into two one-hour classes, break here.

SUPPLIES

- ❑ copies of the "D-Fining Words" handout
- ❑ copies of the "General Rules" handouts (only on the website)
- ❑ markerboard
- ❑ marker
- ❑ paper
- ❑ pens or pencils

PREPARATION: Make copies of the "D-Fining Words" and "General Rules" handouts.

Ask volunteers to read aloud John Wesley's first General Rule for Methodist Societies, "Do No Harm," focusing on the examples of evil that Wesley lists. Then challenge the confirmands to think about what examples of evil Wesley might list if he were writing today. Which items would remain unchanged, which would need to be revised or replaced, and what would need to be added? Record their ideas on a markerboard.

As time permits, ask the group to come to a consensus on a list of 10–15 items. Have a volunteer record these examples of doing harm on a sheet of paper. Ask another volunteer to take the list and to take responsibility for typing up the group's version of John Wesley's first rule, sending it to you so that you can send the document to the rest of the group, post it to a group page on a social networking site, or send it to someone who can post it on the congregation's website.

supplies

- ❑ copies of the "Rejection Letters" handout
- ❑ copies of *The United Methodist Hymnal* or the "Confirmation Vows" handout (used in the "Evil Designs" "Rejection Letters" activities)
- ❑ pens or pencils

preparation: Make copies of the "Rejection Letters" handout.

rejection letters

(15 minutes)

Say: "We often feel powerless in the face of evil and wickedness, but God calls us to take a stand against these forces and to actively reject them. We cannot accept poverty; we must work to eliminate it. We cannot accept prejudice; we must, by our witness, help change people's thinking."

Again, ask a volunteer to read aloud the first confirmation vow from the hymnal (page 34) or the "Confirmation Vows" handout.

Ask:

- Think about the examples of evil and wickedness you identified and of the definitions you read of *renounce* and *reject*. What, do you think, does it mean to "renounce the spiritual forces of wickedness" and "reject the evil powers of this world"?

Invite the youth to write these phrases in their own words on the "Rejection Letters" handout.

Then say: "When you vow to renounce wickedness and reject evil, you are promising to stand up against and actively resist any activities that are opposed to God's will. Some forces of evil may seem too big for us to take on, but God calls us—as individuals and as the church—to stand up and take action against the evil and wickedness that threaten God's children and all of God's creation. But we aren't powerless to do this. As Paul affirms in his letter to the Philippians, 'I can do all things through [Christ] who gives me strength' (**Philippians 4:13**)."

Invite students to spend a few minutes thinking of specific ways they can personally renounce and resist evil, both locally and globally. Have them complete the "Letter of Intent" on the "Rejection Letters" handout. Then ask for volunteers to read aloud what they have written.

Turn Your Life Around

(10 minutes)

Take another look at the first confirmation vow:

> On behalf of the whole church, I ask you:
>
> Do you reject the spiritual forces of wickedness,
> reject the evil powers of this world,
> and repent of your sin?

Ask:

- In addition to *renounce* and *reject,* what is the third "r" word in this vow? (*repent*)

Ask two youth to stand up so that they are facing each other. Have one of the two persons play the role of "sin." Have the other play the role of a Christian. Instruct the Christian to turn from "sin" and walk away.

Say: "This activity may seem strange, but it illustrates the meaning of the word *repent*. Repenting is more than just feeling sorry or regretting something that we've done; it also involves turning away from that behavior."

Ask:

- Why, do you think, is the phrase *repent of your sin* included in this particular confirmation vow?
- How is the phrase *repent of your sin* connected to the other parts of the vow?

Say: "How can we stand up against and fight evil and wickedness in the world if we are allowing it to have power in our own lives? To follow Christ and to call Christ our Lord and Savior means that we must consistently turn from sin. Sin disrupts our relationships with God and others and keeps us from doing the things God calls us to do. When we repent of sin, we turn away from the evil in our lives and turn to face the world as witnesses of Christ's love and redemption."

Hand out copies of *The United Methodist Hymnal,* and ask the students to turn to the "Prayers of Confession, Assurance, and Pardon," numbers 890–893. Ask the students to read through these prayers, paying attention to what the prayers say about repentance and turning away from sin.

As time permits, challenge them to work together as a group to write their own prayer of confession and repentance.

Supplies

- ❑ copies of *The United Methodist Hymnal*
- ❑ paper
- ❑ pens or pencils

Slavery: A Case Study

(5 minutes)

Read aloud the following:

> The denominations that would come together to form The United Methodist Church were established in the United States in the late eighteenth and early nineteenth centuries. At that time the country was divided over the issue of slavery, and many of our founders and early leaders—people such as John Wesley, Philip William Otterbein, Martin Boehm, Jacob Albright, and Francis Asbury—fiercely opposed slavery. But as Methodism spread, the new church attracted many slave owners and others who supported (or did not oppose) the institution of slavery. The debate over whether to renounce or accept slavery split the church.
>
> In the early nineteenth century two African American churches—the African Methodist Episcopal Church and the African Methodist Episcopal Zion Church—split from the Methodists. The issue of slavery also was one reason that the Free Methodist and Wesleyan Churches would split from the Methodists. Meanwhile, the Evangelical and United Brethren Churches, because of their unwavering rejection of slavery, were unable to spread into southern slave states.
>
> The biggest rift came in 1844, when the Methodist Episcopal Church declared that Bishop James O. Andrew, who had acquired slaves through marriage, must free his slaves or no longer serve as bishop. General Conference delegates from the South reacted by leaving the Methodist Episcopal Church and forming the Methodist Episcopal Church, South. The two branches would come back together nearly a century later. Methodists had to repent of their sins of racism and support of slavery, and turn in a new direction. Today The United Methodist Church, while far from perfect, is a strong advocate of equality and human rights; and it opposes human trafficking and slavery around the world.

NOW WHAT?

Closing Ritual

(10 minutes)

Gather the confirmands into a circle. During the first unit, "Know Your Story," you led this time of prayer. During the second unit, "Confirm Your Faith," one of the confirmands took the lead in closing each session. During this unit, "Live Your Commitment," no one person will lead this time of prayer. Instead, go around the circle; and allow each person to offer a prayer thanking God for your time together and all that the group has learned and experienced and asking for God's guidance as you go forth.

Close this prayer time by saying aloud and in unison the benediction, John Wesley's Rule.

Note: Before you dismiss, instruct the confirmands to read, reflect on, and journal about the material in the "Renounce, Reject, Repent" section of the *Credo Confirmation Student Journal* before your next session. Also encourage them to try to do the activities related to "Renounce, Reject, Repent" on the confirmand website.

Supplies
- ❑ markerboard
- ❑ marker

Preparation: Write the benediction, "John Wesley's Rule," on a markerboard; or print it out from the website.

Accept

INTRODUCTION

"Do you accept the freedom and power God gives you to resist evil, injustice, and oppression in whatever forms they present themselves?"

Freedom: It's what adolescents yearn for—freedom to choose their own friends, freedom to make their own decisions (and mistakes), freedom to dress the way they want to dress, freedom to drive a car, freedom to express themselves, freedom to make choices about their future. While this yearning for freedom is a normal part of adolescent development, too often youth get the impression that freedom is just living without rules—or, at least, living by whatever rules *they* choose.

God's Gift of Freedom

Properly understood, freedom is a gift from God. Each person may exercise his or her free will and may use this freedom to accept God's grace or resist God's grace. As expressed in the Articles of Religion of the Methodist Church, "God's initiative in salvation allows for, empowers, and requires a free human response to God's 'amazing grace' " (Article 8). With this freedom, we also choose whether and how we will use the abilities, opportunities, and power that God gives us. Will we use these abilities and opportunities to resist, cooperate with, or ignore "evil, injustice, and oppression in whatever forms they present themselves"?

What good news for young people! Freedom! How can you not be interested in a religion that offers you that? In our United Methodist tradition, we understand that free will is most fulfilling when we temper it with discipline and accountability. Using our freedom in Christ, without being shaped, trained, or nurtured by spiritual discipline, is like being a gifted athlete who demonstrates exceptional strength, speed, and agility but doesn't know how to use his or her gifts to benefit the team and, therefore, struggles with the pressures of competition. For Christians, using one's free will without the training, practice, and accountability that come from spiritual disciplines and a Christian community often results in self-centered pursuits that do not bear fruit. Thus accepting God's freedom also means accepting Christian discipline and accountability.

Accepting the Freedom

Specifically, those who take the vows of confirmation and baptism agree to accept God's freedom to "resist evil, injustice, and oppression." The previous session dealt with rejecting the "spiritual forces of wickedness." We can reject evil because God gives us the freedom and the power to resist evil. Although we live in a broken and sinful world, we can—by the grace of God—choose not to participate in evil, injustice, and oppression.

The word *resist* implies that one is withstanding some sort of force or pressure. And resisting evil, injustice, and oppression is not something that we do passively. Rather, we must train ourselves. Again, faithfully accepting freedom also means faithfully accepting discipline.

John Wesley felt that discipline was essential to Christian living; and he expected those in his Methodist societies to "attend to the ordinances of God" through spiritual practices such as worship, prayer, studying Scripture, celebrating Holy Communion, and abstaining from activities that would separate us from God. These disciplines, among others, give us the spiritual strength and balance we need to resist the pressures of wickedness that we inevitably encounter.

In this session, confirmands will consider the meaning of freedom and the relationship between freedom and discipline. They will examine what it means to resist evil, injustice, and oppression; and they will commit to taking on disciplines that will strengthen them spiritually and draw them closer to God.

SUPPLIES AND PREPARATION

BASIC SUPPLIES		
❑ Bibles of various translations ❑ markerboard or large sheets of paper ❑ markers ❑ pens or pencils	❑ clear tape and/or glue ❑ masking tape ❑ index cards or paper cut about the same size (3-by-5 or 4-by-6) ❑ sheets of posterboard	❑ paper (Use paper that has already been used on one side as much as possible, depending on the activity.) ❑ scissors

ACTIVITY	PREPARATION	OTHER SUPPLIES
WHAT?		
Opening Ritual	Have on hand supplies for the youth to add fruit to the vine.	❑ vine from previous sessions ❑ vine fruit (1 for each student) ❑ copies of *The United Methodist Hymnal*
Call to Worship	Write on a markerboard the responsive reading, make copies of the "Call to Worship" (from the website) to hand out, or download the slide (website) to project.	❑ candle ❑ a lighter or matches ❑ optional: photocopies or slide of "Call to Worship"and a way to project the slide
SO WHAT? PART 1		
Life Without Rules	Gather supplies.	❑ ball (preferably one that isn't associated with a particular sport, such as a soccer ball or baseball)
Words of Freedom (and Discipline)	Make copies of the "Words of Freedom (and Discipline)" handout, from the website.	❑ copies of both pages of the "Words of Freedom (and Discipline)" handout
Freedom Rules!	Make copies of the "General Rules" handout, from the website.	❑ copies of *UM Hymnal* ❑ "General Rules" handout ❑ large sheets of paper or posterboard and art supplies
SO WHAT? PART 2		
Get Fired Up!	Write each of the phrases from 1 Thessalonians 5:16-19 (NIV) on a separate slip of paper. Print out the information about the cross and flame symbol, on the website.	❑ prepared slips of paper ❑ candle ❑ a lighter or matches ❑ copies of *The United Methodist Hymnal* ❑ information sheet about the UM cross and flame symbol
Resistance		
Transformers	Make copies of the "Transformers: Christians Who Chose to Change the World" handout. Write on a markerboard the questions in the activity.	❑ copies of the "Transformers" handout
NOW WHAT?		
Personal Training	Make copies of the "General Rules" and "Training Schedule" handouts.	❑ copies of the "General Rules" handout ❑ copies of the "Training Schedule" handout
Closing Ritual	Write the benediction, "John Wesley's Rule," on a markerboard; or print out the poster from the website.	

WHAT?

OPENING RITUAL

(10 minutes)

As the confirmands arrive, give each of them a cutout of a piece of fruit. Invite the confirmands to reflect on the previous session and to write on their fruit something they learned or experienced during that session. Ask the confirmands to affix their fruit to the vine. Remind them that these fruit represent ways that we, as Christians and United Methodists, live in response to God's grace.

When all of the confirmands have arrived, invite each person to talk briefly about what he or she wrote on his or her piece of fruit. (You might also ask why he or she attached the fruit to a particular branch or near a particular leaf.) Then hand out copies of *The United Methodist Hymnal,* and ask the confirmands to turn to the "Affirmation From 1 Corinthians 15:1-6 and Colossians 1:15-20" (888). Invite a volunteer to read the Leader part. Everyone else, including you, should read the part of the People.

SUPPLIES
- ❑ vine from previous sessions
- ❑ vine fruit (1 for each student)
- ❑ copies of *The United Methodist Hymnal*

PREPARATION: Have on hand supplies for the youth to add fruit to the vine.

NOTE: Take time before you get started to talk with the confirmands about what they read and wrote in the "Renounce, Reject, Repent" section of their *Credo Confirmation Student Journal.*

CALL TO WORSHIP

(5 minutes)

Write the "Call to Worship" (below) on a markerboard, project it using the slide, or distribute the handout. Ask a volunteer to serve as the Leader. The Leader should light a candle then lead the group in the following responsive reading inspired by **Psalm 119:**

Leader: Let praise cascade off my lips.

People: Invigorate my soul so that I can praise you well.

Leader: Let your love, God, shape my life with salvation.

People: And I'll stride freely through wide-open spaces.

Leader: I see the limits to everything human.

People: But the horizons can't contain your commands.

Leader: I'll tell the world what I find, speak out boldly in public, unembarrassed.

People: I cherish your commandments.

Leader: The way you tell me to live is always right; help me understand it so that I can live to the fullest.

People: Amen.

SUPPLIES
- ❑ candle
- ❑ a lighter or matches
- ❑ optional: marker and markerboard, photocopies or slide of "Call to Worship"
- ❑ optional: a way to project the slide

PREPARATION: Write on a markerboard the responsive reading, make copies of the "Call to Worship" (from the website) to hand out, or download the slide (from the website) to project.

SO WHAT? PART 1

supplies
- ❏ ball, preferably one that isn't associated with a particular sport, such as a soccer ball or baseball
- ❏ markerboard
- ❏ marker

Life Without Rules
(15 minutes)

Clear a large space in the middle of the room, and divide the confirmands and adult volunteers into two teams.

Say: "We're going to play a game that you have never played before. I know that you have never played it before because it hasn't been created yet. I am giving you the freedom to design a game that uses this ball."

Show the youth the ball. Then allow the students a couple minutes to brainstorm ideas for their game. Then interrupt them to give them one stipulation: Their game may not have any rules. It must be a freestyle game, because this session is about freedom.

Give the youth some time to wrestle with the task of designing a game with no rules. Remind them about the "no rules" requirement whenever anyone suggests an idea that is actually a rule, such as an idea about how to play or how to score. When the youth start to get really frustrated, invite them to reflect on the activity.

Write the word *freedom* on a markerboard. Then ask:

- What thoughts, feelings, or images come to mind when you hear the word *freedom*? (Write the students' ideas on the markerboard, below *freedom*.)
- What did you think or feel when I told you that you had the freedom to create your own game?
- What was it like to design a game with no rules?
- Consider the game of ________ [insert the name of a game or sport that your confirmands are familiar with]. What are some of the rules of that game?
- What are some of the rules that you have to follow at home? at school? at church? among your friends?
- Why are rules helpful and important in games that we play?
- Why are rules helpful and important in life?

Words of Freedom (and Discipline)
(15 minutes)

Distribute both pages of the "Words of Freedom (and Discipline)" handout. Give the confirmands about 5 minutes to complete the worksheet by reading each of the statements, circling any words or phrases that relate to freedom, and underlining any words or phrases that relate to rules or discipline.

Invite volunteers to talk about some of the words and phrases they circled or underlined. Then ask:

- What does each of these texts say to you about freedom? about discipline? about the relationship between freedom and discipline?
- Which text most rings true with you? Why?
- After reading these texts, how, do you think, are freedom and discipline related?

supplies
- ❑ copies of both pages of the "Words of Freedom (and Discipline)" handout
- ❑ pens and pencils

preparation: Make copies of both pages of the "Words of Freedom (and Discipline)" handout, from the website.

Freedom Rules!

(15–20 minutes)

Hand out hymnals.

Say: "We've been talking about freedom because freedom is a big part of one of our confirmation vows." Read aloud the second vow on page 34 as a group:

> Do you accept the freedom and power God gives you
> to resist evil, injustice, and oppression
> in whatever forms they present themselves?

Refer to the list of thoughts, feelings, and images that the youth listed as being associated with freedom (from "Life Without Rules"). Name any examples that connote permissiveness or living without rules or boundaries.

Then say: "When you tried to create a game without rules, you discovered that freedom without boundaries is a disaster. The texts that you read on the 'Words of Freedom' handout emphasized the relationship between freedom and discipline."

Challenge the confirmands to name some things that they are free to do but that they will not be able to do if they are not disciplined. (For instance, they are free to become collegiate athletes, architects, neurosurgeons, or concert musicians; but they will not achieve any of these goals unless they have extraordinary discipline.) Talk with the students about how a lack of discipline can place limits on what we can do and how it actually make us less free.

Say: "Too often we think of discipline as something that constrains or limits us; it usually is not something that we associate with freedom. But as we've discovered, discipline is really more like training. As Christians who accept God's gift of freedom, we need to understand that the more disciplined (or well-trained) we are, the better equipped we are to do the work that God calls us to do and to live the abundant life that God desires for us."

Explain that discipline, or spiritual training, was so important to John Wesley that he created a list of rules and disciplines that he expected people in his Methodist societies to practice.

Distribute copies of the "General Rules" handout. (Confirmands may recognize this handout from the previous session, "Renounce, Reject, Repent.") Ask the confirmands to name John Wesley's three General Rules ("Do no harm, do good,

supplies
- ❑ copies of *The United Methodist Hymnal*
- ❑ copies of the "General Rules" handout
- ❑ large sheets of paper or posterboard
- ❑ assorted art supplies

preparation: Make copies of the "General Rules" handout, from the website.

and attend to the ordinances of God"); then give them a couple minutes to read through some of the examples that Wesley gives for each rule. (Taking a look at Wesley's examples of doing no harm was part of the previous session.)

Set out the large paper or posterboard and assorted art supplies; and ask the youth to make posters promoting the General Rules. They may create a poster publicizing all three of the rules or focusing on one of the three. Encourage creativity.

While they work, ask:

- How easy or difficult is it to be faithful to these three rules?
- What are some additional examples of doing no harm (beyond the ones Wesley has provided)?
- What are some additional examples of doing good?

Allow each student to present his or her poster. Display the posters in your meeting space or (preferably) elsewhere in the church building where others can see them.

NOTE: If you choose to divide this session into two one-hour classes, break here.

SO WHAT? PART 2

SUPPLIES

- prepared slips of paper
- candle
- a lighter or matches
- copies of *The United Methodist Hymnal*
- information sheet about the United Methodist cross and flame symbol

PREPARATION: Write each of the phrases from 1 Thessalonians 5:16-19 (NIV) on a separate slip of paper. Print out the information about the cross and flame symbol, on the website.

GET FIRED UP!

(10–15 minutes)

Reread the confirmation vow for this session:

> Do you accept the freedom and power God gives you
> to resist evil, injustice, and oppression
> in whatever forms they present themselves?

Say: "We've talked a lot about freedom, but this vow also mentions power. Not only does God give us the freedom to resist evil, injustice, and oppression; but God also gives us the power we need to make faithful choices."

To help the confirmands understand where this power comes from, set out the slips from **1 Thessalonians 5:16-19,** and challenge the confirmands to work together to reconstruct these verses. Offer assistance as needed. When properly assembled, the slips should read as follows:

Be joyful always; pray continually; give thanks in all circumstances, for this is God's will for you in Christ Jesus. Do not put out the Spirit's fire.

Say: "Paul wrote these words at the end of his letter to the Christian church in Thessalonica (THES-uh-luh-NIGH-kuh). He tells the members of this church to practice their faith by always praying and being joyful and thankful, but he also reminds them about the source of their power: the Holy Spirit."

Light a candle and ask the confirmands to name characteristics of a fire. (*It gives heat, provides light, can be used to generate energy, offers comfort, and so on.*) Many of these attributes of fire also are attributes of the Spirit.

Hand out the hymnals and point out that on the cover is the cross and flame, the symbol of The United Methodist Church. Discuss the significance of the flame being part of this symbol. Give the youth more information on the cross and flame from the information sheet from the website.

Say: "Paul tells us not to 'put out the Spirit's fire'; because, among other things, the Holy Spirit gives us the power to resist evil, injustice, and oppression."

resistance

(10–15 minutes)

Have the participants (including adults) pair off so that (as much as possible) partners are approximately the same height and weight. Instruct the partners to face each other, with their legs shoulder-width apart. Have each person hold out his or her arms and press his or her palms against the palms of his or her partner. Tell the confirmands, on your signal, to apply pressure to try to make their partners lose balance. At the same time, they must resist the pressure from their partners and maintain their own balance.

Have partners play several times, as time permits. If some of the youth in your group cannot participate in this activity because of physical limitations, select two volunteers to demonstrate the game for the class.

Ask:

- How difficult was it to resist the pressure from your partner and to maintain your balance?

Say: "Like the game we just played, the confirmation vow we've been discussing involves resistance. As members of the body of Christ, we vow to 'resist evil, injustice, and oppression.' Were you to want to get really good at this game, you could make a habit of doing strength and balance exercises that would help you resist the pressure and stand your ground. Being faithful to our confirmation vows by resisting evil, injustice, and oppression also requires regular exercises, or spiritual disciplines."

Ask:

- What are some forms of "evil, injustice, and oppression"? (The confirmands should recall some examples of "spiritual forces of wickedness" from the previous session, "Renounce, Reject, Repent.")
- How do these examples of evil, injustice, and oppression put pressure on you or tempt you? (Answers might include *pressure to drink or do drugs, temptation to spread rumors or*

bully a peer, pressure to focus on material possessions, temptation to ignore problems such as poverty, hunger, and slavery.)

- What are some ways that you can resist this pressure?

Transformers

(10–15 minutes)

supplies
- ❑ copies of the "Transformers" handout (one for every two confirmands)

preparation: Make copies of the "Transformers: Christians Who Chose to Change the World" handout. Write on a markerboard the questions in the activity.

Distribute the "Transformers: Christians Who Chose to Change the World" handout. Invite a volunteer to read one of the profiles of a Christian who used his or her God-given freedom to change the world. Then discuss the following questions:

- How did this person use his or her freedom to follow Christ?
- What forms of evil, injustice, or oppression did this person resist or reject?
- How do you see the power of the Holy Spirit at work in this person's life?

Continue until you have read about and discussed all four "Transformers."

NOW WHAT?

Personal Training

(10 minutes)

supplies
- ❑ copies of the "General Rules" handout
- ❑ copies of the "Training Schedule" handout
- ❑ pens or pencils

preparation: Make copies of the "General Rules" and "Training Schedule" handouts.

Return to the "General Rules" handout.

Say: "John Wesley believed that real, genuine faith is to be lived out (or 'manifested' or 'fleshed out') in the life of a Christian. His three General Rules guide us by giving us specific ways that we can live out our faith. Wesley didn't intend for these rules to be church law but saw them as a 'way of discipleship' (*Discipline,* page 48). In other words, when we follow these rules, we train ourselves, or *discipline* ourselves, to live our lives in relationship with Christ and to resist the pressures of evil, injustice, and oppression."

Ask volunteers to read aloud the third rule, "Attend to the ordinances of God" from the "General Rules" handout, including all of the examples that Wesley gives. Allow the youth to name other spiritual practices that Wesley did not include. (These might include fellowship with other Christians, devotional reading, serving others, and so forth.)

Have the confirmands read through this rule again—this time silently and prayerfully asking God to reveal to them which ordinances, or spiritual disciplines, that they could devote themselves to as part of their "training" as disciples of Christ.

Give the youth a couple minutes to reflect then distribute the "Training Schedule" handout. Invite them to fill in the

schedule by labeling the days of the month and writing the disciplines that they will commit to on the appropriate days.

Allow a couple minutes for the confirmands to fill in their schedules. (They might need to finish their schedules at home.) Then have them discuss their training schedule with a partner. Encourage the partners to hold each other accountable to their commitments by checking up with each other sometime during the week.

NOTE: Before you dismiss, instruct the confirmands to read, reflect on, and journal about the material in the "Accept" section of the *Credo Confirmation Student Journal* before your next session. Also encourage them to try to do the activities related to "Accept" on the confirmand website.

CLOSING RITUAL

(5 minutes)

Gather the confirmands into a circle. Go around the circle and allow each person to offer a prayer thanking God for your time together and all that the group has learned and experienced and asking for God's guidance as you go forth.

Close this prayer time by saying aloud and in unison the benediction, John Wesley's Rule.

SUPPLIES

- ❑ markerboard
- ❑ marker

PREPARATION: Write the benediction, "John Wesley's Rule," on a markerboard; or print it out from the website.

Confess

INTRODUCTION

"Do you confess Jesus Christ as your Savior, put your whole trust in his grace, and promise to serve him as your Lord in union with the church, which Christ has opened to people of all ages, nations, and races?"

Confessing often makes people nervous. To confess is to openly embrace and associate with something we hold to be true. When we confess a belief or an allegiance, we reveal something important about ourselves and invite others to hold us accountable. Our confessions may range from trivial to life changing: We confess to liking a color or a musical artist; we confess opposition to certain political practices; we confess an affinity for a sports team. In all of these cases, confessing removes from us the opportunity to say, "Well, I never actually said. . . ."

Our society puts a premium on our giving and keeping our word. In criminal justice, confessing to a crime closes a case. When a criminal confesses, no further investigation is necessary. In journalism, reporters are trained to gather information from individuals through careful questioning, eliciting confessions through conversation. Confession indicates a deep commitment to a belief, a truth, or a way of life.

a positive and proactive confession

Within the "Renunciation of Sin and Profession of Faith" portion of "Baptismal Covenant I" (page 34 of *The United Methodist Hymnal*)—the first vows in the confirmation service, following the introduction and "Presentation of Candidates"—we find a call to confession. This service does not ask those being confirmed to confess their sins; rather it asks them to repent of their sins. The confession is positive and proactive: "Do you confess Jesus Christ as your Savior, put your whole trust in his grace, and promise to serve him as your Lord, in union with the church which Christ has opened to people of all ages, nations, and races?"

With difficulty, we must accept that the simple words "I do" are capable of containing our answer to this question: to proclaim Jesus Christ as God and Savior; to trust his grace to draw us toward Christian perfection; to join with all believers—regardless of age, nation, or race—in service to God.

Having rejected and accepted, we can now confess

This confession is the culmination of our previous rejection of wickedness, evil, and sin and of acceptance of God's power to resist the same. Having repented of sin and accepted God's freedom, those taking these vows can confess Christ and their reliance on God's grace and promise to join with others in doing the work of God's kingdom. The final phrase in this vow "people of all ages, nations, and races" echoes Paul's teaching in **Galatians 3:26-29:**

> For in Christ Jesus you are all children of God through faith. As many of you as were baptized into Christ have clothed yourselves with Christ. There is no longer Jew or Greek, there is no longer slave or free, there is no longer male and female; for all of you are one in Christ Jesus. And if you belong to Christ, then you are Abraham's offspring, heirs according to the promise.

This session will help you guide the youth as they confess Christ as Savior, learn to trust in his grace, promise to serve him as Lord, and cooperate in union with the church that surrounds them. The power of our given word is substantial. As we confess Christ with our mouths, may we also learn to confess him with our lives.

SUPPLIES AND PREPARATION

BASIC SUPPLIES

❑ Bibles of various translations ❑ markerboard or large sheets of paper ❑ markers ❑ pens or pencils	❑ clear tape and/or glue ❑ masking tape ❑ index cards or paper cut about the same size (3-by-5 or 4-by-6) ❑ sheets of posterboard	❑ paper (Use paper that has already been used on one side as much as possible, depending on the activity.) ❑ scissors

ACTIVITY	PREPARATION	OTHER SUPPLIES
WHAT?		
Opening Ritual	Have on hand supplies for the youth to add fruit to the vine.	❑ vine from previous sessions ❑ vine fruit (1 for each student) ❑ copies of *The United Methodist Hymnal*
Signed, Sealed, Delivered		
The Last Thing You Expected	Prepare posterboard strips with unusual facts about yourself.	❑ prepared posterboard strips
SO WHAT? PART 1		
Trust: The One Who Knows	Optional: Make copies of the "Confirmation Vows" handout, from the website.	❑ copies of *The United Methodist Hymnal* or of the "Confirmation Vows" worksheet
Trust: Simple Math	Prepare posterboard or construction paper as described in the "Preparation" in the margin next to the activity.	❑ sheets of posterboard or construction paper prepared according to the instructions
Promise: Pinkie Swears		
Promise: Real Promises		
SO WHAT? PART 2		
Unity: Closer Than a Brother		
Unity: Put Me in, Coach	Gather items specific to your congregation, showing its connectedness to other UM congregations.	❑ items specific to your congregation, showing its connectedness to other UM congregations
NOW WHAT?		
Closing Ritual	Write the benediction, "John Wesley's Rule," on a markerboard; or print out the poster from the website.	

WHAT?

Opening Ritual

(10 minutes)

As the confirmands arrive, give each of them a cutout of a piece of fruit. Invite the confirmands to reflect on the previous session and to write on their fruit something they learned or experienced during that session. Ask the confirmands to affix their fruit to the vine. Remind them that these fruit represent ways that we, as Christians and United Methodists, live in response to God's grace.

When all of the confirmands have arrived, invite each person to talk briefly about what he or she wrote on his or her piece of fruit. (You might also ask why he or she attached the fruit to a particular branch or near a particular leaf.) Then hand out copies of *The United Methodist Hymnal,* and ask the confirmands to turn to the "Affirmation From 1 Corinthians 15:1-6 and Colossians 1:15-20" (888). Invite a volunteer to read the Leader part. Everyone else should read the part of the People.

Supplies
- ❑ vine from previous sessions
- ❑ vine fruit (1 for each student)
- ❑ copies of *The United Methodist Hymnal*

Preparation: Have on hand supplies for the youth to add fruit to the vine.

Note: Take time before you get started to talk with the confirmands about what they read and wrote in the "Accept" section of their *Credo Confirmation Student Journal.*

Signed, Sealed, Delivered

(15–20 minutes)

Begin by asking the confirmands:

- What comes to mind when you hear the word *confession*?

Say: "Often people associate the word *confession* with guilt, apology, or penitence. And honestly admitting our mistakes *is* an act of confession. But confession is much more than just telling people that we messed up."

Hand out paper.

Say: "Imagine that you have been arrested because of your faith, and you have decided to write a full confession of your 'crime.' As clearly as possible, write what you believe to be true about your faith and your relationship with God. When you have finished, sign your name to your confession."

Read aloud your confession as an example.

Be patient with the youth during this exercise. This may well be the first effort by some of them to express their faith in words, and some of them might struggle. Some youth might not be ready to write out such a confession. Be clear that this is a "no wrong answers" activity. It is not a trap or an attempt to coax them into saying things that they do not believe or understand. The purpose of the activity is merely to help the confirmands gauge where their relationship with God stands.

Give the confirmands plenty of time to write their confessions. Invite them to read aloud what they have written.

Option: Instead of asking the youth about the word *confession,* write it on a markerboard. Invite the youth to write on the board some words, phrases, and images that the word brings to mind.

Supplies
- ❑ paper
- ❑ pens or pencils

Preparation: Do this activity yourself. Be prepared to read to the confirmands the confession that you write.

Then ask:

- How difficult was it to put your beliefs into words?
- Before you did this activity, how much thought had you given to what you believe and why?
- Did you come to any new realizations about your faith while writing your confession? (Invite confirmands to explain these realizations if they feel comfortable doing so.)

SUPPLIES

- ❑ posterboard strips on which you have written unusual facts about yourself (See "Preparation," below.)
- ❑ masking tape

PREPARATION: Identify 5 things that are true about you. One to 4 of them should surprise the youth (such as "I am a former ballet champ," "I co-wrote the song 'Pac-Man Fever,' " "I was the 1988 Tiddlywinks World Champion"). Write each of these statements in large letters on posterboard. Then cut the posterboard into 5 strips so that each fact is on a separate strip.

THE LAST THING YOU EXPECTED

(10–15 minutes)

Tell the group the 5 things about yourself that you prepared beforehand. (See the note in the margin.) Use masking tape to post the strips on the wall. Tell the youth to rank these statements in order from easiest to believe to most difficult (with the easiest to believe at the top).

Give them plenty of time to work, then ask:

- How did you decide which statements were most and least believable?

Reveal which of the statements are true. (*all of them*)

- Did any of these truths about me surprise you?

Then ask a volunteer to read aloud **Acts 9:17-22,** Saul's initial reception by other Christians.

Ask:

- If Saul had greeted the Christians in Damascus with the statements below, how, do you think, would the Christians in Damascus have ranked his statements in order of believability?

  __ My name is Saul.
  __ I am from Tarsus.
  __ On my way here, I had a vision of the risen Christ.
  __ I have renounced my former ways and become a Christian.
  __ I am here to proclaim the gospel of Christ.

- How, do you think, did Saul's faith change so radically, from his being a persecutor of Christians to becoming a preacher of the gospel?
- When have you been surprised to learn about someone else's faith? Why were you surprised?

SO WHAT? PART 1

TRUST: THE ONE WHO KNOWS

(10–15 minutes)

Hand out hymnals or the "Confirmation Vows" worksheet. Ask a volunteer to read aloud the third vow (below and the third non-bold paragraph on page 34 of the hymnal):

> Do you confess Jesus Christ as your Savior,
> put your whole trust in his grace,
> and promise to serve him as your Lord,
> in union with the church which Christ has opened
> to people of all ages, nations, and races?

Say: "This vow is a confession. When we take this vow, we confess that Jesus Christ is our Savior, that we trust in his grace, and that we will join with other Christians to serve Christ. Let's look at each part of this vow, starting with the word *trust*."

Ask:

- What does it mean to trust someone?
- How do you decide how much you will trust someone?

Ask the confirmands to spend a few moments thinking about the people they trust most. Ask a volunteer to describe whom he or she trusts most and to tell why. Were there specific actions that made a certain person trustworthy?

Then ask the youth to narrow their list of trustworthy people to a single person.

Ask:

- Who is the one person you trust more than anyone else? (The confirmands need not tell the name of the person whom they trust more than any other person.)
- Is there anything with which you would not trust the person you identified? (If the youth are reluctant to talk about what they will or will not trust this person with, spark conversation with examples from your own experience.)

Then ask a volunteer to read aloud **Proverbs 3:5-6.** Ask:

- How is putting trust in God similar to and different from trusting another person?
- How much do you trust God with the day-to-day details of your life?
- What, if anything, keeps you from fully trusting God with every aspect of your life?

SUPPLIES

- ❑ Bibles
- ❑ copies of *The United Methodist Hymnal* or of the "Confirmation Vows" worksheet

PREPARATION: Make copies of the "Confirmation Vows" handout, from the website. Think about examples from your own life about what kinds of things you would or would not trust with your most-trusted person. Make these general examples.

SUPPLIES
- ❑ Bibles
- ❑ sheets of posterboard or construction paper prepared according to the instructions below

PREPARATION: Write the following mathematical equation onto separate pieces of posterboard or construction paper: ME + GRACE = PERFECTION in GOD. ("ME" should be on one piece; "+" on a second; "GRACE" on a third; "=" on a fourth; and "PERFECTION in GOD" on a fifth.) To make things more interesting, you might choose to add more mathematical symbols, such as "–" or "x" or "÷" or "<" or ">."

NOTE: If possible, use posterboard or construction paper that has already been used on one side.

TRUST: SIMPLE MATH

(15–20 minutes)

Set out the pieces of posterboard or construction paper on the floor. Ask the confirmands to work together to form an equation. When they have finished, ask them to explain their equation. Allow for creativity, but try not to let things get too silly. Eventually guide them to the equation "ME + GRACE = PERFECTION in GOD."

Say: "As United Methodists, we strive for Christian perfection—loving God with our whole hearts, loving our neighbors as ourselves, and making every effort to live a righteous and holy life. But we don't achieve perfection on our own. As our confirmation vows say, we put our 'whole trust' in God's grace."

Remind the confirmands of what they learned about God's grace in the "Way of Salvation" session in the "Confirm Your Faith" unit.

Refer to the equation they made. Ask:

- What might be wrong with trying to reduce our experience of God's grace to a simple math equation?

Ask a volunteer to read aloud **Ephesians 2:8-10.**

Say: "Paul, who wrote this letter to the Ephesians, makes it very clear that we cannot achieve salvation or perfection on our own. So confessing Jesus Christ as our Savior and putting our 'whole trust in his grace' go hand in hand."

Ask:

- According to this passage from Ephesians, how will we respond to God's grace? *(by doing "good works")*

SUPPLIES
- ❑ Bibles

PROMISE: PINKIE SWEARS

(15 minutes)

The youth—and any adults who are present—will be doing a "pinkie promise" exercise, linking pinkie fingers in an outward expression of agreement or covenant. As you read a series of statements, one by one, each youth and adult volunteer should find someone with whom he or she is willing to "pinkie promise." The activity should follow this form:

You read the statement: "I will call you to say, 'Hey,' every day for a week."

Have the youth pair up. One person in each pair will repeat the statement. Then the second person in each pair will repeat the statement. After each has voiced the promise, the two will say together, "Pinkie promise?" If both agree, they will each extend the pinkie finger on their right hands, link pinkies, and shake them in agreement. The confirmands should find a different

partner (including adults) each time you read a statement. Following the form above, read these statements as the confirmands form pairs and make pinkie promises.

- I promise to never steal your shoes.
- I promise to not toilet-paper your house this year.
- I promise to pray for you all week.
- I promise to save you a seat in [Sunday school, youth fellowship, or worship] next week.

At the conclusion of the exercise, ask:

- Were these difficult promises to make? Why, or why not?
- Have you ever had to make a truly difficult promise? (Allow volunteers to name such promises, but be clear that they should not betray anyone's trust.)

Ask a volunteer to read aloud **Mark 14:29-31.** Then ask:

- What did Peter promise Jesus? Do you think that this was a difficult promise?
- Was he able to keep his promise? (See **Mark 14:66-72.**)

Have another volunteer read aloud **John 21:13-17.** Then ask:

- How does Jesus treat Peter in this passage, despite the fact that Peter had broken his promise?

Say: "As we promise to serve God with our lives, we must remember that God's grace works to restore us even when we stumble."

promise: real promises

(15 minutes)

supplies
- ❑ Bible
- ❑ markerboard or paper
- ❑ marker

Work with the confirmands to compile a list of the most ridiculous promises that they can remember making. Write these on a markerboard or paper. Encourage the youth to think of promises from early childhood, if they can recall them, such as, "I'll clean my room every day for a year if we can go to the amusement park," or "If you get me this present for Christmas, I won't ask for any presents for my birthday or for next Christmas," or the classic "I'll be your best friend for life."

When you have a good-size list, have the confirmands vote for the best promises categories such as *most absurd, easiest to fulfill, most likely to be a complete bluff, probably broken,* and other categories that the confirmands come up with.

Then ask:

- What does it mean to promise to serve God as your Lord?
- Whom do you know who serves God with his or her whole life? How do you know that is true?
- What is challenging about being faithful to a promise to serve God?

Have volunteers read aloud **Ruth 1:1-18.** Ask:

- How would you describe Ruth's level of dedication to Naomi?
- How can you show that same level of dedication to God?

NOTE: **If you choose to divide this session into two one-hour classes, break here.**

SO WHAT? PART 2

UNITY: CLOSER THAN A BROTHER

(10–15 minutes)

SUPPLIES
❑ Bibles

Ask the confirmands and any adults who are present to stand in as small of a circle as they can manage.

Ask:

- How did you go about getting into the circle?
- Was there any organization? Was anyone "in charge"?
- On a scale of *1* to *10,* how successful would say you were in creating a circle?
- If all future circles were to be based on the quality of your circle, what would the future of circles look like?

Have the youth within the circle read aloud **Acts 2:37-47,** each reading a verse at a time until the entire passage has been read.

Ask:

- How organized does this "first circle" of the church seem?
- What does this "first circle" of the church look like?
- What sorts of things does this "first circle" of the church do? (*hold all things in common, teach and have fellowship, break bread, pray together*)
- Which of these things does our congregation still practice today?

Have the confirmands form a new circle. This time, instruct them to stand with their left hands outstretched to the middle of the circle, making a fist with their thumbs up (like a hitchhiker). Have them turn their left hands so that their thumbs are pointing to the right. Each person then should, with his or her left hand, grab onto the thumb of the person to his or her left and allow his or her left thumb to be grasped by the person on his or her right. The result will be a uniform circle of knuckles. The circle may still be imperfect, but a symmetry will have formed. While the confirmands are still in the circle, ask:

- How is this circle similar to or different from our previous circle? Does this circle feel more organized than our first circle?
- What are some big differences between the way the first "circle" of church happened in Acts and the way we "circle" for church today?

UNITY: PUT ME IN, COACH

Ask a volunteer to read aloud **1 Corinthians 12:12-27.**

Say: "This Scripture emphasizes the importance of teamwork in the Christian faith. But this sort of cooperation involves more than just individuals working together as a congregation. It also involves congregations joining together to do God's work."

Discuss the connectional nature of The United Methodist Church. Explain how each congregation belongs to an annual conference, and tell the confirmands which annual conference your church belongs to.

Discuss jurisdictional conferences, central conferences, and general conferences and how lay and clergy delegates gather to elect bishops and vote on resolutions and legislation.

Talk about how each congregation pays apportionments, which support the ministries of the annual conference and the global church. Introduce the youth to some of the agencies, boards, and ministries of the church; and explain how congregations support and benefit from these ministries. (Examples follow.)

Explain that The United Methodist Church is a connectional denomination. While each congregation is unique and has different strengths, individual congregations do not stand alone. They are accountable to the global church; they join together with other congregations to do God's work; they support ministries in their community and around the world; they send delegates to conferences and volunteers to participate in denominational mission work; they benefit from and contribute to resources provided by denominational boards and agencies.

Examples of denominational boards, agencies, and ministries:

United Methodist Committee on Relief (UMCOR): UMCOR is a ministry of the General Board of Global Ministries devoted to responding to natural disasters, alleviating hunger and poverty, supporting refugees and immigrants, and supporting health initiatives in impoverished nations. It relies on apportionment money and the donations and hard work of individual United Methodists and congregations.

United Methodist Volunteers in Mission (VIM): VIM, another ministry of the General Board of Global Ministries, equips volunteers to serve in their communities, elsewhere in their home country, or elsewhere in the world. VIM provides a wide variety of volunteer opportunities to fit a volunteer's spiritual gifts and availability. VIM receives support from apportionment money and from congregations that commission members as volunteers.

United Methodist Publishing House (UMPH): UMPH—through Abingdon Press, it's publishing arm—publishes a wide variety of books, Christian education resources, and leadership resources in print and digital formats. Cokesbury, its retail arm,

SUPPLIES

- ❑ items specific to your congregation, showing its connectedness to other UM congregations

PREPARATION: Gather items specific to your congregation, showing its connectedness to other UM congregations.

Before class begins, tell one confirmand that he or she will be the "captain" of a game. Explain that, during the first stage of the game, his or her job will be to toss the ball across the room, even though there will be no one on the other side to catch it.

NOTE: Maps and information about annual conferences are available at *www.umc.org*. Additional materials are available at the website.

NOTE: Before you dismiss, instruct the confirmands to read, reflect on, and journal about the material in the "Confess" section of the *Credo Confirmation Student Journal* before your next session. Also encourage them to try to do the activities related to "Confess" on the confirmand website.

SPECIAL NOTE: Ask the youth to bring their student journal with them to the next class.

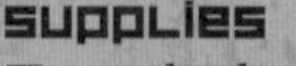

- ❑ markerboard
- ❑ marker

PREPARATION: Write the benediction, "John Wesley's Rule," on a markerboard; or print out the poster from the website.

offers churches an even wider array of books, United Methodist-specific curriculum materials, leadership resources, and church supplies. Many of the people responsible for writing and developing UMPH products serve as clergy, staff persons, and ministry volunteers in United Methodist congregations.

General Board of Discipleship (GBOD): GBOD is an agency devoted to Christian discipleship and spiritual formation in The United Methodist Church. It equips and trains leaders in the areas of worship, Christian education, evangelism, stewardship, and age-level ministries, among others.

The Upper Room: The Upper Room is a publishing ministry of the General Board of Discipleship that provides resources for spiritual formation. It is best known for *The Upper Room* magazine, a daily devotional magazine that is published in several languages and distributed throughout the world. Upper Room also publishes *Devo'Zine,* a devotional magazine for youth. Many United Methodists from several countries have contributed devotional readings to either *The Upper Room* or *Devo'Zine.*

United Methodist Communications (UMCom): UMCom, the church's media arm, is responsible for UMC.org (the denominational website) and the United Methodist News Service, which provides news stories, photos, and video news segments to assorted media outlets. UMC.org and the United Methodist News Service lift up the ministries of congregations and annual conferences throughout the United Methodist connection. Among other things, UMCom also produces television commercials for The United Methodist Church.

Ask:

- How does our connectional system help us remain unified?
- How does the fact that United Methodist congregations are different but related help us open our doors to more people?
- How does our congregation work cooperatively with other churches? How does our congregation participate in the ministries of the global United Methodist Church?

NOW WHAT?

CLOSING RITUAL

(10 minutes)

Gather the confirmands into a circle. Go around the circle and allow each person to offer a prayer thanking God for your time together and all that the group has learned and experienced and asking for God's guidance as you go forth.

Close this prayer time by saying aloud and in unison the benediction, John Wesley's Rule.

I Believe

INTRODUCTION

Has someone ever approached you and asked, "What does The United Methodist Church believe about _______?" Were you ready with an answer? If you didn't know the answer yourself, did you know where to turn? Thanks to technology, young people today have unprecedented access to a diverse range of ideas and beliefs from many different traditions and schools of thought. When faced with so many perspectives and beliefs, how can youth discern what is true and right? or what is important? or what cannot be known for sure and is part of the mystery of God?

We Believe . . .

For centuries, Christians have used creeds, formal statements of belief, to articulate essential truths and core doctrines. Youth who have grown up in The United Methodist Church are likely familiar with the Apostles' Creed, which is part of the baptism and confirmation services in *The United Methodist Hymnal*. As early as the second or third century, Christians were saying a version of the Apostles' Creed as a profession of faith before they were baptized. (The Apostles' Creed assumed its current form in the eighth century.)

In the fourth century, a church council developed the Nicene Creed, which some youth also will be familiar with (especially if they have ever attended a Roman Catholic mass). It was created to resolve disputes about doctrine, particularly regarding the divinity of Christ. The Apostles' Creed and Nicene Creed are two of the many creeds that Christians today recite as affirmations of faith.

The beliefs that we articulate in creeds give us a foundation on which to build our faith and practice. Consider for a moment the structure of a house. Many households give little thought to the foundation beneath their house nor the length of time their house has stood on top of this foundation. Yet the stability and longevity of their house relies on the excellence of the foundation. If the house settles or the foundation begins to show fault, the consequences can be disastrous.

BUILDING THE FOUNDATION

Your confirmands are likely in the foundation stage of building their spiritual homes. They have been led to the land by God's prevenient grace. No doubt they are at different stages of readiness to build; some probably have broken ground, while others are still surveying the lot. This confirmation experience has been an opportunity for confirmands to put down such a foundation by learning about and claiming the essential Christian beliefs expressed in the creeds.

In **Matthew 7,** Jesus spoke of the importance of building a foundation:

> "Everyone then who hears these words of mine and acts on them will be like a wise man who built his house on rock. The rain fell, the floods came, and the winds blew and beat on that house, but it did not fall, because it had been founded on rock. And everyone who hears these words of mine and does not act on them will be like a foolish man who built his house on sand. The rain fell, and the floods came, and the winds blew and beat against that house, and it fell—and great was its fall!"
>
> **—Matthew 7:24-27**

We all go through storms that test our faith. If we have a solid foundation, we can weather these storms and emerge from them stronger than before.

The fourth stanza of the hymn "How Firm a Foundation" attests to how the trials we face can make us stronger: "When through fiery trials thy pathways shall lie, my grace, all sufficient, shall be thy supply; the flame shall not hurt thee; I only design thy dross to consume, and thy gold to refine" (*The United Methodist Hymnal,* 529).

As you look at the creeds and statements of faith of our Christian forebears, remind the confirmands that they are part of an eternal story—involving many people who came before and many who will follow—that is rooted in the essential truths found in the creeds.

SUPPLIES AND PREPARATION

BASIC SUPPLIES		
❑ Bibles of various translations ❑ markerboard or large sheets of paper ❑ markers ❑ pens or pencils	❑ clear tape and/or glue ❑ masking tape ❑ index cards or paper cut about the same size (3-by-5 or 4-by-6) ❑ sheets of posterboard	❑ paper (Use paper that has already been used on one side as much as possible, depending on the activity.) ❑ scissors

ACTIVITY	PREPARATION	OTHER SUPPLIES
WHAT?		
Opening Ritual	Have on hand supplies for the youth to add fruit to the vine.	❑ vine from previous sessions ❑ vine fruit (1 for each student) ❑ copies of *The United Methodist Hymnal*
All In		
The String Around Your Finger	Find photos of a *tefillin,* a *mezuzah,* and *mezuzah* cases.	❑ spool of string ❑ photos of a *tefillin,* a *mezuzah,* and *mezuzah* cases
SO WHAT? PART 1		
Father, Son, Spirit	Make copies of the "Nicene Creed" handout, from the website.	❑ copies of the "Nicene Creed" handout, from the website ❑ copies of *The United Methodist Hymnal* ❑ three different colors of highlighter markers (several of each color)
SO WHAT? PART 2		
For Such a Time as This	Gather supplies.	
The Faith of the Church	Gather supplies.	❑ copies of *The United Methodist Hymnal* ❑ copies of *The Book of Discipline*
A Creed Apart	Make a copy of "Apostles' Creed" handout, from the website, for each confirmand. Cut each copy of the creed into strips. Keep an uncut version of the creed so that you can check the students' work.	❑ "Apostles' Creed" strips (See "Preparation," left.) ❑ optional: envelopes ❑ optional: small prize or prizes
Heard It All Before	Gather supplies.	❑ taped-together Apostles' Creed handouts from previous activity ❑ highlighter markers
NOW WHAT?		
I Believe	Ask the youth to bring their *Credo Confirmation Student Journal* to class with them.	❑ the students' *Credo Confirmation Student Journals*
Closing Ritual	Write the benediction, "John Wesley's Rule," on a markerboard; or print out the poster from the website.	

WHAT?

supplies
- ❑ vine from previous sessions
- ❑ vine fruit (1 for each student)
- ❑ copies of *The United Methodist Hymnal*

preparation: Have on hand supplies for the youth to add fruit to the vine.

note: Take time before you get started to talk with the confirmands about what they read and wrote in the "Confess" section of their *Credo Confirmation Student Journal.*

opening ritual

(10 minutes)

As the confirmands arrive, give each of them a cutout of a piece of fruit. Invite the confirmands to reflect on the previous session and to write on their fruit something they learned or experienced during that session. Ask the confirmands to affix their fruit to the vine. Remind them that these fruit represent ways that we, as Christians and United Methodists, live in response to God's grace.

When all of the confirmands have arrived, invite each person to talk briefly about what he or she wrote on his or her piece of fruit. (You might also ask why he or she attached the fruit to a particular branch or near a particular leaf.) Then open this session by reading aloud and in unison the Apostles' Creed (*The United Methodist Hymnal,* 882).

supplies
- ❑ Bible
- ❑ paper
- ❑ art supplies

all in

(15–20 minutes)

Begin by reading aloud **Deuteronomy 6:4-6.** This Scripture, which begins, "Hear, O Israel," is called the *Shema*. The word *Shema* means "hear" in Hebrew.

Ask the youth:

- What did you hear in this Scripture? What stood out to you?
- What does it mean to do something with your whole heart? with all your soul? with all your might?

Set out art supplies and give each person a sheet of paper. Instruct the confirmands to draw a picture of themselves doing something with all of their heart, souls, and mind. Tell them that this does *not* need to be a spiritual activity; it can be playing a sport or an instrument, engaging in a hobby—anything in which they feel fully engaged.

Give the confirmands plenty of time to work, then allow each person to present his or her picture and explain what makes him or her so passionate about the activity he or she has drawn. Have the youth talk about the lengths to which he or she will go—skipping dinner to get to practice, spending less time with friends and family, and so on—to participate in those activities.

Give the confirmands some time to reflect on these questions:

- Are you as passionate about your faith as you are about the activity you drew?
- If not, how would your life be different if you were that passionate about your faith?
- What, do you think, influences how passionate you are about your faith?

The String Around Your Finger

(10–15 minutes)

Stick your finger in the air so that the youth can finally see it, and ask:

- Does any of you know why I have this string tied around my finger?

Explain: "Although it's not as common as it once was, the practice of tying a string around one's finger is used as a memory trigger. The idea is that the visual of the string on your finger reminds you of the thing you're actually trying to remember."

Ask:

- What do you do when you need to remember something important? Do you ever do anything odd, such as tying a string around your finger?
- Are there things that are so important that you just remember, even without leaving yourself reminders?

Have a volunteer read aloud **Deuteronomy 6:7-9.**

Ask:

- Why, do you think, would the ancient Israelites go to such lengths to keep visual reminders of **Deuteronomy 6:4-6** before them?
- What do we do in our worship services to remind ourselves of the words we need to keep "in our heart"? (Examples include reciting creeds, saying the Lord's Prayer, singing the Doxology.) Why, do you think, do we include these things in our worship services?

Explain that many Jewish people still follow the instructions in verses 7-9 in very literal ways. *Tefillin* are small, leather boxes containing Scripture that observant Jewish persons "bind" with straps to their hands (and arms) and wear on their foreheads. A *mezuzah* is a piece of parchment on which verses of Scripture are written that Jewish families affix to their doorframes; often it is contained inside a small, decorative case attached to the doorframe. As time and resources permit, show the students photos of *tefillin* and a *mezuzah*.

Give each student a length of string to tie around a finger. After each confirmand has received and tied his or her "reminder string," close by reading again **Deuteronomy 6:4-6.**

Supplies

- ❑ Bible
- ❑ spool of string
- ❑ scissors
- ❑ photos of a *tefillin,* a *mezuzah,* and *mezuzah* cases

Preparation: Find photos of a *tefillin,* a *mezuzah,* and *mezuzah* cases.

Before the session, tie a piece of string around one of your fingers. Try to keep it out of sight before this activity so that the youth will not ask you about it.

SO WHAT? PART 1

Father, Son, Spirit

(10–15 minutes)

supplies

- ❑ copies of the "Nicene Creed" handout, from the website
- ❑ copies of *The United Methodist Hymnal*
- ❑ three different colors of highlighter markers (several of each color)

preparation: Make copies of "Nicene Creed" handout, from the website.

Have everyone turn to number 880 in *The United Methodist Hymnal.* Point out the Nicene Creed. Ask the confirmands whether they are familiar with this creed. (Even if your congregation seldom recites the Nicene Creed, some of the youth might have heard it at a Roman Catholic mass or an Episcopal or Orthodox service.) Explain that a church council wrote the Nicene Creed in the fourth century to make clear its beliefs about each person of the Trinity and to resolve disputes about doctrine."

Assign one person of the Trinity—Father, Son, and Holy Spirit—to a different person or pair. And give each person or pair a different colored highlighter. Distribute copies of the "Nicene Creed" handout, and have the confirmands read aloud the creed: The person or pair assigned the Father will read the first section; the person or pair assigned the Son will read the second; and the person or pair assigned the Holy Spirit will read the third.

Ask:

- Why, do you think, did the authors of this creed organize it into three sections? Why was it so important for them to establish the concept of the Trinity?

Then have each person or pair read through the entire creed, highlighting all references to their person of the Trinity. Give them a few minutes to work, then have each person or pair present what was highlighted.

Say: "At first it might have seemed like the creed's statements about the Father, the Son, and the Holy Spirit were independent of one another. But after doing this exercise, we can see a lot of overlap. When the authors of the Nicene Creed wrote this statement of faith, they not only explained the roles of the persons of the Trinity, but they also showed the complex relationship between the Father, the Son, and the Holy Spirit."

NOTE: If you choose to divide this session into two one-hour classes, break here.

SO WHAT? PART 2

For Such a Time as This

(10–15 minutes)

This activity calls for sensitivity on your part, because it involves the confirmands' revealing experiences of pain and doubt. Some youth will freely talk about such stories, while others might want to run from the room at the thought of revealing a personal hurt. Be gentle as you move through this exercise, being clear all along that no one need say anything beyond his or her comfort level.

Hand out paper and pens or pencils. Instruct the students to write a short paragraph about a situation that left them needing affirmation or an explanation from God, from family, or from friends. Tell them to answer these questions in their paragraph:

- What happened?
- How did this experience cause doubt, fear, or insecurity?
- Where or to whom did you turn for comfort?

Before inviting confirmands to tell their stories, read aloud **John 11:17-27.** Ask:

- What situation were Mary and Martha facing? (*Their brother had died.*)
- What beliefs might this situation have called into question for them?
- Where did they turn for comfort?
- How did Jesus comfort them?

Then invite the confirmands (or those who feel comfortable doing so) to tell their stories. Emphasize and encourage their answers to the above questions.

Then say: "**John 11:25-27** isn't exactly a creed, but it is a statement of faith."

Ask:

- How did this statement of faith give Martha comfort after Lazarus's death?
- Have you ever found comfort in a statement of belief such as a creed, an affirmation of faith, or a Scripture such as **John 11:25-27**?
- Why might reminders of who God is and what we believe as Christians give us comfort in difficult times?

SUPPLIES
- ❑ Bibles
- ❑ paper
- ❑ pens or pencils

THE FAITH OF THE CHURCH

(15–20 minutes)

Ask the confirmands to turn to **Philippians 2:5-11.** Have a volunteer read aloud this Scripture.

Then say: "These verses likely come from an ancient Christian hymn and are one of the earliest examples we have of Christians composing a statement of faith to express their beliefs about Christ."

Ask:

- What does this ancient hymn say about who Christ is?

Hand out hymnals, paper, and pens or pencils. Ask the confirmands to look over the various creeds and affirmations of faith found in the hymnal, beginning with the Nicene Creed (880) and ending with the "Affirmation From 1 Timothy 2:5-6; 1:15; 3:16" (889). Have the youth work

SUPPLIES
- ❑ Bibles
- ❑ paper
- ❑ pens or pencils
- ❑ copies of *The United Methodist Hymnal*
- ❑ copies of *The Book of Discipline of The United Methodist Church*

individually to jot down phrases and expressions of faith from the creeds that stand out to them. Encourage the confirmands to write 5 or 6 words or phrases.

Then set out a copy of *The Book of Discipline*. Tell the youth to turn to the Contents, and point out to them some of the various sections, or parts, of the book. Also point out how to find particular paragraphs, which are identified by number. (See "Note" at the top of the Contents page of *The Book of Discipline*.)

Then instruct the youth to turn to the paragraph entitled "Our Doctrinal Standards and General Rules" (¶ 103). Ask them to scan the section, making note of article and section titles that are of interest to them. This section includes The Articles of Religion of the Methodist Church and The Confession of Faith of The Evangelical United Brethren Church as well as John Wesley's General Rules for Methodist Societies.

Ask:

- Were you aware that this much thought had gone into describing the beliefs that our denomination holds true?
- What do these statements of faith say about what our tradition believes and values?

supplies

- ❑ "Apostles' Creed" strips (See "Preparation," below.)
- ❑ tape
- ❑ optional: envelopes
- ❑ optional: small prize or prizes

preparation: Make a copy of "Apostles' Creed" handout, from the website, for each confirmand. Cut each copy of the creed into strips. Keep an uncut version of the creed so that you can check the students' work.

option: Put the strips for each creed into a separate envelope to keep them together.

a creed apart

(10–15 minutes)

Your confirmands may be familiar with the Apostles' Creed. It is part of the Baptismal Covenants in *The United Methodist Hymnal*. Perhaps your congregation recites this creed each Sunday in worship. But even if the youth do not know the Apostles' Creed, they will be able to participate in this exercise.

Hand out a set of slips from the Apostles' Creed to each confirmand. On your mark, have the students race to reassemble the creed. Have a hymnal (or an uncut printout of the Apostles' Creed) handy to check their work. Consider awarding a small prize to the first person to correctly assemble the creed. Or just for fun, give a small prize to everyone as they complete the assembly.

Once the youth have reassembled the creed correctly, instruct them to tape together the slips of paper, putting the tape on the back (non-printed side) of the page. (In the next activity, they'll be highlighting phrases; and most highlighter markers don't write well on clear tape.)

Then ask:

- How difficult was it to reassemble the Apostles' Creed?
- What method did you use to assemble the creed? Did you work from memory?
- How familiar are you with the Apostles' Creed? If you are, where and in what settings have you heard this creed?

Heard It All Before

(10–15 minutes)

Ask the confirmands to read the Apostles' Creed aloud together. Then have the confirmands highlight (with highlighter markers on the taped-together creeds from the previous activity) any words or phrases that they have questions about or would like to have explained. Give the youth a few minutes to highlight.

Then read aloud the first line of the creed and see whether anyone has it highlighted. If so, spend some time discussing it. If not, continue to the next line. Continue until you have read through the entire creed.

Supplies
- ❑ taped-together Apostles' Creed handouts from the previous activity
- ❑ highlighter markers

Now What?

I Believe

(20–25 minutes)

Throughout the Credo Confirmation program, confirmands have been writing in their student journal statements of belief about each topic you have studied. When placed together, these statements form a personal credo, or creed, that your youth will be able to look back on for years to come.

The creeds you've studied in this session were the work of communities of faith coming together and, through God's grace, naming the beliefs and values they have in common. Spend the rest of your time in this session working together as a group to create a creed. (If you have more than 6 confirmands, divide them into small groups for this exercise; and have each small group create a creed.)

Start by inviting the confirmands to read aloud the statements of belief they have already written in their student journal. Then work together to craft statements that everyone in the group is comfortable with. Organize these statements as the group sees fit.

Review—and, as necessary, tweak—your class creed during the remaining sessions.

Supplies
- ❑ the students' *Credo Confirmation Student Journals*

Preparation: Ask the youth to bring their student journal to class with them.

Note: Before you dismiss, instruct the confirmands to read, reflect on, and journal about the material in the "I Believe" section of the Credo Student Journal before your next session. Also encourage them to try to do the activities related to "I Believe" on the confirmand website.

Closing Ritual

(5 minutes)

Gather the confirmands into a circle. Go around the circle and allow each person to offer a prayer thanking God for your time together and all that the group has learned and experienced and asking for God's guidance as you go forth.

Close this prayer time by saying aloud and in unison the benediction, John Wesley's Rule.

Supplies
- ❑ markerboard
- ❑ marker

Preparation: Write the benediction, "John Wesley's Rule," on a markerboard; or print it out from the website.

Prayers, Presence, Gifts, Service, and Witness

INTRODUCTION

Let's take a moment to look at the difference between joining The United Methodist Church and the local congregation. To the average person in the congregation, the charge to a new professing member to support the church with his or her prayers, presence, gifts, service, and witness might just sound like the next in a series of questions (to which the new member inevitably answers, "I will"). But when we look closely at the covenant in *The United Methodist Hymnal* (part of "Baptismal Covenant I," on page 38), we notice that this vow to support the church isn't just another question. It gets its own section, with a title in all capitals and everything: "RECEPTION INTO THE LOCAL CONGREGATION." Why? One answer is that this section allows a distinction between persons joining the congregation from another United Methodist congregation and those joining from another faith tradition or no faith tradition. Yet these words point to a deeper, more personal commitment; they are a call to a life of faith, of hope, and of love in a particular faith community.

Our relationship with God demands that we live in relationship with our fellow human beings. But how? What does it look like to live in relationship with others as part of a Christian community? What does God expect of us? One way to answer that question would be to say that God expects us to support the ministries of the church—and particularly those of our local congregation—through our prayers, presence, gifts, service, and witness. (Note: The 2008 General Conference added *witness* to the vows, thus it is not included in the vows as they appear in *The United Methodist Hymnal,* which was published in 1989.)

prayers

We find in the Gospel of John, in the closing chapters, Jesus saying prayers for his disciples and all to follow. And the New Testament Scriptures are replete with instructions for and examples of how to pray (see **Matthew 6:5-13** and **James 5:13-18**). By praying with and for our local congregation, we draw closer to our fellow believers and to Christ.

presence

Presence may seem like the most obvious component of church membership, but there's more to "presence" than showing up at the church building once a week. Sometimes "presence" visits people at the hospital or reaches out to someone who hasn't attended worship or Sunday school for a while. On occasion, "presence" has to restore a broken relationship. Young people who are always on the go and have several things constantly competing for their attention might struggle to be fully present in a community of faith. But if they devote themselves to setting aside time for God and for others, they will find the experience liberating. **Psalm 139** shows the enduring presence, knowledge, and depth of care that God has for us. In the story of Ruth, Scripture illustrates what human devotion to presence looks like.

Gifts

Many of us struggle to claim the gifts that God has given us—sometimes, because we don't recognize these gifts or because we don't want to sound boastful—but the evidence of such gifts in our lives is overwhelming. There is no arrogance in realizing that we possess talents, abilities, and personality traits that can be of service to the church. Paul tells us in **1 Corinthians 12** that certain gifts are held in higher esteem than others but that each person possesses abilities that are vital to the body of Christ. Many adolescents are unaware of or are reluctant to acknowledge their own gifts. As Christian ministers to young people, we must affirm their gifts and help them find ways to return these gifts to God in the form of love—love for God, others (including enemies and strangers), and self.

Service

We put our gifts to use by living a life of Christian service. We serve our congregation and, together with our congregation, we serve God's children in our community and around the world. Our service points to the example of Christ and bears testimony to God's work in our lives. Young Christians need to be made aware of the many opportunities they have to serve, whether by being an acolyte, helping an elderly neighbor, or being part of a Volunteers in Mission team.

Witness

Our witness brings together all of these expressions of faith. When we use our prayers, presence, and gifts in service of God to others, we act as witnesses to God's redeeming love through Christ and as examples of how to live a life of Christian discipleship.

As confirmands consider their confirmation vows and consider making a covenant relationship with the church, they should examine how they have supported, and will continue to support, the ministries of the church, through their prayers, presence, gifts, service, and witness.

SUPPLIES AND PREPARATION

BASIC SUPPLIES

❑ Bibles of various translations ❑ markerboard or large sheets of paper ❑ markers ❑ pens or pencils	❑ clear tape and/or glue ❑ masking tape ❑ index cards or paper cut about the same size (3-by-5 or 4-by-6) ❑ sheets of posterboard	❑ paper (Use paper that has already been used on one side as much as possible, depending on the activity.) ❑ scissors

ACTIVITY	PREPARATION	OTHER SUPPLIES
WHAT?		
Opening Ritual	Have on hand supplies for the youth to add fruit to the vine.	❑ vine from previous sessions ❑ vine fruit (1 for each student) ❑ copies of *The United Methodist Hymnal*
SO WHAT? PART 1		
Prayers: From the Rising of the Sun	Gather supplies.	❑ copies of *The United Methodist Hymnal*.)
Prayers: Power of Prayer	Gather supplies.	
Prayers: Can I Get a Witness?	Gather supplies.	
Presence: Marked Present	Gather supplies.	
Presence: There for You	Gather supplies.	
Presence: Can I Get a Witness?	Gather supplies.	
SO WHAT? PART 2		
Gifts: Taking Inventory	Make copies of the "Spiritual Gifts Inventory," from the website.	❑ copies of the "Spiritual Gifts Inventory"
Gifts: One to Grow on	Gather supplies.	
Gifts: Give It Away Now	Gather supplies.	❑ simple child's puzzle
Gifts: Can I Get a Witness?	Gather supplies.	
Service: Follow the Leader	Gather supplies.	❑ small basin of water ❑ hand towels
Service: Living It	Gather supplies.	
Service: Can I Get a Witness?	Gather supplies.	
NOW WHAT?		
Closing Ritual	Write the benediction, "John Wesley's Rule," on a markerboard; or print out the poster from the website.	

WHAT?

opening ritual

(10 minutes)

As the confirmands arrive, give each of them a cutout of a piece of fruit. Invite the confirmands to reflect on the previous session and to write on their fruit something they learned or experienced during that session. Ask the confirmands to affix their fruit to the vine. Remind them that these fruit represent ways that we, as Christians and United Methodists, live in response to God's grace.

When all of the confirmands have arrived, invite each person to talk briefly about what he or she wrote on his or her piece of fruit. (You might also ask why he or she attached the fruit to a particular branch or near a particular leaf.) Then open this session by reading aloud and in unison the "Reception Into the Local Congregation" from page 38 in *The United Methodist Hymnal*.

supplies

- ❑ vine from previous sessions
- ❑ vine fruit (1 for each student)
- ❑ copies of *The United Methodist Hymnal*

preparation: Have on hand supplies for the youth to add fruit to the vine.

note: Take time before you get started to talk with the confirmands about what they read and wrote in the "I Believe" section of their *Credo Confirmation Student Journal.*

SO WHAT? PART 1

prayers: from the rising of the sun

(15–20 minutes)

Say: "Prayer is obviously an important part of the Christian experience."

Ask:

- What are some examples of prayers that we use in our worship services? (*a pastoral prayer, the Lord's Prayer, a prayer of confession, any liturgical prayer for special services*)

Hand out hymnals. Instruct the students to open their hymnal to page 876, "Orders of Daily Praise and Prayer." Read aloud the opening section.

Ask:

- Did you know that there is an order of service intended for daily use by United Methodists while away from church? Have any of you ever participated in such a service?
- Why, do you think, does our hymnal include such a service?

Then have the confirmands read the "Prayer of Thanksgiving" (877) from "An Order for Morning Praise and Prayer," followed by the "Prayer of Thanksgiving" from "An Order for Evening Prayer and Praise" (878).

supplies

- ❑ copies of *The United Methodist Hymnal*

Ask:

- What stands out to you in each prayer?
- How are these two prayers similar? different?

Ask the youth whether they have a practice of beginning and ending their day in prayer. (They need not answer aloud.) If they aren't in the habit of praying in the morning and evening, challenge them to take on this practice.

SUPPLIES
❑ Bibles

PREPARATION: Ask a volunteer to loudly and proudly read the prepared prayer.

PRAYERS: POWER OF PRAYER

(10–15 minutes)

Have a volunteer open this activity by reading aloud the following prayer:

> O Great and Glorious Lord of Hosts and the embodiment of all that is holy, I thank thee this day for the great honor and privilege of addressing you before all these gathered here. May they be blessed as I have already been blessed in my life; may their love for you grow to be as large and sincere as my own. Be with any of them who are struggling; because, although I am not struggling myself, I can tell by the look in their eyes and also by the way some of them dress that some of them have sadness in their hearts. Thank you for loving me as much as you do so that I can sometimes, perhaps, share that love with others. Amen.

Pause to allow the confirmands to react. Then ask them to talk about their impressions of the prayer and whether the prayer seemed sincere.

Ask a youth to read aloud **Matthew 6:5-6** and **Luke 18:9-14.** Then ask:

- What do Jesus' instructions on prayer tell us about the prayer we just heard?

Ask volunteers to read aloud Jesus' prayer in **John 17,** each person reading a few verses at a time. Then ask:

- For whom is Jesus praying in this passage? (*his disciples*)
- When has someone prayed aloud for you in your presence? How did this make you feel?
- Have you ever prayed aloud for someone in his or her presence? What was that experience like?

PRAYERS: CAN I GET A WITNESS?

(5 minutes)

This activity will repeat throughout the session. Emphasize that our witness, the final word of our commitment to the local church, stems from all of the other elements. Those elements, perfectly lived out, become our witness.

Read aloud **John 13:34-35.** Then ask:

- How can our prayers bear witness to our love to others, in obedience to Jesus' command in this passage?

Read aloud **Romans 1:16-17.** Then ask:

- How can our prayers show others that we are not ashamed of the gospel?

SUPPLIES
- ❑ Bibles

PRESENCE: MARKED PRESENT

(15–20 minutes)

Have the youth begin, with one color of marker, to draw rectangular blocks on a sheet of paper. These blocks should represent all of the various parts of their lives: family, school, church, and so on. Give them plenty of time to work, then invite each person to present his or her drawings. Point out blocks that make each person unique as well as blocks that several people have in common.

Then have the confirmands use a second color to fill in the blocks that represent parts of their life where they experience God's presence. Talk about ways in which God is present in each of these parts of their life.

Read aloud **Psalm 139:1-10.** Then ask:

- How aware are you of God's presence in your life?
- In what ways is God present with us?
- According to this psalm, when and where is God present?
- After reading this psalm, would you color in any more of your blocks? Why, or why not?

SUPPLIES
- ❑ markers of various colors
- ❑ paper

NOTE: Each youth should have access to three different colors of marker for this activity and the next.

PRESENCE: THERE FOR YOU

(10–15 minutes)

Ask:

- When in your life has someone "showed up" for you at a time when you really needed support?

Invite the youth to think about any friends or family members they can count on, no matter what. Then ask them to think about any times when their relationships with these persons were tested.

Ask a volunteer to read aloud **Ruth 1:1-19*a*** (ending with "until they came to Bethlehem"). Then ask:

- Are you as devoted to anyone as Ruth was to Naomi? Are you as devoted to God as Ruth was to Naomi and the God of Israel?
- How can you show the same level of devotion to the church—your faith family and your friends in Christ?

SUPPLIES
- ❑ Bibles
- ❑ markers of various colors
- ❑ students' papers from previous activity

Return to the drawings of the blocks that the youth made in previous exercise. Now have the confirmands use a third color to mark the blocks that represent the parts of their lives in which they show up for God. This may require some clarification. The students shouldn't look for areas in their life where they feel like they'll listen to God; rather, they're looking for areas where they feel motivated to act on God's behalf—such as by helping a person in need, praying with a friend, or singing a song of praise. For many of the confirmands, this may be a new way of looking at their relationship with God.

Spend some time discussing the discrepancy between the times and places where God shows up for them and the times and places where they show up for God.

Ask:

- What does this exercise tell you about your relationship with God?

supplies
- ❑ Bibles

presence: can i get a witness?

(5 minutes)

If necessary, review **John 13:34-35** and **Romans 1:16-17.**

Ask:

- How can we demonstrate through our presence with others in our congregation the love that Jesus talks about in **John 13:34-35**?
- How can we, by being fully present with God and with others, show that we are not ashamed of the gospel?

note: If you choose to divide this session into two one-hour classes, break here.

SO WHAT? PART 2

supplies
- ❑ copies of the "Spiritual Gifts Inventory"

preparation: Make copies of the "Spiritual Gifts Inventory," from the website.

gifts: taking inventory

(15 minutes)

Hand out copies of the "Spiritual Gifts Inventory." Ask the confirmands to complete it and identify their spiritual gifts. (If you choose or if time is a concern, you might have them complete this inventory beforehand on the website.)

Invite each person to name his or her spiritual gifts, as identified by the "Spiritual Gifts Inventory."

gifts: one to grow on

(10–15 minutes)

Gather the youth into a circle. Begin by turning to the person on your left and use only one word to affirm something about that person. The affirming word should not be related to a person's appearance but to his or her positive character and personality traits. The person you affirm should offer a one-word affirmation to the person to his or her left. Continue around the circle until you receive a one-word affirmation.

Then make a list on a markerboard or paper of all of these one-word affirmations. Ask:

- How did it feel to be affirmed?
- Were you nervous as your turn approached? Why, or why not?

Ask a youth to read aloud **1 Corinthians 12:4-7**. Then ask:

- Why is it so important that God gives us a variety of gifts?
- What, do you think, did Paul (the author of this letter) mean by "for the common good," in verse 7?
- How have you been able to use your gifts for the good of others and for God? (Refer to the gifts identified in the "Taking Inventory" activity.)

supplies
- ❑ Bibles
- ❑ markerboard or paper
- ❑ marker

Gifts: Give It Away Now

(10–15 minutes)

supplies
- ❑ Bibles
- ❑ simple child's puzzle (the fewer pieces the better)

Hand one piece of a child's puzzle to each person in your group. Ask the youth to guess, by looking at their piece, what the entire puzzle will look like. Then set out the remaining pieces and allow the youth to assemble the puzzle.

Ask:

- Were you able to guess correctly what the puzzle was going to look like from the piece (or pieces) you had?
- How many of the pieces were necessary to complete the puzzle?

Say: "Each puzzle piece is far more meaningful and important when it is joined with the other pieces than it is by itself. In the same way, our God-given gifts are far more meaningful when they are combined with the gifts of others in the community of faith."

Have a youth read aloud **1 Corinthians 13:1-13** (sometimes known as Paul's Love Chapter).

Say: "**1 Corinthians 12** teaches us about our spiritual gifts. Chapter 13 teaches us that, no matter how we are gifted, our lives and gifts are puzzle pieces that come together with the gifts of others to show God's love to the world around us. And without our gifts, this larger picture is incomplete."

Ask:

- How do you (or can you) use your gifts to show God's love?

Refer to the one-word affirmations from "Gifts: One to Grow on" (above) and the gifts identified in "Taking Inventory" (above). Talk about these gifts and character traits, and encourage the confirmands to think of ways that these gifts could be given back to God.

SUPPLIES
- ❑ Bibles

GIFTS: CAN I GET A WITNESS?

(5 minutes)

If necessary, review **John 13:34-35** and **Romans 1:16-17.**

Say: "The way we use our gifts to show God's love is one of the most important ways in which we witness to others."

Ask:

- How can you use your gifts to fulfill Jesus' commandment in **John 13:34-35**?
- How can using our gifts to express love for God and others show people that we are not ashamed of the gospel?

SUPPLIES
- ❑ Bibles
- ❑ small basin of water
- ❑ hand towels

SERVICE: FOLLOW THE LEADER

(15–20 minutes)

Read aloud **John 13:3-15.** (Jesus washes his disciples' feet.)

Say: "In Jesus' day, foot washing was something that a servant did as a courtesy for a house guest. Back then, the average person's feet were almost always filthy from walking barefoot or in sandals. Foot washing was a dirty job, and it certainly wasn't something that a teacher did for his disciples."

Ask:

- Why, do you think, did Jesus wash his disciples' feet even though doing so was unusual and unconventional?

Say: "In remembrance of the example that Jesus set by humbly serving his disciples, we're going to wash one another's hands."

(Be clear that this exercise is symbolic. There is no need for anyone to go overboard by scrubbing another person's hands.)

Dip a towel into the bowl of water, wipe the hands of the person to your right; then dry his or her hands with a second towel. This person should wipe and dry the hands of the person on his or her right. Continue until someone washes your hands.

Say: "The custom of foot washing, while common in Jesus' time, has fallen out of practice in our culture of pavement and closed-toed shoes."

Then ask:

- What are some similar acts of humble service that we could perform in our culture today?
- By washing his disciples' feet, Jesus humbly served others in his community of faith. How can you serve people in our faith community and the faith community as a whole? (This could include acolyting and participating in music ministries.)

Service: Living It

(10–15 minutes)

Supplies
- ❑ Bibles
- ❑ markerboard or paper
- ❑ marker

Have a student read aloud **Isaiah 1:16-17.**

Then ask:

- Who are the oppressed, the orphans, and the widows in our community? (Focus on all persons who are vulnerable, not just people who are literally oppressed or are literally orphans or widows.)

Ask the youth to call out acts of service that could be performed in your community. See how long they can keep coming up with ideas without repeating any or without any periods of silence. Continue to a designated time or until the youth run out of ideas or until it gets silly. Write down on a markerboard or paper the acts of service that the youth call out.

Following the game, read through the acts of service that you've listed. (Feel free at this point to discard any silly ones that you may have accepted for the purpose of keeping the game going.)

Discuss each act of service, having the youth consider how your congregation is already involved in each or how the congregation might become involved in each. As a class, choose one act of service with which your church is not already involved, and develop an action plan for your group to perform this act of service.

Ask:

- What did this exercise teach you about our church's involvement in service in our community?

Then invite the confirmands to reflect on which acts of service they are involved in or have been involved in and which they could take on in the coming weeks and months.

Service: Can I Get a Witness?

(5 minutes)

Supplies
- ❑ Bibles

Say: "Service is the most visible way in which we witness to people in our community and give them an experience of God's love."

If necessary, review **John 13:34-35** and **Romans 1:16-17.**

Ask:

- How can our acts of service show love to those around us, in obedience to Jesus command in **John 13:34-35**?
- How can acts of service in our community demonstrate for others that we are not ashamed of the gospel?

NOTE: Before you dismiss, instruct the confirmands to read, reflect on, and journal about the material in the "Prayers, Presence, Gifts, Service, and Witness" section of the *Credo Confirmation Student Journal* before your next session. Also encourage them to try to do the activities related to "PPGSW" on the confirmand website.

SUPPLIES

- ❑ markerboard
- ❑ marker

PREPARATION: Write the benediction, "John Wesley's Rule," on a markerboard; or print out the poster from the website.

NOW WHAT?

CLOSING RITUAL

(5 minutes)

Gather the confirmands into a circle. Go around the circle and allow each person to offer a prayer thanking God for your time together and all that the group has learned and experienced and asking for God's guidance as you go forth.

Close this prayer time by saying aloud and in unison the benediction, John Wesley's Rule.

Going Forth

INTRODUCTION

IN CONCLUSION . . .

"Amen." "In Jesus' name." "Selah." "The Lord bless you and keep you." "We'll keep in touch."

How often do the words that conclude a time or place in our life lose their depth of meaning? When we hear "in conclusion," our first instinct often is to reach for our car keys. We reduce blessings and benedictions to space-holders that simply release us from one space to the next. Guard against that tendency in your preparation this week. Your students are on a life-changing journey, and you must honor the steps they've taken already and offer them continued guidance for the road ahead. Completing confirmation is a mile marker, not the end of the road.

Our thoughts this week will be guided by the closing words of the confirmation service in *The United Methodist Hymnal*:

> The God of all grace,
>   who has called us to eternal glory in Christ
> establish you and strengthen you
>   by the power of the Holy Spirit,
> that you may live in grace and peace.

Your students have walked the path of these words during their confirmation experience. They have met the God of grace through Creation; through sin, brokenness, and estrangement; and in redemption. They have heard the call of God as they have learned about renouncing the "spiritual forces of wickedness," accepting "the freedom and power" that God offers, and confessing Jesus Christ as their Savior on their way to becoming a "New Creation." As they have learned about church, the way of discipleship, and sacraments; and as they have professed the Christian faith, they have been established and strengthened. Now they are free to begin to live in grace in peace, using what they have learned from studying the Wesleyan quadrilateral; worship; holiness; and how to faithfully participate in the ministries of the church by their prayers, presence, gifts, service, and witness.

A Continuation, Not an Inoculation

Too often in The United Methodist Church, we misconstrue confirmation as a one-shot theological inoculation or a graduation into the local church's youth ministry. Confirmation is the continuation of a journey that begins at baptism and continues throughout the rest of one's lifetime. The worship service in which young people take the vows of confirmation is not a final ceremony but an opportunity for the local congregation to further embrace, guide, and welcome in Christian love the young people being confirmed.

In **John 14:25-31,** Jesus speaks peace over his disciples, preparing them for the life they are about to live beyond his immediate influence. Jesus tells his disciples that—although he will die, rise, and ascend to heaven—he is sending the Holy Spirit to guide them as they do the work Jesus has called them to do. Similarly, as your youth leave the immediate influence of you and the other confirmation leaders, they will find comfort in knowing that, in addition to the leading of the Spirit, they will be accompanied by their fellow travelers in faith. Bear all this in mind as you prepare for and lead this final session; speak toward their future in all that you do.

Bearing Fruit

Throughout this program, your confirmands have grown spiritually. You have illustrated this growth with a root and trunk that grew branches. These branches grew leaves and eventually yielded fruit. Rejoice in the fruit that God has produced in the lives of these young people during your time together. Where you are able, speak to your confirmands of specific spiritual fruit that you've seen growing in their lives; and help them identify specific spiritual fruits growing in one another's' life.

This lesson is an opportunity to dwell on the benediction of the confirmation service, but it also serves as a benediction for your confirmation program. Take time, during this session and as you prepare for this session, to reflect on the time you've spent with your confirmands and to point them toward a life spent in the grace and peace of the Holy Spirit.

SUPPLIES AND PREPARATION

BASIC SUPPLIES

❑ Bibles of various translations ❑ markerboard or large sheets of paper ❑ markers ❑ pens or pencils	❑ clear tape and/or glue ❑ masking tape ❑ index cards or paper cut about the same size (3-by-5 or 4-by-6) ❑ sheets of posterboard	❑ paper (Use paper that has already been used on one side as much as possible, depending on the activity.) ❑ scissors

ACTIVITY	PREPARATION	OTHER SUPPLIES
WHAT?		
Opening Ritual	Have on hand supplies for the youth to add fruit to the vine.	❑ vine from previous sessions ❑ vine fruit (1 for each student)
In the Image of God	Gather supplies.	❑ colored pencils ❑ crayons
Disconnected	Use a hammer and nail to punch a hole in the bottom of each can. The hole has to be large enough for the string to pass through it.	❑ 4 clean liquid laundry detergent cups or steel cans (preferably soup cans with a pop top or that were opened by a safety can opener) ❑ sturdy toothpicks ❑ 2 lengths of string, each long enough to stretch across your room ❑ hammer ❑ nail
SO WHAT? PART 1		
Sole Purpose	Gather supplies.	❑ shoeboxes ❑ craft paper
Terms of Endearment	Gather supplies.	
Fertile Soil	Gather supplies.	❑ potted plant
Remembrance	Gather supplies.	❑ bowl ❑ water ❑ Communion elements
SO WHAT? PART 2		
Somewhere in the Middle	Gather supplies.	❑ balance board(s) ❑ optional: foam balls or other soft items that could be thrown at people without hurting them
Living in the Presence	Gather supplies	
NOW WHAT?		
Closing Ritual	Write the benediction, "John Wesley's Rule," on a markerboard; or print out the poster from the website.	

WHAT?

SUPPLIES
- ❑ vine from previous sessions
- ❑ vine fruit (1 for each student)
- ❑ copies of *The United Methodist Hymnal*

PREPARATION: Have on hand supplies for the youth to add fruit to the vine.

NOTE: Take time before you get started to talk with the confirmands about what they read and wrote in the "Prayers, Presence, Gifts, Service, and Witness" section of their *Credo Confirmation Student Journal*.

OPENING RITUAL

(10 minutes)

As the confirmands arrive, give each person a piece of fruit for the vine. Invite the confirmands to reflect on the previous session and to write on their fruit something they learned or experienced during that session. Ask the confirmands to attach their fruit to the vine. Remind them that these fruit represent ways that we, as Christians and United Methodists, grow in our faith and more fully experience God's grace.

When all of the confirmands have arrived, invite each person to talk briefly about what he or she wrote on his or her piece of fruit. (You might also ask why he or she attached the leaf to a particular branch or near a particular leaf.) Then open this session by reading aloud and in unison the "Welcome" from page 39 in *The United Methodist Hymnal* (beginning with "The God of all grace").

SUPPLIES
- ❑ Bibles
- ❑ paper
- ❑ pens
- ❑ markers
- ❑ colored pencils
- ❑ crayons

IN THE IMAGE OF GOD

(10–15 minutes)

Ask:

- Scripture tells us that God has created us in God's likeness. What does it mean to you to be created in the image of God?

Set out paper and pens, markers, crayons, and/or colored pencils. Ask the youth to draw their image of God. Encourage the youth not to filter their response but just to draw what they see in their minds. If some confirmands aren't comfortable drawing a picture of God, give them the option of expressing their image of God in writing. Give everyone plenty of time to work, then invite each person to present the image he or she has created.

Ask:

- What characteristics of God did you focus on as you drew (or wrote about) your image of God?
- What are some things that you liked about your friends' images that you didn't include in yours?
- What does your drawing (or writing) say about your perception of God and your relationship with God?
- Do you see yourself in the image of God you created? If so, how?
- Has this activity changed your understanding of what it means to be created in God's image?

Say: "Jesus' disciples had a very clear image of God. They had been working closely with Jesus, who was God in human form. But they were about to be separated from their image of God."

Ask a volunteer to read aloud **John 14:25-31.** Then ask:

- With Jesus leaving them, how, do you think, would the disciples interact with God?
- What are some ways in which we interact with God, even though God is not present with us in the flesh?

disconnected

(15–20 minutes)

Guide the students in the construction of a set of can phones. Feed one end of the string through the hole into the interior of the can. Tie the string end around a toothpick that you've broken to fit the inside bottom of the can. Repeat this procedure with a second can at the other end of the string. The string should be as long as possible, given the constraints of your meeting space.

Allow the confirmands to use the can phones to communicate by speaking into the cans and holding the cans up to their ears to hear the person on the other end of the line. Have the youth experiment to see how quietly they can speak and how far apart they can stand while still being understood on the other end of the line. After a few minutes, use the scissors to cut the string while a conversation in progress.

Ask:

- What made the ability to talk with each other on these phones possible?
- Is this ability to communicate ruined now that I have cut the string?

Say: "During our time together, we've discussed the role of communication in our relationship with God."

Ask:

- What are some of the things that "cut the string" of our communication with God? When have you felt disconnected from God?

Tie the strings of the can phones back together that you had cut, and ask the confirmands to once again communicate, using the phones. Then ask:

- How can we restore our connection to God when we feel as though our communication has been cut off?

supplies

- ❑ 2 clean liquid laundry detergent cups or steel cans (preferably soup cans with a pop top or that were opened by a safety can opener)
- ❑ sturdy toothpicks
- ❑ 2 lengths of string, each long enough to stretch across your room
- ❑ scissors
- ❑ hammer
- ❑ nail

preparation: Use a hammer and nail to punch a hole in the bottom of each can or cup. The hole has to be just large enough for the string to pass through it.

SO WHAT? PART 1

sole purpose

(15–20 minutes)

Give the group a shoebox; and set out craft paper, scissors, glue or tape, and markers. Instruct the youth to work together to create a diorama or shadow box of one of their favorite

SUPPLIES
- ❑ a shoebox
- ❑ craft paper
- ❑ scissors
- ❑ glue or tape
- ❑ markers

passages of Scripture. Don't direct their choice of Scripture, but have them work together to select a passage.

Allow plenty of time for the youth to work. Then invite them to show and talk about their diorama.

After the presentations, ask:

- What did this box originally contain?
- What kind of shoes might it have contained?
- How has the shoebox changed since it was used to hold shoes? Is it still a box?

Then ask:

- How are we like the shoebox?
- What did our lives look like before we were aware of God's presence in our lives?
- How have our lives changed as a result of living in relationship with God? (You might talk specifically about how lives have changed during this confirmation experience.)

Conclude this activity with a prayer such as: "God, thank you for the grace that transforms our hearts and lives. Help us be, like these boxes, forever changed by the story within us."

Terms of Endearment

(10–15 minutes)

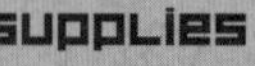

SUPPLIES
- ❑ paper
- ❑ pens or pencils

Begin with some discussion about true-to-life situations in the lives of the confirmands, situations where they have felt wronged. Be clear that they should not mention any names. (Keep an eye on your time; this activity can run over if you don't keep a tight rein on the storytelling.)

After everyone has had a chance to express his or her experience of being slighted, divide the confirmands into pairs.

Instruct the pairs to create a contract specifying what a person must do to gain their forgiveness. (For example: "In order for _________ [hereafter, known as "the offending party"] to gain forgiveness from _________ [hereafter known as "the wronged"], the offending party must _________.")

Tell the pairs not to focus much on the legal language but, instead, to emphasize what it will take to forgive a wrongdoing.

Check on their progress as they work, helping where you can. As the youth finish, have each pair read aloud its terms for gaining forgiveness.

Ask:

- What is most difficult about the terms of your contract?
- How does your contract resemble or differ from the way God forgives us?
- What are God's requirements for forgiving someone?

Ask the confirmands what they remember from the sessions on sin and redemption (sessions 2 and 3), from the "Know Your Story" unit. (As needed, use the information in the introduction to the "Sin" and "Redemption" sessions to refresh the youth's memories.) Emphasize that we are all sinners in need of redemption and that God's grace is available to all.

Say: "God, through the death and resurrection of Christ, forgives our sins. We need only to claim and embrace God's forgiveness. Part of claiming God's forgiveness is forgiving others as God has forgiven us."

Lift up the portion of the Lord's Prayer that says, "Forgive us our trespasses, as we forgive those who trespass against us."

Fertile Soil

(10–15 minutes)

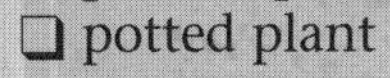

- ❑ Bibles
- ❑ scratch paper
- ❑ pens or pencils
- ❑ potted plant

As an illustration of how God strengthens and establishes us through a nurturing Christian community, show your group a potted plant. Instruct each person to create a list of outside elements that would help ensure the plant's growth and vitality (*water, light,* and so forth). Also have each person prepare a list of outside elements that would likely contribute to the plant's demise. When they've all had a few minutes to write their lists, allow them to read aloud their lists for comparison.

Ask a volunteer to read aloud **Galatians 5:22-26.** Then ask:

- What elements ensure that you will grow spiritually and bear the kind of fruit we read about in this Scripture? (Encourage the confirmands to be specific.)
- Which of these elements are active in your life right now? Which are you missing?
- What elements have a negative effect on your spiritual growth? How can you eliminate these elements or keep them from hurting you?
- After you are confirmed, how can you surround yourself with persons who will help you grow in faith?

SUPPLIES
- ❑ basin
- ❑ water
- ❑ Communion elements, including bread and grape juice

REMEMBRANCE
(10–15 minutes)

The celebration of the sacraments is one of the most powerful ways that we, both as individuals and as members of the body of Christ, connect with God.

Gather the confirmands around the basin of water and the Communion elements.Invite each youth to dip his or her fingers into the basin and to say the first word related to baptism that pops into his or her head. (As time permits, review the material on baptism from the "Sacraments" session.)

Ask the youth to talk about their baptism, whether they were baptized as infants or as older children or if they have made a decision to be baptized before being confirmed. If they have already been baptized, ask whether they remember their baptism or whether their parents have told them about their baptism. (Perhaps they have a candle, a certificate, or a copy of the order of worship from when they were baptized.)

Then ask:

- What does being baptized mean to you? (This question applies to all—those who have been baptized and those who have not.)
- How does our United Methodist understanding of baptism differ from other traditions' understandings of baptism? (Here you might choose to review the material about the infant and believer's baptism, from the "Sacraments" session, in the "Confirm Your Faith" unit.)

Then pass around the bread and the grape juice. This time have the confirmands say the first word that comes to mind when they think of Holy Communion. (As time permits, review the material on Holy Communion, from the "Sacraments" session.)

NOTE: If you choose to divide this session into two one-hour classes, break here.

Ask:

- What does Holy Communion mean to you?
- Why, do you think, do Christians take Holy Communion?
- What is the significance of the Communion elements—the bread and grape juice?
- How does our United Methodist understanding of Holy Communion differ from other traditions' understandings of Communion?

Conclude this portion of the session with a prayer such as: "Lord, we praise you and thank you for your provision. Thank you for the sacraments of baptism and Holy Communion, through which we remember your sacrifice and our introduction to your grace."

SO WHAT? PART 2

Somewhere in the Middle

(15–20 minutes)

Have the confirmands take turns balancing on a balance board. See who can stay balanced longest; if balancing proves to be too easy, see who can stay balanced longest while dodging projectiles such as foam balls. Adults should serve as spotters and should be available to hold the hand of the person who is balancing to help keep him or her from falling and getting hurt.

Say: "This activity is about physical balance, which can be pretty important."

Ask:

- What are some areas in our lives that require physical balance?
- What other kinds of balance do we need in our lives? (*emotional balance, balancing things that compete for our time and attention,* and so on)
- What do you have troubling balancing in your life?

Ask:

- What are the four "sides" of the Wesleyan quadrilateral (*Scripture, tradition, reason,* and *experience*)

Discuss how these four elements are important for a balanced Christian life and for balanced Christian decision-making.

Then spend some time discussing how these four elements are key in a balanced Christian life.

Ask:

- What would happen if any one of these four elements were to become too dominant? (For example, talk about the problems of reading Scripture without applying reason or drawing from the wisdom of Christians throughout the centuries; talk about the dangers of applying reason and experience without having Scripture as a foundation.)
- How do you apply all four elements when making decisions?

Supplies
- ❑ balance board(s)
- ❑ optional: foam balls or other soft items that could be thrown at people without hurting them

Note: If you choose to have the youth throw soft items at those balancing on the balance board, be sure that the items don't have parts on them that could hurt people. For example, if you choose to use pillows, be sure that they don't have exposed zippers on them.

Living in the Presence

(10–15 minutes)

Direct confirmands to come up with a working definition of the word *worship*. After a few minutes, ask volunteers to read aloud their definitions. Then divide a markerboard into two columns, entitled "Essentials" and "Nonessentials."

Supplies
- ❑ markerboard
- ❑ marker
- ❑ scratch paper
- ❑ pens or pencils

NOTE: Before you dismiss, instruct the confirmands to read, reflect on, and journal about the material in the "Going Forth" section of the *Credo Confirmation Student Journal* before your next session. Also encourage them to try to do the activities related to "Going Forth" on the confirmand website.

Have the confirmands list in the first column the things that they think are essential to any worship experience. Then have them list in the second column the things that are not essential but are common in worship.

Go over the lists, and ask the youth to talk about how your congregation incorporates the essentials into its worship services. Then talk about some of the nonessential parts of your congregation's worship services.

Say: "There is no single, correct way to worship. Different communities of faith connect with God through worship in different ways. A lot of the nonessentials we listed are very powerful and important parts of many worship services."

Spend some time talking about how God works through different elements of the worship service to produce the fruit listed in **Galatians 5:25-26.**

NOW WHAT?

SUPPLIES
- ❏ markerboard
- ❏ marker

PREPARATION: Write the benediction, "John Wesley's Rule," on a markerboard; or print out the poster from the website.

CLOSING RITUAL

(10 minutes)

Gather the confirmands into a circle. Lead the youth in prayer, giving thanks to God for your time together and for all that the group has learned and experienced. Then go around the circle, inviting each person to pray aloud one word or phrase that describes something he or she learned during the past week of confirmation. After every person has had a chance to contribute a word or phrase, say a brief closing prayer. Then invite the confirmands to say aloud and in unison the benediction, "John Wesley's Rule."